DATE DUE

~~DE 8 98~~			
NO 6 99			
NO 26 '01			
~~DE 8 01~~			

BOTH RIGHT AND LEFT HANDED

BOTH RIGHT AND LEFT HANDED
ARAB WOMEN
TALK ABOUT THEIR LIVES

BOUTHAINA SHAABAN

INDIANA UNIVERSITY PRESS
Bloomington and Indianapolis

First Midland Book Edition 1991

First published by the Women's Press Limited, London, UK, 1988

© 1988 Bouthaina Shaaban

The paper used in this publication meets the minimum require-
ments of American National Standard for Information Sciences —
Permanence of Paper for Printed Library Materials, ANSI Z39.
48-1984.

Manufactured in the United States of America

Library of Congress Cataloging-in-Publication Data

Shaaban, Bouthaina.
    Both right and left handed : Arab women talk about their lives /
Bouthaina Shaaban. — 1st Midland book ed.
        p. cm.
    Reprint. Originally published: London : Women's Press, 1988.
    ISBN 0-253-35189-8. — ISBN 0-253-20688-X (pbk.)
    1. Women — Arab countries — Social conditions. 2. Women,
Muslim — Arab countries — Attitudes. I. Title.
HQ1784.S47   1991
305.48'6971 — dc20   91-10866

3 4 5 95 94 93

Contents

BOTH RIGHT AND LEFT HANDED

Introduction: An Arab woman saying No

The idea for this book came to me during a visit to London in 1982. That was the long, intense summer of the Israeli invasion of Lebanon, when every day our television screens seared our sight with the spectacle of women and children dragged dead and dying from the rubble of Beirut. It was also the summer when I was pregnant with my first child, and as the baby moved in my belly I looked forward so passionately to becoming a mother myself, yet feared desperately for the future. My grief for the mothers of Beirut, for the Lebanese in the bombarded city and the Palestinians in the refugee camps set me thinking about the fate of women in struggles which they do not control, and as victims of a violence they do not initiate.

Then, a year later, I saw Lebanese and Palestinian women dry their tears, dress their wounds and pick up guns, to surprise the world with their heroic effort to fight back. Those women defied every stereotype of the passive, compliant Arab woman. They were not the dutiful wives and daughters that, we had been taught, the Prophet demanded, and that the law demands in many Arab countries. I resolved to learn something about my own people and out of that impulse grew the writing of this book.

I travelled from Algeria (where I was working) to Syria (where I grew up and where I now live) and to Lebanon. I interviewed women in all these places, and in Syria and Lebanon I also met Palestinian women. My purpose was to let all these women speak for themselves, to tell their own stories in their own way, and to reveal, if they would, their truest, innermost feelings. I hoped by this means to enable other Arab women and Western women to share something of my experience, and to hear for themselves the voices of these women – fighters and professionals, politicians and peasants, devoted wives and faithful mothers of martyrs. I intervened very little in these interviews; I saw myself as an enabler only, a microphone through which my speakers could speak and my readers could hear, through barriers of class, race and culture. And I was confident throughout that the women I spoke to were opening their hearts to me, speaking with an astonishing frankness, and sometimes telling me what they would not tell their closest kin.

The accounts of these women filled me with love and admiration for my own sex. I found women to be brave fighters, bold thinkers, uncompromising partisans, affectionate mothers, great friends, and mostly unselfish in their attitudes and beliefs. Behind the façade of a 'weak' sex I discovered courageous, original minds and principled moral values. What we women need, most of all, I concluded, is the chance to discover each other, in order to take our true place in this world that has so far been moulded by men. And this struggle – for mutual self-discovery among women – is surely a universal one, to which this book may be one contribution.

So *Both Right and Left Handed* is not a sociological study. It deals very little with statistics of any kind; it does not attempt to analyse the political, social or historical place of women in the Arab world; nor does it reflect the 'official' picture promoted by governments anxious to claim women's liberation for themselves. It is a personal book, an attempt to enable a number of women caught up in a burning moment of history to share their experience with others.

My sample of women comes from four different national groups, and I have tried to include women from various social classes. But the sample is by no means a scientific one.

It has also to be stressed that the views expressed by the women in this book have not been mediated through my own opinions: those opinions are theirs alone, and do not necessarily reflect mine, which are described in the account of my own life that follows.

An Arab Woman Saying No

It was a bright morning early in 1968. The pupils were streaming from my village in groups of twos and threes towards the only secondary school in the area, situated at the entrance to the next village just past a garage and the police station. It was a mixed school. We had never heard, then, of the luxury of a school for boys and another for girls; when we heard about this possibility a few years later we still preferred our mixed school.

About three miles separated my home from my school, the distance I had to measure with my feet twice a day for six happy years. Through winter and summer alike, on cold mornings and hot after-noons, we walked to and from school, grateful for having a school so close – some were much farther afield – to share the fruits of know-ledge with the boys.

I had just reached the police station, heading towards the school, when I saw my class-mate Aziz joyfully descending a hill in the centre of the village, waving a dagger dripping with blood and chanting, 'I've killed her and saved the family's honour!' He ran up to two policemen who were standing outside the station, handed them the dagger and said in a voice loud enough for everyone around to hear, 'I have killed my sister and have come to hand myself over for justice.' The three of them strolled slowly into the police station, chatting amicably.

With that scene etched upon my mind, I got to school. The first les-son that morning was taught by a young teacher who happened to be a Christian. When he came into the class he looked deathly pale, his hands were trembling and he avoided the pupils' eyes, until he lighted on two sisters sitting just in front of me, Sahar and Samar, and began to question them: 'How did he kill her? Where was your father? Did she cry out?' Reluctantly the two girls described how they had been sleeping in the same bed as Yemen, the sister of Aziz, and had woken up to find her murdered, in a pool of blood.

Yemen was sixteen years old. At that time a trade in women ser-vants flourished between our village and some of the wealthy families of Beirut. People in the village started calling such girls 'officers' because army officers were known for their high income. Some lucky families had three or even four 'officers' in Beirut. Their fathers would go once a year to collect their wages and see them. On coming back they would proudly talk about the wonderful life in Beirut. For the first time, perhaps, fathers were delighted to have girls, for every new girl in the family meant a thousand Lebanese lira per annum. When girls came of age, however, they would be brought back to wait for their prospective husbands.

Yemen's father had died, and left her at the age of seven with three older brothers and their mother. Having no source of income after their father's death the three brothers agreed to send their sister to Beirut so they could use her wages to pay for their education. At the age of 15 Yemen was finally brought back home. Her two elder brothers had by then finished their A levels and the youngest, Aziz, had only one year to go. I still distinctly remember when she first arrived in the village. She was wearing a blue skirt and white blouse and holding a small, round radio in her hand. She had a blue ribbon in her hair and blue sun glasses hid her eyes. By village standards she was extremely smart. Most of the girls who went to see her were looking at her smart clothes and listening with envy to her urban accent. This was how the girls of the village responded to her arrival. I had no idea how the boys felt. Some calculating ones, at least, might have seen her as easy prey.

Only a few months after Yemen's arrival, underground gossip erupted with the news that she was pregnant. Her young, single aunt was our next-door neighbour. She came to my mother and said there was no smoke without fire: 'Yemen's tummy and breasts are swollen and her nipples and the area surrounding them are dark. Does this mean that she is pregnant?'

'Very likely,' my mother answered. 'Take her to a doctor straight away.'

On the same day, Yemen's aunt and mother put her on a hired motorcycle and took her to the neighbouring town, Salamia, where the doctor confirmed the pregnancy. Her mother didn't dare bring her back home, fearful that her brothers might kill her. So she took her to the house of *Al Mokhtar* (village master or chief) in the next village and asked him to protect her from her brothers. According to our Arabic traditions, anyone who enters one's home and asks for protection should be protected. Traditionally, the host would sacrifice his life rather than let *Al Dakhiel* (the one who has asked to be protected) be assaulted in his home. *Al Mokhtar* put her with his two young daughters and, by all accounts, was looking after her well until, on a moonlit night, Aziz climbed walls and roofs and managed to reach the room where the three girls were sleeping. With a sharpened dagger he cut Yemen's throat. Unlike most criminals who try their best to leave no trace of themselves, he dipped his hands in the warm, innocent blood and went out triumphantly to celebrate publicly the cleansing of his honour.

Burial ceremonies are usually not allowed for the victims of such 'crimes of honour';[1] any respect shown towards the dead body would be construed as condoning the victim's ignoble act. Thus, *Al Mokhtar* had no choice but to invite young children in and ask them to pull the body to the graveyard at the other end of the village. Children were pulling her by the hair, throwing big stones at her misshapen, pregnant abdomen and spitting at her. On our way back from school we saw the naked body still lying in the graveyard like a dead sheep. None of us dared show the slightest sign of pity, but most of the girls didn't go to school the next morning to avoid the appallingly sad scene. Two days later the news reached us that the body had been removed, either by wild beasts or by someone who had taken pity on her and buried her at a time when he or she would not be seen.

Aziz was imprisoned for only six months. What is more, he emerged from prison with a mysteriously heroic air. Somehow he became one of the most notable personalities in the village. Shortly afterwards he left for the Gulf States, where he worked to get some money together. When he came back he opened up a bakery in the village and started feeding the village people with bread made with the same hands that had cut his sister's throat and had been dipped in her blood.

One year after this horrible incident I passed my baccalaureate and was awarded a grant to continue my education at university. I was the first girl to leave the village on her own, unaccompanied by a male relative, to study in Damascus. Yet there was no question, either at home or in the village, about my going. On the contrary, the village people were talking about my performance and my will to pursue my studies with admiration and pride.

With the coming of President Assad to power in the early 1970s, and the progressive policy of national development which he pursued, education advanced very rapidly. Schools were built everywhere and education was offered free to the smallest and most remote villages. To most people, education became a magic key which opened all doors to employment, careers and highly regarded social and political posts. Thus, when I got my BA and was offered a grant to do a postgraduate degree in Britain, I was one of quite a few women who left to do postgraduate degrees in different parts of the world, an unprecedented phenomenon. Families, friends and colleagues responded by lending us their support and encouragement.

That was in 1976. In less than a year I got my MA from Warwick University and registered for a PhD course there. At Warwick I came to know an Iraqi who was doing a PhD in physics. We were working in the Arab Society together and got on extremely well. When we decided to get married I felt obliged to consult my father first as he had taken on a social responsibility by granting me his approval to travel. I couldn't, of course, have told him I was getting married in Britain, because that would have been considered as serious a crime as that which Yemen had committed. Stunned and overawed by the possibility of defiance on my part, my father refrained from discussing such a serious issue in letters and asked both of us to pay him a visit in Syria to which we acceded. After this visit and during the summer of 1979, through 1980 and up to the summer of 1981, my family and I were continuously engaged in a heated battle over personal rights and family duties. After meeting the man I chose they desperately wanted me to abandon him, ostensibly because of the difference in our nationalities and religions. These two issues, however, were only the pretext for something much more serious. The real problem was that I was the first woman they had known to choose her husband quite independently of her father's and brothers' wishes. My father reiterated that people in the village were going to say I had brought my husband with me and that, like a coward, my father had had to endorse my choice. Although all my older brothers got married to women of their own choice, and invited my father as a guest to their wedding ceremonies, they all denied me the same right because of the stark fact that they were men and I was a woman. This I deprecated and rejected. Although my younger brothers and sisters supported me, all discussions and heated arguments failed to bridge the huge gap between our two diametrically opposed points of view: the male and the female. Eventually, my father gave me an ultimatum: either to leave the man of my choice or to leave home and never see my parents again. I hated to make the choice but I was forced to do so. So I bade my family a last goodbye and went in to Homs where my husband and I were married in a simple civil ceremony. That was in the early summer of 1981; I have not seen my parents since.

Thus, only a decade after Yemen's death, my father and elder brothers didn't even contemplate inflicting physical harm on me to stop me from living my life the way I wanted to. The most they could do was exert moral and psychological pressures on me – which didn't work. Furthermore, in a way I became a pioneer for a younger generation which reaped the fruits of my sacrifice. One of my younger sisters, for example, just had to name the man she chose to be given my father's blessing and many wonderful presents besides.

If the battle with my family over my marriage was the most bitter and decisive, it certainly was not the only one I had to fight as a woman. All the battles I had to fight were strictly related to my being a woman. The supposedly warm and supportive family atmosphere at times turns into a male inferno. The pleasure of discovering a talent for writing becomes an act of mischief one has to hide and defend oneself against; an appointment with a man in an office, who ostensibly can provide the salvation for a young woman's dilemma, turns out to be an opportunity for sexual abuse; and the last, safe hope – the women's union – is discovered to be run by men rather than women.

Being a member of a then average family of nine children (five boys and four girls – with three older brothers and two younger ones, and one elder sister and two younger ones) I was always made conscious of my sexuality and the potential danger this might bring to the honour of the family. Sex education was absolutely non-existent, both at home and at school; it was only thanks to lessons about the Islamic religion that I first learnt how our bodies function and how this function changes on reaching puberty. Even so, when I first saw blood dripping out of me my imagination was gripped with the nightmare that I must either have been raped or mysteriously impregnated with a baby. Having no access to, and no experience in, using sanitary towels I woke up the next morning to find a huge spot of blood colouring not only my nightdress but my two younger sisters' pyjamas as well. My father peered into the big blood spot, looked me straight in the eyes, and asked me angrily and accusingly: 'What is this?' Without saying a word, or even daring to lift my eyes, I collected my shameful attributes, took them to the bathroom and had a long crying session there. I thought of asking my mother about what was happening to me, but didn't dare to, for fear that she might confirm my worst doubts. I felt as if the eyes of my three elder brothers were chasing me around the house and that I was at the centre of a muted, terribly heavy atmosphere at home. To make things worse – and presumably due to my extremely anxious state – my period lasted for two weeks exactly. With a two-roomed house and four adult men around, all of whom seemed to be fully aware of the precise date my period started, I felt as if my blood was all over the place and I was wrapped in shame and disgrace.

Before that, however, it had seemed that I was my father's favourite child. He always called me 'Maliki' which means 'queen', and asked me either to recite poems or imitate a queen sitting on her throne in front of visitors. He did his utmost to ensure his daughters had an equal education to his sons. It was only when I reached puberty that he started to be suspicious about my movements. Whenever a young woman was discovered on her wedding day not to have been a virgin I could see his resentful eyes silently telling me that I could be a similar source of shame to him. Although he never tried to stop me continuing my studies, first in Damascus and then in Britain, there was a tacit agreement between us that boyfriends were not allowed. When he heard that some women in Britain sleep with men without being married to them he warned me against such evils; even so, he didn't think the threat was serious enough to stop my going there. On saying goodbye, he whispered in my ear that he trusted I would never do what English women did (that is, have a boyfriend). I couldn't betray his trust.

When I now think of my father it is amazing how many different, even contradictory, pictures of him cross my mind. He is the loving, affectionate father of my early childhood, keen and interested in my education. He is also the potentially violent master for whom a natural event such as puberty was a misery that necessitated taking full control of my life. He never agreed to marry me off to anyone who proposed to me, despite my desperate pleadings at times. Judging from the way he looked and behaved, I could see that he was not able to contemplate handing me over to another man. He once said to me about a man I had fallen in love with during my university years and wanted to marry: 'How could you kiss him? His lips are so thick!' I had never thought of that detail, but he seemed to have thought about it on my behalf. The most frightening image of him is the one I have of him when in love with my husband, Khalil. I was in London when I had the most terrible nightmares about what he planned to do to me. After we had first visited him in 1979, and he had stubbornly refused to bless our union, he started to admonish me with an unstoppable flood of horrid letters. I remember leaving his letters for two days on the table, unable to pick them up until my friend Jules would come up cheerfully saying, 'Oh ho! A letter from home.' I would thank her and put the letter aside, unable to open it for a week or so. It would take me at least a week of strenuous effort to be able to read one of his letters. They were mostly threats that he would kill me wherever I was if I didn't obey his injunction to give up Khalil. My brothers and sisters wrote me letters begging me to leave this man, because my father started to threaten my younger sister Nahid (who was close to me) that he would kill her instead of me if she didn't manage to convince me to give up the idea of marrying Khalil. It is in acknowledgment of what she suffered on my behalf that I named my daughter after her.

Yet, it wasn't as if I had freed myself from my culture's fetters. In Britain, I only ever had Khalil as a boyfriend. Because of the way I was brought up, I was never able to imagine sleeping with a man who was not my husband. I only wanted the right to choose my husband.

Of course, puberty highlighted the significance of virginity in my life as a woman. More than once I heard my mother warning my elder sister, on seeing her talking to boys in the neighbourhood, that loss of virginity meant the loss of her life. I was so terrified of losing my virginity I often thought to myself that if ever I discovered I was not a virgin I would throw myself into the Mediterranean. However, I had no idea what this virginity was. My elder sister enlightened me, and explained that it was a thin skin covering the opening to the vagina. I desperately wanted to have tangible proof that I was a virgin, to the extent that I wished virginity were a physical deformity that could be seen in full view on a woman's body. When I first fell in love, with a young relative of mine at the age of 17, I was not able to sleep the night when he held my hand and squeezed it between his, for fear of having lost my virginity.

A friend of mine who had a loving relationship that culminated in marriage came all the way from Paris to London by herself to tell me about the catastrophe that had befallen her; she had got married three days previously, but had found no evidence of her precious virginity. She was extremely perturbed because she knew she had never slept with a man before and yet she did not bleed on her wedding night. Her husband, she said, was relieved that she had not bled because he hated the sight of blood and he was sure she had never slept with a man before. But she was very upset and suffering from a true psychological crisis, and kept on pressurising me until I took her to my GP. My GP explained to her that not all women bleed and that in fact if men were gentle with their brides a very small percentage of women would have to bleed. On our way back home, she quite rightly asked me: 'If this is the case, why do we have an Article in our law that guarantees the man an immediate divorce and full reclamation of the dowry if his bride turns out not to be a virgin; the only proof of virginity being the few spots of blood shown during the first occasion of love making?' According to our law her husband would have had the right to hand her divorce papers immediately and she would have been the object of social disgrace. Today, young men's attitude to virginity is changing (though no man would openly admit this), and is becoming quite relaxed and understanding; nevertheless the Article in the law is still there in case any male chauvinist would like to make use of it.

This fear I felt was not just about my virginity but even extended to my writing. When I was a little girl I used to scribble a few words on paper every time I felt ill at ease with my family, or society, or both. I used to hide what I had written in a safe place because I had a vague idea that my father and brothers would not approve of it. What mattered most was that every time I wrote something I felt much better afterwards. At high school I began to understand that what I was writing was poetry, and started enjoying both the reading and the writing of it. At university, my relationship with poetry became a lot easier, partly because I was away from home, which meant more freedom from the immediate threat of being caught out writing it, and partly because I had a better literary knowledge. In my second year at university I entered a poetry competition and won first prize. When I went home for my summer holiday some of my school friends and secondary school teachers came to visit and asked me to read them the poem which had won the prize. I saw no reason to object to such a simple request. I was half way through reading the poem when one of my brothers (who had evidently been eavesdropping outside the door) burst in, tore the text away from my hand, and called my father to come and see what his daughter had been doing at university. Admittedly, the poem was about the double standards of the morality of brothers, and how they often apply one standard to their sisters which is completely different to the one they apply to themselves. My brother took the poem as a personal attack on him (which it partly was) and started taunting me and raving in front of all my guests. My guests sneaked quietly away, one after another, leaving me alone with a raucous brother and sullen father. My papers were torn up, my beloved, precious poems were thrown out of the window, and I was beaten hard. I can't recall how much physical pain was actually inflicted on me but I do remember only too well how I was dying of humiliation.

On hearing my screams, my sister-in-law rushed in, pulled me out of my brother's arms, and pushed him out of the room. Once she had closed the door after him she looked me in the eyes and said: 'You know their mentality; why do you write poetry? You are not living in London, you know; you are in Al Massoudiah. Look at me: I never write poetry and none of my sisters ever wrote poetry, either.'

'What do you mean?' I shouted at her, 'Could you write poetry even if you tried? Could my brother who is beating me up for writing a poem write one himself?' I was trying to stop crying but my tears were still tumbling over my dry, swollen lips.

'Hush, hush,' she repeated in an effort to restrain me. 'Don't let them hear you say such a thing; don't challenge them; don't be arrogant!' My brother, who was still listening to what was going on outside the door, kicked it open with his foot and in a second was standing in front of me like a black column struck by an earthquake, quivering with rage. 'You will never go to university again,' he screamed at me, mad with anger. 'You think you are something; I shall prove to you that you are nothing.'

Although I managed to complete my university education and do a PhD on poetry I still feel that on that day something deep down inside me was torn apart which I have never been able to put together again as far as writing poetry is concerned.

One year my best postgraduate student left her course half way through the year. I was disconcerted and wanted to know the reason for her decision – and was even more shocked when I learnt why she had done this. 'I am married with two young boys,' she started off as soon as her colleagues had left us alone to talk. 'My husband is a very rich man and is extremely fond of his food and comfort. His family has never approved of work for women. They even feel embarrassed that their daughter-in-law should be keen to pursue her studies. If the neighbours knew, my mother-in-law believes, they might well think there is something seriously wrong at home which has incited me to such strange pursuits. "What do you need this study for?" my father-in-law asked me the other day. "Do you need money, social status or prestige? You have all these and a bit more besides; you are the wife of Tarik Mahmoud. You shouldn't want to be seen with your colleagues, or have tea at the university, or look for books in the British Council like a small girl.'' '

She told me that she would very much regret missing the opportunity of doing something in literature. 'Although I had my two boys during my university study, I got my BA with first class honours and was the first in the whole department. It seems as if it was okay for me to do a BA but not to carry things any further and start dreaming of an MA and, perhaps, a PhD.'

'Has your husband got a university degree?' I asked.

'No, he hasn't. Neither does he believe it is worth the effort. He has given me an ultimatum: either leave my home and children or leave university. This is no choice, really. I have two children and I adore them; I can't realise my ambition at their expense.'

'But how can you love him after he has thwarted your efforts to do what you want to do most?' I exclaimed. 'How can you feel close to him, kiss him or make love to him? You are his victim!'

We talked at length, but still the end result was the same; she abandoned the course. A few months later I heard she was expecting a baby.

This was the second shock I had received since my arrival in Damascus in 1984 after seven years absence, spent in Britain and Algeria; the first shock had been caused by an old friend of mine with whom I was, by chance, reunited.

In the hairdresser's I was reading Dante's *Divine Comedy* and considering that women's lot on earth is far worse than that which sinners have to face in the 'Inferno', when I saw a very familiar face in the mirror. In the manner of Dante's way of thinking, I remembered masses of details related to my dear friend before I could recall her name. Many images and snippets of long-lasting friendship rushed into my mind which, instead of helping me to remember her name, blocked it out altogether. Although I hadn't seen her for a number of years, I still treasured the precious, intimate moments I had spent with her. When she lifted her head she saw my startled eyes fixed on the mirror in front of her. She blinked, looked round at me, jumped off her chair, and in one move her head was buried in my breast. We embraced, kissed and started catching up with mutual news of six eventful years of our lives. No more than ten minutes had passed, however, when she looked at her watch and said in a voice which almost shook: 'I've got to have my hair done and rush home to prepare a meal before my husband arrives.'

'Let him do that for you today,' I said, looking into her eyes and trying to detect her response.

'You must be joking,' she said. 'That doesn't happen in reputable families, and my husband is a descendant of one.'

'This is not the Najwa I knew,' I replied. (The name came back to me so easily that it seemed strange I had had any problem recalling it.)

'It surely isn't,' she answered. 'It is a reduced, distorted version of myself which you wouldn't care to know.'

A few days later I went to see her at her workplace. In her office she was without question the most brilliant, dynamic and personable engineer. She was very smart and obviously in full control of her profession. She seemed confident, happy and quite fulfilled. The enthusiasm with which she approached her work seemed to be like that of an athlete at the starting line.

'This is more like the person I knew,' I muttered to myself. 'I'm so glad I came to see her here.'

When I tried to leave, she pressed me to have lunch with her and meet her husband. Meanwhile, it was a pleasure watching my friend being a successful, happy chairwoman of an engineering company.

The moment we got into her car and drove towards her home her face started to change. She suddenly looked anxious. On the way she tried to buy some tomatoes for the salad; when she couldn't find any decent ones she looked even more worried.

'My husband likes salad with his lunch and here I am unable to buy any tomatoes.'

'He'll just have to do without his precious salad today,' I said to her, unable to believe that she might be really worried about this. As soon as we arrived at her flat she put an apron on, set the table, heated the lunch (cooked the previous evening), and started going round in circles – clearly anxious about whether she had forgotten anything. The doorbell rang; she ran to the mirror, looked at her face, put her hand through her hair and ran towards the door.

'Hello darling,' I heard her greeting her husband with a loud voice, and guessed his answer from a snapped 'Hello' which just reached my ears.

'Lunch is ready,' she added confidently, which must have been answered with a nod. He went to the bedroom to change and passed by the bathroom to wash his hands, giving her another chance to examine the table again.

Having been introduced to each other and exchanging preliminary niceties we started to eat and I could see her anxiously following his mouth and eyes, eager to find out what he thought of the food. It wasn't compliments she was seeking, I was sure, just bare approval. The maximum he deigned to offer her was a nod of approval, without wasting one of his expensive words on such a trivial matter. After lunch he buried his head behind his newspapers which he brought with him from his office while she did the washing up and prepared the tea. We drank tea together, during which she managed to extract a few words about his office, and then he excused himself to lie down for a bit before resuming his work in the afternoon.

Later I learnt from her that he was also an engineer, working for a firm other than hers, and trying to work his way up in the business. I also learnt that she loved him dearly, and that that was why she was trying to help him become a successful engineer. But why was she petrified at home?

'Because he is a nervous person and has got quite a violent temper. I am a much calmer person, so I try not to give him reasons for being nervous.' She reminded me of one of my neighbours who at 4 p.m. every afternoon came down the stairs with her four children to find somewhere to go to make sure her husband had a peaceful siesta. 'He needs that to feel refreshed in the afternoon and evening,' she always maintained.

Having closely watched these examples of married women I no longer wonder why Um Yassin, an attractive widow and a very good friend of my mother back in our village, flatly refused to get married again, even though her husband died when she was only 20 years old, leaving her with a two-year-old son. I still remember how her expression changed completely when my mother once asked her whether she wanted to get married again. 'No, no, no,' she answered. 'Never, ever again! Why should I? For the sake of a man? I have my son and I'll bring him up the best way I can.' She was an illiterate woman who had no property of her own but who worked as a daily labourer and managed to obtain a good standard of living for both her son and herself. And she was not the only widow in the village who refused to get married after her husband's death, worked hard for her child or children and thus commanded everyone's respect. It was noticeable that there were many widows in our village – but not a single widower. When I once asked my father about the reasons for this he told me that it was because men do dangerous jobs such as fighting wars, digging up wells, cutting stones and driving cars, so they were more prone to accidents and more susceptible to early deaths than women. His theory began to crumble for me, however, when two women died in childbirth and two more of cancer, and the husbands could hardly wait until the end of the traditional 40 days of mourning to get married again. Everyone in the village felt deep sympathy and sorrow for these men, who could not cook, clean, wash or look after their children!

If the widows in the village had never been the object of sympathy, that was because they did not need it. They always looked as though they were happy, strong individuals, in full control of their own lives and the lives of their children. I always enjoyed the company of widows rather than that of other women, because they always seemed to be more cheerful, more confident, and even more fulfilled than other members of their own sex. With some married women in the village I noticed that the husband's presence would strangle the wife's usual smile and produce fear which shook her self-confidence and reduced her to a feeble, hesitant creature.

Indeed, the word *fear* is quite central to my feminist analysis; through personal experience and close observation of others I have become certain that fear is the thing that most distorts women's characters. I was often living in a state of fear – lest I was discovered bleeding, writing a poem, choosing a husband. I even lived in fear of becoming pregnant with a girl rather than a boy. Why, I ask myself, are our lives as women reduced to spells of dread, anxiety and apprehension? It might well be that because men detect something terribly strong in us they become obsessed with the effort to suppress this, whether by reducing us to obedient servants or turning us into sexual objects. It is certainly for fear of the power of female sexuality that circumcision is practised. It could also be due to their fear of true female strength that men always present women as the 'weaker sex'. This analysis might at least explain some cases of rape, battering and sexual abuse.

However, I certainly was in no position to contemplate such issues when, at the age of 17, I went to see the governor of our province; the first time in my life I had encountered such an important man. To my utter horror I discovered that this important man, who held salvation in his hands for streams of anxious, waiting people, had nothing to offer my ambitious soul; he was only interested in my young flesh.

In 1971 I passed my baccalaureate with good grades. I came top in my home province (Homs) and the fourth in Syria as a whole. Yet, immediately after the announcement of the results I went into a state of semi-mourning because I could see how impossible it was going to be for me to go to university. My father was hard up and it was difficult for him to send me to Damascus. So I was advised to do a two-year teaching course which would qualify me to be an elementary school teacher. But I so desperately wanted to study English literature and to go on to postgraduate studies afterwards that I absolutely refused to do anything else. Pressure was exerted on me to do the teaching course and get a job, so that I could help my father bring up my younger brothers and sisters. This would have been the very thing for a good girl to do – but I wasn't the good girl which everyone expected and wanted me to be.

Just by chance the governor of Homs and the secretary of the Baath Party (the ruling party in Syria) paid a visit to our village in the course of their inspection tour of the area. Our school had prepared a full programme in their honour, including putting on a play performed by school children. I played the main role in the play and the show was a great success. Subsequently I gave a speech on behalf of the women's union there in which I listed the demands of women in the area. After the official programme was over I met the governor who was with a delegation from the women's union and held a working session with him during which we explained to him the very bad plight of women in the area and demanded the opening of nurseries and kindergartens. At the conclusion of the meeting he asked whether any of us had a personal problem which we wanted to talk about. I jumped at this opportunity and told him about my problem of wanting, but being unable, to enrol at university. He was very sympathetic, suggested a grant which he could give me, and gave me an appointment to go to see him in his office in town within a week.

My father and I were seated in a huge lounge – it seemed to me that everyone in town had come to see the governor – when the porter called me and stood by a huge, wooden door ready to usher me in. My father walked with me, expecting to be allowed in too, but the porter stopped him, saying, 'The appointment is for this little (sic) girl only;

your name was not mentioned at all by the governor.' I could see my father was terribly upset by this and that he was even considering not letting me go into the room on my own. I thought he was much too particular and quickly escaped his disapproving looks by disappearing through the huge door.

I was wondering why my father had behaved in such an uncivilised fashion when I saw the governor smiling and signalling to me to come and stand by him near the table. I blushed, stood shyly opposite him and made an effort to release some of the pressure and embarrassment which were bottling up inside me. Without saying a word he stretched his left hand, held my right hand tightly, squeezed it, and pulled me in a half-circular movement towards him. Once I stood by him he put his hands out, embraced my waist and rubbed his head against my belly. I tried to resist and withdraw but he wouldn't let go.

'Be a sensible girl,' he mumbled. 'I like you immensely; you will get all what you want; just relax with me a little.'

'I don't want anything,' I said in a trembling voice. 'I just want to go out.'

'You will in a minute,' he said. 'But first you tell me when I can see you again; would you come out to have lunch with me tomorrow?'

'No, I am afraid I can't; may I ask about the grant?'

'Don't worry about that. I'll see to it that you get one, but don't bring your father with you next time you come so that we can go out together, just the two of us. Can you imagine how nice it is going to be?'

I walked away feeling humiliated and worthless, and yet waving him goodbye and saying 'thank you' in an effort to restore an official air to our meeting. I must have looked as pale as death once I got outside the door, because the moment my father's eyes fell on me he screamed, 'What the hell is wrong with you? What has happened?'

'Nothing,' I answered in a faint voice. 'He just told me it was not possible to give me a grant.'

'To hell with grants,' he shouted, his voice betraying him and showing the state of deep pain he was in on my behalf, 'Let's go to your women's union; I am sure they will try to help you.'

The head of the women's union was polite but nowhere as enthusiastic as I had expected her to be. When I pressed her to give me a definite answer she said I would have to go to see her brother who acted as an adviser for the women's union on such matters. She offered to go with me and I gratefully accepted the offer.

Her brother's office was luxuriously furnished, with a huge, beautiful pine desk, behind which the fat man seemed immovable. In his movements, voice, gestures and manners he assumed such an air of importance that he put his sister (who was officially his boss) in second place. After exchanging cool greetings with us he started to lecture us about women's rights and duties, pointing out to us the significant fact that Arab women should never become as selfish as European women. 'As for you,' he addressed me in a patronising tone, 'I think you'd better do the teaching course which guarantees you a job afterwards so that you can help in bringing up your younger brothers and sisters.' I tried to make my point but soon decided that it was all in vain. So I thanked him and went out feeling disenchanted by all men, to whom we women are either a lump of flesh which they would like to use or potential mothers who should sacrifice what they want most in life for the sake of their fathers, brothers or younger sisters. What disturbed me most was that even the women's organisation was run by a man.

Now, 15 years after that incident, most Arab women still suffer from the grim consequences of the lack of genuine organisations for women. Almost all the existing women's unions, organisations, associations, etc. are tightly controlled by male-dominated bureaucracies, government or political parties. Official women's unions, even to the left of the political spectrum, are more interested in winning women recruits to their political parties, in propagating their policies and defending their own partisan positions than in feminist issues. Arab women, therefore, are still forced to fight their battle by proxy, under the patronage of the exclusively male central committees of the left wing parties. A token woman minister in an otherwise male-dominated government seems to be more cosmetic than genuinely representative of governments' much flaunted secular and progressive programmes.

What is most vexing and disappointing is that even the small percentage of women politicians who get ministerial or parliamentary posts are often anxious to prove that they are as good as men in ignoring women's issues. No sooner do they take a post than they fall into the same mould as men, speak their language and present their points of view. They are made to feel that raising women's issues or giving them priority is proof that they are women rather than ministers or MPs. That is why we find political women, or women who are involved with politics through their fathers or husbands, always stress women's traditional role and often advocate giving it priority over profession and career under the pretext of protecting the family or preserving our national heritage. They totally ignore women's issues, in order to be taken for moderate, sensible politicians. What are needed are some strong, aggressive feminist politicians who are able to turn the current concept of a woman politician on its head.

After my graduation from the English department of Damascus University in 1975, and my almost immediate appointment as a research assistant there, I had to leave the student campus and start the long, agonising search for a flat. For everybody the accommodation problem in Damascus is terrible, but for a single woman it is almost insoluble. The house has to be without men, the neighbourhood extremely respectable and the family must have a well-known name. I was beginning to despair when someone casually mentioned that a friend of his sister whose husband was away might very well welcome a female lodger. I lost no time in catching a taxi to the school where this woman taught.

It was about eleven o'clock on a sunny, bright, but frosty February morning when I arrived and found all the teachers sitting in a circle around two big plates of *homos* and *foul*. After greeting them I glanced quickly at their faces, trying to recognise Ghada but failing to do so. I realised I had to explain immediately the reason for my unexpected visit and asked who Ghada was. A mass of very black, beautiful long hair lifted itself from the plates of food, while two big black eyes with a serene but subdued smile were looking at me with astonishment bordering on fear.

'What do you want from me?' she asked nervously, and then added, 'I am Ghada.'

'I would like to see if you would . . . ' I began, but before giving me a chance to finish my sentence her face brightened up, as if she suddenly knew what I was after, and she interrupted me with:

'I'm afraid I have to rush to my class now. Could you come to see me at my flat around four o'clock this afternoon?'

As we sat sipping our small cups of Arabic coffee in her flat after we had introduced ourselves, I immediately felt that all the usual barriers that exist between strangers had somehow dissolved. We were talking warmly like two old friends.

'To start at the beginning,' she said with a friendly and very intelligent smile. 'I have no room to let; there is only that bedroom' – which I could see through a door that had been left ajar – 'where I sleep with my two daughters. But if you like us enough, and would like to live with us, you are welcome. There is always room for good friends. This sofa which we are sitting on opens out into a bed at night, so you could sleep on it – or I could sleep on it and you sleep with my daughters in the bedroom. My husband is away, you see, and I feel very lonely, particularly in the evenings, and I would very much like your company. I'm just sorry I don't have a comfortable place to offer you. I really like you and would love you to stay with us. I don't want any money or anything from you – just come and stay.'

Her immediate trust in me, which had no justification beyond an intuitive liking, puzzled and almost shocked me. Like me, I thought to myself, this woman acts intuitively, which is lovely, but sometimes dangerous. Only women, I reflected, believe in intuition; men call it nonsense.

'When is your husband due back?' I enquired.

'God knows,' she answered, with a deep, subdued sigh. 'It's a very long story which I can tell you in instalments in the evenings if you decide to stay with us.'

Even then I felt I had no choice. I was feeling so much at home that it would have been ridiculous to have pulled myself away from this lovely woman.

'When can I bring my things?' I asked abruptly. 'I only have clothes and books.'

'Any time,' she answered happily. 'Here is the key to the flat. Come and rob me tonight if you like!' she said, in the tone of someone who knows she'll be understood.

'I will come tonight, but not to rob you; I'll be coming to stay with you,' I said.

'That's great!' she replied, and embraced me warmly.

My evenings with Ghada were the most enjoyable I had ever known and I experienced a most intensely loving and caring relationship with a female friend and a sister, except that Ghada was more than a friend and sister. One evening she began to tell me about her husband, obviously very dear to her, who was a poet, dramatist and an excellent letter-writer, but, even so, an unworldly man and father.

'At the age of eighteen I met this mysterious, young, slim, sexy and very beautiful Egyptian who was producing a play at my school in which I had been given a leading role. I fell head over heels in love with him, and desperately wanted to marry him. My family, however, is Kurdish and would have been prepared to bury me alive rather than marry me off to a non-Kurdi. So I decided to elope with him to Beirut (at that time the free zone of the Arab world), where we got married. After short visits to Jordan and Iraq where we tried (but failed) to find jobs, we came back to Syria. My family were then trying to find me to kill me and cleanse their honour from the shame I had brought upon them. I changed my name and the way I dressed, did a teacher training course, and came to live with my husband here in Damascus, which my family hardly, if ever, visit. Once married, I discovered my husband had no qualifications whatsoever and that he had been on the tour to my village as a juvenile, rather than as a professional, producer. But I still loved him. I told him that I was prepared to work to support him until he got some qualifications. But he was not interested. He would sleep until noon and leave our home to play chess and drink with his friends until midnight. He was jobless and penniless. In a week he would spend what I earned in a month, and then spend the rest of the month bullying me to get more money for him. When he got desperate he would beat me – and a few hours afterwards would write me a poem apologising for what he had done. When our life reached a very low ebb he came up with the idea of flying to London to work for the BBC. He said that as soon as he had settled down there he would send for me. In less than a week's time he had got himself a ticket. He left me five months pregnant with my elder daughter.

'That was four years ago. In that time he paid me one ten-day visit during which I got pregnant with my younger daughter, Safa, who is now a year old.'

Ghada told me disconcerting stories of how she had had to give birth to her two daughters with no one to look after her except her next door neighbour, who had cut the baby's umbilical cord with her sewing scissors. She hadn't dared to visit a hospital for fear of being discovered by her brother, who was still intent on killing her. She discovered later that her mother would have loved to have come to her, but didn't dare to.

'Three hours after giving birth,' she said to me, 'I was starving. So I had to get up, soaked in my blood, to cook myself something to eat. During those years I received many cards and love letters from my husband, but not a single penny. He's never even seen his younger daughter. To be fair to him, he is an intelligent, sensitive man, and very exciting to be with, but he has no sense of responsibility. I think his problem is that he has never grown up, but how many men *do* grow up? None of my colleagues or neighbours know this, not even my elder daughter, Rasha. I'm always telling her that her father is great; that he is away for her sake; that he is sending her money, presents and his love. Despite everything, I still love him; I don't believe I did anything wrong, but perhaps I made the wrong choice.'

'My only regret,' Ghada would say to me, time and time again, 'is that I can't see my elderly mother, whom I adore. I'm not allowed to. She's been put under virtual house arrest by my brother, who would kill me this very moment if he found out where I was. My mother secretly manages to send me messages of love, a lock of her hair or a piece cut from her dress which I keep here in my bra to feel with every heartbeat. She knows nothing about the reality of my life. I always assure her that I am very happy and that my husband is the best husband in the world.'

Shortly after I moved in with Ghada I got a part-time job as a translator. To my surprise, my colleague at work was from Ghada's village. I asked for news of her family and was able to brighten Ghada's dark evenings by bits of news about the person dearest to her.

'Why don't you go to see your mother when your brother is at work?' I asked her one day.

'I don't dare to. No, never!' she replied. 'Supposing he were there for some reason or other, he'd kill me on sight. But I have an idea. Why don't you go with your colleague and see her for me?' I said I would.

My colleague and I drove through valleys and golden fields of wheat and barley, brighter than the pale afternoon sun. We stopped in front of a low, extremely humble building with only two rooms; no courtyard, kitchen or bathroom were in evidence.

'This is where Ghada's mother lives,' my colleague said. 'I'll leave you here for a while, and come back to collect you to take you back to Damascus.' The word 'collect' sounded very apt, for I felt like a little girl who is afraid of being abandoned and desperately waiting for her parents to 'collect' her.

'What shall I do?' I asked in a voice which betrayed all my fears and anxiety.

'Just knock on the door, go in and say what you want to say,' said my colleague to encourage me.

Before I had reached the door it opened to reveal a thin, elderly, clearly nervous woman who leaned, trembling, on a stick. She looked aggressively at me and asked in a shaky voice, 'Who are you? What do you want from me?'

Her nervousness and fear were catching and I found myself mumbling in low, dejected tones, 'I am a friend of Ghada; I just came to tell you how much she loves you and misses you. She asked me to come and see you, to fill my eyes with looking at you, to kiss your eyes and hands, to smell you and carry your smell back to her.'

'Oh my God,' she said wretchedly, in a voice full of defeat, turning her face away from me in an effort to escape my insistent, enquiring gaze. 'Go, please go!' she begged, as she tried to stop herself falling by clutching her stick. 'If her brother sees you here he will kill you; he might walk in at any moment. Go, please go.' Then, turning her deeply sad, tearful eyes towards me, she asked, 'How is she? Is her husband good to her? Is she happy? Is she still as beautiful as she used to be? Has she still got that black hair which I miss washing and combing? *Please* go! You must be mad to have come here. Why did she let you risk your life like this?'

'Listen,' I said almost angrily, having collected my wits together. 'Ghada is still as beautiful as ever. She has two gorgeous daughters and is managing quite well. She loves you. She adores you, and would love to see you or even live with you again. Why don't you leave this place and come to live with her in Damascus? I could arrange that for you, don't worry.'

'Go, please go!' she kept repeating frantically. 'Tell Ghada that I love her and that I'd love to see her, too, but for the moment all that matters is that I know she is happy. I'm imprisoned here. Don't think this is where Ghada was born and brought up. Oh, no! We are respectable people. We have a lovely house over there,' she pointed in the direction of the village centre, 'but this is the cell which my son has chosen for me to live and die in, all alone like a lonely beast. Ghada's brother is cruel and bloody. Please tell her to keep out of his way. He still vows daily to kill her and cleanse his honour with her blood. Don't ever come to see me again and don't let Ghada even think of such a crazy thing. I'm fine. I'm an old woman; I've lived my life and I don't care what happens to me now, but I want her to live hers. Oh, God, I just wish I could see her. Go, please go! Just *move*!'

When I looked at her face I saw that floods of tears were streaming down her cheeks. Our eyes met, perhaps for the first time, and she took my hand and with a sudden, astonishing strength, pushed me out of the door. 'Don't stand there looking at my door! Run to the village, hitch-hike, do anything you like, but just disappear from this place before he comes. He would shoot you immediately if he knew who you were.'

'Oh my God!' I thought to myself as I was pushed out of the door. 'What an ordeal both mother and daughter are going through – and for what? The daughter has committed the crime of getting married to a man of her choice in a way she saw fit, but what has the mother done? Do the mistakes of the daughters visit themselves upon the mothers?'

How her mother looked, what she had worn, what she had said, and how she had smelt, were the ever interesting topics which brightened up Ghada's melancholy and tormented mind for weeks.

'Don't ever make my mistake,' she sometimes burst out in a fit of tears. 'Marry a Syrian; someone tangible you can hold on to for financial support, at least. No man is worth the sacrifices I've made for my husband. My mother will die, I am sure, in her dreary loneli-ness, and I won't even be able to see cold death on her once warm, affectionate features. And for what? For a husband whom I loved and still love but who doesn't give a damn about the way I feel, or even the way his daughters feel. Why can't we be selfish, egotistical, dump our feelings to one side and look for a convenient, comfortable life? Perhaps we wouldn't be happy like that, either.'

Then she would rest her head on my shoulder, have a good cry, and fall asleep soaked in her tears.

'Nahid Jawad,' the voice of a woman doctor was calling, obviously not for the first time. These were the only two words that I was able to register, amidst a meaningless and irritating noise. I was vaguely aware of being extremely tired and very wet. I moved my head, which was resting heavily on an unfamiliar pillow and tried to open my eyes to see where I was. 'Nahid Jawad,' the doctor called again, more loudly and insistently this time, perhaps cross with my lack of response. Half consciously recalling that 'Jawad' was my husband's surname and having failed to open my eyes, I tried to raise my hand and managed to say in a faint, hardly audible whisper, 'ici, ici.'

'Oh what a gorgeous daughter you've brought us!' the woman doctor said in a cheerful, jolly voice.

'Daughter? Have I got a daughter?' I said. I was burning with curiosity. I wanted to see my daughter.

The woman doctor was bending over my head, turning towards me a beautiful, tiny face with distinct black eyebrows, black eyelashes, black hair and very tiny mouth and nose. 'My God,' I thought to myself, 'what a beautiful daughter I've got.' Now I could see my baby I was overcome with joy.

Back home, even before congratulating me for my safe delivery, people would say they hoped it was a boy next time. Theories were immediately voiced that my daughter's face looked a bit masculine, which meant I would have a boy to follow. Without looking at my girl or showing any interest in her whatsoever, women were advising me what to eat and on which day of the month I should sleep with my husband in order to make sure I would have a boy next time. The next time came and I had another lovely girl; the pressure this time was so much worse, particularly when people knew I already had a girl. Sisters in the delivery ward were looking at me with pity, unable to look me in the eyes, and none of them volunteered to go out to tell my husband he had a girl. Topical stories at the hospital were of poor mothers who had three or four girls and were desperate for a boy. When my friend's husband looked upset on hearing he had a boy – it was actually his third – sisters breaking the news to him thought he was really odd.

Back in the neighbourhood all announced their sympathy for poor me for having a second girl. In a social gathering of the neighbours in my flat the most outspoken chauvinist among them, who himself had recently had a girl, didn't make any effort to hide his resentment. 'Come on,' he said to me. 'If you don't manage a boy, all this fuss about having a family is useless. All that girls bring you is concern and worry; there is nothing like having a boy and feeling confident that he can go to the end of the earth and come back safely.'

'I couldn't agree more,' I said. 'In a male chauvinist society like this women are bound to have a hard time; as for me, I've had my family and I am quite happy with what I've got.'

As we were sipping our coffee the news broke of a next door neighbour who had given birth to triplets – boys – that very morning in hospital (she already had two sons at home). Our chauvinist friend said to my husband, 'Let's bury our heads in the sand you and I, only Abo Iad [the father of the five boys] performed well; we are certainly not as good.'

'Oh my God!' I screamed at him instantly. 'When it is a girl it's the woman who has had it, but when it's a boy it's the man who has made it. How awful of you!'

My elder daughter is now in her fifth year; she is sensitive and affectionate. For some reason she keeps enquiring about her grandparents and how much she misses them – though she has never seen them, of course. During the *Eid*, the major Muslim festival of the year, she listens to her friends talking about the holiday they have spent with their grandparents and the presents they have been given. She comes home and starts asking why I don't go to see my parents; don't I love them? Don't I say to her everyone must love his or her parents, so why don't I love mine? Or don't I know where they live; have I ever been there, etc? It is unfortunate for her that her father's mother is dead and that his father lives in Iraq; we don't even receive letters from him. So she has never seen any of her grandparents and she really shows that she feels quite deprived. In a country where family relations are tightly knit and where grandparents play a major role in bringing up children she finds herself an exception to the rule.

I, too, would love to see my parents, despite all that has happened, and I have made several attempts to see them, but my father has flatly refused either to receive me or to let my mother – who, I am told, would also love to see us – come to visit me. He has reiterated to all mediators that, as I decided to choose my husband independently, he took the independent decision to consider me dead and he no longer wants to know whether I am dead or alive. My older brothers, who are university graduates, have never seen me since my separation from my parents either. As for other people, most believe that I turned out to be a thoroughly bad girl after my family tried to give me the best education possible; I paid them back by abandoning them at the age of 28 and marrying a man of my choice.

Needless to say, I have no regrets and if I were to re-live my life I would do precisely what I have done. But I am angry with male hypocrites – and that includes almost all men – who try to propagate the idea that, just because women go out to work, to school or to university, they are now fully liberated and independent. The aim of these hypocrites is to make women feel grateful for the slight progress they have made and stop them going beyond this. Yet the real battle has only just begun. In my study for this book, I found that although women have become professionals and politicians and have excelled in many fields, at home they are still considered the weaker sex, and are expected to act as servants. In fact, the more successful the woman is in her profession, the greater is the pressure exerted on her at home to prove that she is still a 'woman' with connotations of 'weak, docile and feminine'. I also found out that these women, who, for the most part, had rich experiences and valuable thoughts, were fettered by their own fears of seeming odd or ridiculous or of jeopardising their chances of a happy family life if they didn't behave according to inherited social traditions.

Note

1. The crime of honour is a legal term covering the murder of women suspected of having had premarital sexual relations. The killers are usually male next of kin. The legislation is non-religious but panders to some of the most backward male chauvinist sentiments that still exist in certain rural areas. The word 'honour' is used because Arab men relate their personal and family honour to the premarital sexual behaviour of their nearest women kin.

1 Syria: Guaranteed Rights for All, Except at Home

Syria is today one of the major powers in the Middle East. Like Lebanon, it was mandated to France after the First World War (while Palestine and Jordan went to the British), and independence did not follow until 1945. Between 1958 and 1961 it was part of a United Arab Republic with Nasser's Egypt. Since then it has been almost continuously governed by the Baath Socialist Party, which has over the years introduced a comprehensive programme of social reform: a mixed economy, with centralised co-operative and state-owned sectors; national education programmes, for girls as well as boys; and 'guaranteed' rights for all citizens regardless of sex, colour or religion. As in Algeria, mass organisations of workers, women and students are expected to play a role in the national political life.

Thus there is no doubt that women have benefited immeasurably from Baathist progressive social policies. But social attitudes change more slowly than official policies, as the following interviews show very clearly. Syrian women remain subject to a body of religious family law which places their daily lives under the control of fathers and husbands.

Guaranteed Rights for All, Except at Home

As our plane probed the glittering sky above Damascus at about 1 a.m. in late August, I could almost feel the cool, gentle breeze which normally accompanies these moonlit nights. I came to appreciate Damascus August nights which are cool, serene and poetic in contrast to the brilliant sunshine of the unbearably hot days. I looked out from the window and saw the shadow of the plane flying over Ghota with its endless green fruit trees. Back in our small village near Homs, August used to be the month of night festivities and parties. Come

August, the night is no longer claimed by sleeping, but by walking, meeting people and jubilation. Jubilation over what it is hard to tell; perhaps over nature at its best, at its most pleasant. Along the Roman canal which ran through my village boys and girls would spend the best part of the night walking in groups of three or four, sometimes washing salad in the crystal-clear water, laughing and chattering about school, village and discreet love affairs.

Between 7 and 8 in the evening a lively hum would start in the village, gradually getting louder and louder until the sounds of talking, singing and traditional dancing could be distinguished. Almost everyone would go out for a walk, while mothers of very young babies and elderly men and women would take chairs out and sit in front of their homes chatting about their daily concerns.

After listening to the stories of my favourite people I would hurry to join my friends, who would sometimes leave the village for the hills and valleys nearby. Nothing disturbed the tranquillity of the village except the sound of small portable radios. There was no traffic, of course, except the one minibus which left the surrounding villages to go to town at six o'clock in the morning and came back with much welcomed travellers at about four o'clock in the afternoon.

For me and for my ex-school mates this world now lives only in memory: the Roman canal has dried up and the August moonlight has been overpowered by the electric street lighting. I wonder whether young people any longer go out in spontaneous gatherings.

Two hours before my appointment with Abla was due I decided to go to the hairdresser, for whenever a Syrian woman steps out of her home she has to look as if she is going to the opera at Covent Garden. The atmosphere in the hairdresser was that of *Harem*, where it is permissible for women to do whatever they like so long as they are at a safe distance from male intruders. Women who wore *Al Hijab* in the streets and looked quite conservative were in see-through dresses, revealing blouses, and their hairstyles and make-up were *à la mode*. One woman with long hair attracted my attention. Three women were bending over her, pulling, plaiting and curling her hair – one felt that the woman's head had metamorphosed into a wig which was being chemically and mercilessly treated by these professional hairdressers. When they eventually finished, her hair was as decorated as a Christmas cake. Yet before leaving the shop she stood in front of the mirror and covered her head completely with a huge scarf, making her long, pale face look even longer and paler. What is the point, I wondered, of spending all that time and money on having a hairstyle which she is going to cover up? When I expressed surprise at what I saw I was told she was to attend a women's party that evening. Then I recalled that women in my country go to a great deal of trouble to be as elegant and presentable as they can be, even when no men are going to attend their parties – in fact, especially when no men are allowed to attend. The women enjoy each other's elegance and beauty and seem to give expression to their love and even sexual feelings amongst each other.

In the back of the shop where I went to the lavatory, there was a sink, a small cooker, food shelves and an old bunk bed. On that bed there were two women in their petticoats, embracing and kissing each other. One of them held the other's head in her hands, looked straight into her eyes and said to her, 'Oh, you are beautiful'. I must have been looking askance, trying to understand an unusual scene in the most unexpected of places when I was struck by another, equally puzzling episode. As the woman with the hairstyle was leaving the shop, another veiled woman who wore *Al Hijab* was coming in speaking loudly and addressing herself to no one in particular, just like a rich man at an Arabic wedding who starts throwing money up into the sky without looking into anyone's eyes, knowing full well that people around him are both grateful and admiring. '*Salem, Salem*', she was almost shouting as she entered the shop and before she could lay her eyes on the owner she added hastily: 'Do you have a girl whom you would like to marry off to a rich Saudi?' Her eyes roved over the shop and she added in an even louder voice, 'What do you think, girls? Hey! Would any of you like to get married to a Saudi?' The shop owner's eyes glittered at hearing the phrase and she gave me the impression that had she been a little bit younger (she was over 60) she wouldn't have minded taking up the offer. Indeed, she was as excited and as anxious as a fisherman who has netted a golden fish.

'Can't we see him?' asked one of the girls, laughing.

'Well,' the woman answered wryly. 'First you must know that he is not young but he is rich and is prepared to pay. Think about it, anyway,' the woman gave a last call before leaving the shop as briskly as she had entered it. Detecting my embarrassment and disgust the shop owner pulled her chair nearer to me and started whispering in my ear: 'Look, my dear girl. My own daughter is married to a rich Saudi who is 30 years her senior, yet she is very happy with him. The important thing for the woman, I believe, is to secure her rights before getting married; she should make the man buy her a flat and put a large sum of money into her bank account and let him go to hell afterwards. Look at this woman,' she said, pointing to a young, lovely-looking woman sitting next to her. 'She is married to a Syrian who has been working in Saudi Arabia for the last ten years during which time she has had four children.'

'How did you manage to have these four children, then?' I asked the woman jokingly.

'Oh, he visits us sometimes,' she replied. 'In fact, every summer he comes to spend a month with us. During this month I realise how much nicer it is to live without a man; I can't wait to see the back of him. He is, of course, our only source of income, but other than that his absence is better than his presence. During this one month which he spends with us I feel like an ill-used slave. I go round the clock cleaning, washing, cooking and serving tea and coffee to his uninterrupted stream of guests.'

Are these women lesbians, I wondered to myself. What I saw a few minutes ago in the back of the shop seemed to suggest that and what I was hearing now seemed to confirm this. Do they just express their feelings to one another as their only outlet in a sexually oppressive society where woman's sexuality never seems to matter or even exist? One thing seems certain, however, and that is that these women don't seem to see any relation between marriage and love, or even between marriage and making love. They seem to get married to old, rich Saudis to secure a comfortable and socially desirable material life and then to go about satisfying their sexual desires the way they see fit. Not bad logic, perhaps.

Both the posh, quiet avenue and the building's entrance told of upper-middle-class inhabitants. Children were playing in the gardens or in the hall built especially for them on the ground floor. It was a five-storey building of what seemed to be an elegant block of flats.

I was invited into a huge room. The floor was almost completely covered with colourful, fine Persian carpets, and a mahogany cabinet and china closet added the final, elegant touch to the place.

'You've changed a lot,' Abla started. 'You are wearing your hair short; it suits you better than long hair. You also look terribly well for a pregnant woman in this heat.'

'Oh, yes,' I said. 'I never feel as good as when I am pregnant. Pregnancy seems to improve me physically and to provide me with some extra energy.'

'Where have you left your little daughter?' Abla continued to interview me before granting me the chance to do the same to her.

'With her father, of course,' I answered, fully aware of the tinge of surprise which my tone betrayed.

'Oh, good.' Her rising tone intimated that that was the exception rather than the rule. 'None of my brothers-in-law,' she added, 'babysits for their wives. They just don't want to know about their children. But, of course, you are married to an Iraqi; Iraqi men are much better with their women than Syrian men. My aunt is married to an Iraqi. He does everything at home. He is a better cook and better housekeeper than she is. Generally speaking, Iraqi men take women more as equals than do Syrian men.'

While it took some time to catch up on mutual news for the last ten years, eventually Abla and I began the informal interview which ran as follows.

'I was born in 1928 and was the eldest of eight children in a happy family headed by quite an enlightened father. It was the norm in those days that girls, especially the eldest, be kept at home to help with the housework and eventually be married off between the ages of 12 and 14. Aware of his humble financial position and of what was then considered to be the duty of the father to secure a good future for his children by leaving them money or land, my father decided to provide us with good education instead. Thus he sent us all, boys and girls, to school, which was quite unusual. I did very well at school and loved all subjects, particularly history. Unusually privileged by my father's constant backing, I was glad to invest my hard work and energy in acquiring the formal education provided at that time. From elementary school I moved to the secondary school which was the only one for girls in the whole of Damascus and maybe in Syria. My academic career culminated happily in 1947 with my joining the history department at the University of Damascus.

'So I was one of the very few privileged girls of those days to have both opportunities and choices and to face absolutely no social or family problems in acquiring an education – generally thought to be an exclusively male domain. Most girls had to suffer the boredom of spending their time in total isolation at home waiting for eligible husbands to knock on their doors. Some of the better off girls could study for a few years if only to escape illiteracy, and others who managed to continue their studies had to put the Islamic veil on whenever they left the house. I knew such girls as friends and colleagues at the university. Clearly they put on the veil as a result of social pressures rather than from conviction – they used to take it off whenever they were at the university or out of risk areas.'

'How were you received by your male colleagues at the university?'

'Our male colleagues' attitudes towards women's new ventures were ambivalent. Generally, we were received calmly and Platonic relationships were soon established. Yet a suspicious question was evidently forming in their heads: "Since men are the bread winners what the hell are these women doing here?" We had to be reticent, decently dressed and socialised circumspectly. Furthermore, we had to take part, wittingly or otherwise, in a bizarre race against the social pretence of male superiority. Indeed, we had to prove our intellectual merits all the time; needless to say we had great energy and were able to provide everybody, both in and out of the university, with the proof that we were equal to, if not better than, men. I remember once when, against the advice and apprehension of many of my friends, I stood the challenge of a public lecture with a male colleague and fared better than he did. Many women would not have dared to do such a thing. When I graduated from the university I gave another blow to the pretence of male superiority as I came out first in my class.

'Immediately after university I started looking for a job, and here again my advance proceeded unhindered. I got a teaching job almost straight away after my graduation. I had no difficulty in going to work and, indeed, faced no trouble at all as a teacher. Somehow, it came to be socially accepted that teaching was an apt profession for women. Even today, teaching is still considered a traditional province for women.

'However, being a woman, my progress was bound to be doomed eventually by the social constraints of the 1950s. The first setback I had to suffer and accede to as a woman was the termination of any chance to study abroad for a higher degree. I was actually offered a grant to do a PhD in Egypt. If I had been a man my father wouldn't have hesitated to send me. I still resent not having gone; it is my greatest regret in life. My father trusted me but, taking the advice of other men, including my teachers at the university, he decided that I should not go abroad alone to face all the social problems which that would inevitably bring, even though there was clear evidence that I was an independent, strong and successful woman. The second setback came shortly after this when I had the chance to move to a much better job. I was offered a job at the Museum of Ancient History which was in line with my training, and this was the very thing I would have loved to have done. Here again my father asked me to turn the offer down in order, as he put it, to prevent any possible gossip which might erupt about me or my family. It is such a shame when I think of it now. I could have been in a completely different place, now, and I would have done something worth doing with my life. What makes me more angry is that I lost these two precious chances solely because I was a woman.

'My family always gave me the impression that I was allowed to have emotional relationships, but as I never tried to I am not sure how far I could have gone. My male colleagues considered me as their sister. On the whole, we, as women, were far more mature and rational than they were. To us they were only boys, immature boys, so none of us ever thought of any of our colleagues as a prospective husband. I didn't get married then because whenever anyone came to ask for my hand my father would ask me, "What do you think?" "What can I think?" I would answer. "I don't know the man."

'It is true I was able to see the man once or twice before making up my mind, but that was not enough. Two men with PhDs proposed to me. I found them so immature; I admired neither of them. I so desperately wanted a man whom I could admire and respect. I have still to meet that man. I found the men whom I happened to meet through work or social meetings very shallow and almost silly; perhaps if I had loved someone I would have married him, regardless, and there would have been no problem. But I was never in love. In our family we have complete freedom to choose the partner we want, but I found this total freedom the wrong kind of freedom. One should at least have some hints from one's parents, but my father never interfered and I was not mature enough, in this sense perhaps, to make the right decision. On the other hand, my family's circumstances weren't helpful. Being the eldest of my brothers and sisters, I felt deeply responsible for them when my father died, leaving them all of school age. I used to think: How can I leave my brothers and sisters with no one to support or look after them? I couldn't. And I didn't meet the man who was worth the sacrifice. I never thought, of course, that I wouldn't get married at all and that I would find myself one day as an elderly, single woman. Still, I have no regrets.'

In saying this she no longer could restrain the tears which had been on the point of streaming over her face for quite a while. On the one hand I felt glad that she liked me enough to be able to cry in front of me and on the other I felt so sorry that she had to put up with so much for the sake of others.

I was totally absorbed with my thoughts when I suddenly realised that Abla had stopped crying. Her eyes were fixed on my face waiting for me to look at her. When I did so she asked me what I was thinking about. 'Nothing much,' I replied. 'Perhaps about the different problems of other women. But do you live here on your own?' I hastened to ask. 'What do you think of the problem of Arab women who say that if we have the freedom to live on our own we won't accept living with our husbands or with our families?' Abla smiled gently and replied:

'I shall tell you a story about this. I saved enough money in a building society to buy myself a flat, and eventually I bought one. I said to my uncle, "Come, I want to show you my new flat."

'He looked aghast and asked me why I should want to buy a flat. "For whom?" "For myself," I replied. "Do you think I would live with any of my married brothers or sisters?"

'My uncle gave me a very strange look and said, "Is that possible? Can you possibly think of living on your own?"

' "Of course, I can," I answered.

' Our society does not accept the idea of women living on their own; what we need is a few brave, strong women who challenge this notion and break it once and for all. We need to make people realise there is no reason why women shouldn't live on their own since they are just as qualified to have their own independent homes as men are. I want to tell you another little story, too. Many years ago, after my father's death, I wanted to go to Beirut. Such an endeavour, in the past, required official permission for women intending to travel on their own. I applied for the exit permit. The man in charge there asked me for the permission of my guardian. "I haven't got one," I said. "My father is dead and all my brothers are younger than me. I have a young brother," I added, "who doesn't dare leave the house without asking me. You want *him* to give me *his* permission to travel?"

'He hesitated and said, "But this is the law!"'

' "What law?" I almost screamed in his face. "How am I to invent a guardian for myself when I am the head of the whole family?" Finally, I managed to get the okay, but with great difficulty. As women, we have to fight such degrading and outdated laws. The purpose of this law was to prevent women travelling without their husbands' consent. I always believed that women should be free to travel wherever they liked whenever they liked, and, indeed, women nowadays are free to travel. Although this law still exists no one dares mention it or ask a travelling woman if she has such permission because things have changed so much over the last two decades.'

'As someone who has lived women's problems from the 1950s until now, what do you think of the changes which have occurred regarding women's position in Syria?'

'In reality, women's position here has improved beyond recognition, particularly in the last two decades. Take as an example the entrance of women to the university in huge numbers and to all faculties of their choice. The proportion of women at universities now is at least 50 per cent. Even religious, uneducated and poor men work day and night to pay for their daughters' higher education. Teaching jobs at primary and secondary schools are mostly occupied by women. We hardly have any male teachers at primary school level. In a few years' time we expect primary school teaching to be undertaken exclusively by women. The present educational policy of the government is to turn all schools into mixed ones. This target has almost been achieved at primary school level. Even in secondary schools you find women teachers working at exclusively boys' schools. On the whole working women constitute at least 50 per cent of the working population in Syria. Just wait in the centre of town at 2.30 p.m. when employees leave work and you will see that most of them are women, and a good many of these are veiled women too. Women make up half the students in medical and engineering colleges and probably 70 per cent in pharmacy colleges. As for other professions, most workers in the factories are women. Part of the reason for this is that a huge number of men enrol in the army, so the country is in need of women workers. Essentially, however, the reason is that women started to fight for a better life and for their independence. Women want to be economically independent; they no longer want to rely on fathers, brothers or husbands for their living. The woman teacher who has four children is having a rough time; she is exhausted but she wants to raise her standard of living; she wants to work to be somebody of much value to herself, even if this has to be at the expense of her leisure or health.'

'Do you think the Syrian woman of today is more of an equal to the Syrian man now that she is educated and has a job?'

'The economically independent woman is not totally free in her private life. Of course she is in a better position now. She can keep herself, afford to buy things for her children and has more confidence in herself. But some men still try to control their wives by administering their salaries. She goes out to work all day to come back home exhausted and then has to do all the housework. As usual, she has to cook, clean the house, wash, do the washing up and look after the children. So she has to work a double day. What is more, she has to iron better, cook better and clean better – because she is educated. In this sense, the opportunities for formal education and work have only achieved moral equality for women, not a real equality. The real achievement has meant exhaustion and extra work besides the traditional housework. To have a job, run a house, look after a family and bring up children certainly needs a superwoman. We have nurseries and kindergartens for babies and children but they are not enough. The government is trying to open nurseries at all job centres which have more than five women working in them. The Women's Union[1] also runs its own nurseries. Even so, the increase in the number of women going out to work every year by far exceeds the number of nurseries which are opened and are supposed to cater for the children of these women. The ministry of education has started opening nurseries at schools, the ministry of electricity, the research centre and quite a few factories now have their own nurseries. The women there are very happy with the conditions. Mothers are very pleased to be able to come to work with their babies, to have a look at them during lunch breaks and to go back home with them after work. It is expected that all other ministries and job centres will provide such nurseries very soon. For mothers need to go to work feeling sure that their babies are in safe hands and well looked after rather than be torn apart by worry and anxiety. It is not an easy task, of course, but what can safely be said is that the country and government recognise the importance of cheap and efficient nurseries and are encouraging all institutions to try to provide these for working women.'

'Do you think that women's achievements in most fields will be quite different if they have equal opportunities and real equality with men?'

'Certainly. They will indeed be more original and more inventive than men. Women have more patience, more ambition, more dreams and more imagination than men. All that men have is physical power. But a woman, given equal opportunities, will definitely do better. It is true that the Koran said, concerning inheritance, that a man's share should be twice as much as a woman's, but that was because the man used to be the sole bread winner in the family. As a woman's income is nowadays equal to a man's, I can't see the justification for such legislation.'

'Do you think it would be possible to update our Islamic laws to suit women's emancipation?'

'Islamic law can be understood and interpreted in a way which serves women and helps them achieve their equality with men, but men don't want this: rather, they strongly resist it. Also, women are not working hard enough to bring such change about. Women have to fight and be persistent in their determination in such matters. The equality they have achieved has become a burden to them because of the many new responsibilities it has brought with it. Our men are selfish and they want to be in constant control of our lives. They might like their wives, but they love themselves and their leisure better. There are some men who help at home but most men don't. Women are not going to stand this for ever. They will soon reach a point where they can't take any more and then they are going to fight for a change.'

'What do you think is best for women: to fight personal battles or to fight through their own organisations?'

'I believe that personal struggle is crucial as well as struggle through women's organisations. Women should fight for their rights and our women's organisations should be more serious about women's struggle for liberation and equality. There are women in the Women's Union who are very serious about all this but they are still a minority. The first obligation of the Women's Union is to attract young, intelligent and enthusiastic women who are keen to fight for women's rights. I used to be a member of the union but I left because I could not do anything worthwhile. What we need is a gradual invasion of the organisation by young, ideologically mature and feminist women who are willing to work persistently, because personal struggle is not really enough.'

'How do you compare the position of the Syrian woman with that of the European woman?'

'I believe the European woman is not quite happy, either; she must also be exhausted for similar reasons as outlined above. But she has got more social rights than we have. Personally, I would like to see the Syrian woman treading her own path rather than following in the European woman's footsteps. I would like to keep the positive aspects of our family relationships; it is very nice to have an intimate family and I think it must be painful to lose this security which the European family has mostly lost. It must be hard for the individual to survive without the support and backing of a family. There are good things in our culture which we should try hard to keep. We are capable of finding our own way without imitating the European woman in everything and I believe we have already started doing that, and quite successfully, too.

'Women should be able to reach complete independence; they should reach the job and the station they want without being thwarted because of their sex.'

I was still feeling elated by the intimate and sisterly discussion which I just had with Abla when I found myself at the bus stop trying to catch a bus back home. My thoughts were suddenly distracted by the quite audible conversation of two women who were standing near me.

'It has been a long time since we saw you last,' the first woman said to her friend almost reproachfully.

'What can I do?' answered the second, 'I never know the sunrise from the sunset. I have six children and none of them lifts a finger in the house except my eldest daughter who, like myself, is already exhausted.'

'You still haven't found *Ibn Halal* (a good, respectable man) for her?' the first woman enquired in a concerned tone. 'She is no longer young, you know, she must be 25 years old already, I guess, mustn't she?'

'Yes,' the second woman admitted, and then added in a rising tone, 'but I'm not in a hurry to marry her off; we are not incapable of feeding her and providing for her, so why should I worry?'

I lifted my head, turning it towards the first woman as politely and unobtrusively as I possibly could. She was a middle-aged woman in her late forties. Her strong and somehow attractive expression told of an experienced and self-confident character. Her small, dark eyes were radiant with a challenging look which was mellowed by the sincere concern it showed for her friend.

'People don't marry their daughters off because they can't feed them,' she stated in answer to her friend's argument. 'Marriage is every girl's right and ambition.'

'Even so,' the second woman naïvely resumed her argument, 'I never put my girls in auctions. All the neighbourhood knows that my daughters are good cooks, excellent housekeepers and very polite. But these silly young men of today no longer like this type of girl; rather, they go after loose girls – even if they don't know how to fry an egg. I will not marry my daughter to anyone who is unworthy of her.'

'Don't be stupid,' the other interrupted her hurriedly. 'Fathers and mothers don't live for ever. You are going to die one day, and then what will happen to your daughter? She will either have to stay as a servant in her brother's house or live in penury and shame. Can she live on her own and have her own place like a man? Of course not. This is why you have to act responsibly and marry her to the first decent chap who comes along to ask for her hand.'

I was getting on the bus when these last few words reached my ears. Unfortunately, the two women seemed to have been waiting for a different bus. I looked at them from the bus window, feeling like someone who has just been looking at a very telling 'No comment' cartoon.

In 1941, Makboula Shalaq made history by being the first Syrian woman university student. She graduated from the law department in 1945, the year of Syria's independence from France. Her published short-story collections include *The Bird's Wedding*, *The Adventures of a Hen* and *Stories from my Country*, as well as various articles and poems published in Arab literary magazines. When I met her she was working on a novel based on the social history of Syrian women from 1930 until the present day.

At the age of 64 she still felt passionately about the issues around which her whole life and work were centred, mainly women's rights and emancipation. Although a lawyer by training, she was evidently more interested in literature and the literary history of her country. She spoke to me as follows:

'When I was born in 1921 the Syrian people were tasting the bitter humiliation of yet another foreign occupation. Our young and inexperienced army was defeated by one of the victorious European armies of the First World War, the French army, and our first ever defence minister was murdered by the invading army. Our first independent State in modern history collapsed under the brutality of imperial France. A beautiful dream, relished for centuries, was shattered by what the freedom-loving Syrian people used to consider to be the bastion of liberty. In a new book which I am currently writing I shall record the social history of Syrian women of that period. Our first national liberation movement lasted three years, 1925 to 1928, when it was finally crushed by a combination of a heavily armed modern French army and a savage retaliation policy which our society had never experienced before, even under the brutal, mediaeval Ottoman army. The French used to bury Syrian prisoners alive in a public show to frighten the rest of the population. Women fighters were something quite new in those days but there were a few women martyrs who are regarded as national heroines. That really was the first serious crack in the high wall of the traditional view of women's role in society. I don't remember a great many details about those days of national awareness, but I was quite well informed about them as I was brought up in a house which prided itself on its involvement with the national resistance against that foreign occupation army. When I came of age I became closely involved with the passive civil resistance which was to continue during all the years of French occupation. Henceforth our streets were to witness something remarkably novel: women demonstrators and women marchers on equal footing with their male fellow citizens.

'My father, a judge, and well educated himself, sent us all off to school. At school the teachers were French missionaries, and the women teachers in particular used to treat us with contempt. They tried really hard to make us feel inferior, but the more they insulted our national and private pride the more determined we were to continue our education and prove to them that we were equally good. I once wrote a poem in French and handed it to my French teacher asking for her opinion. She returned it to me, saying in her colonial, obdurate manner: "First go and learn dictation before trying your hand at poetry."

'To add a new dimension to the inherited social prejudice French soldiers used to pester us on the streets, and this was so degrading to women that we became reluctant to go out of the house. Once a friend of mine went out and was followed by a French policeman. French police used to call any Syrian woman they saw on the street by the Arabic name "Fatima". This friend of mine was, of course, veiled, and the French policeman followed her calling, "Fatima, Fatima". He chased her from one street to the next until he was whacked, and finally when she arrived on her own doorstep she turned to him and lifted the veil off her face. He looked at her and apparently found her face no match for his Parisian taste because he exclaimed: "Oh God! To hell with you, Fatima," and turned away.

Damascus women participated in the revolution of 1925 by passing arms and weapons to the fighters. In Damascus the main revolutionary operations used to take place in Al Ghota. Once a friend of mine was informed that her brother and son (later to be killed in action by the French) in Al Ghota needed weapons. To reach them she had to cross a checkpoint on a bridge where men as well as women were being searched. A Frenchman would search the men thoroughly and a French woman did the same for women. She wrapped the arms round her newborn baby and managed to carry them together, acting like an innocent, terribly anxious mother. Women found ingenious ways to pass through the strictest checkpoints and carry ammunition and arms from one part of the town to another. When the revolution was savagely aborted in 1928 and our people decided on a passive resistance campaign Syrian women became even more active and participated heavily in demonstrations.

'Women from women's societies[2] started giving very mild speeches almost in support of the colonial government. Suddenly a woman called Thorea Hafez, a member of our society, got up and said: "My dead father visited me in a dream last night. He said to me: 'Oh my daughter, the people who killed me have come back to steal a piece of my country. Don't let them: fight them with whatever means you have. Awake women, awake. Resist the enemy and abort their plans to tear our country to pieces.' Come on women! Let us try to do something; let us try to be heard; let us go on demonstrations." She went to the door and asked women to move and go out to demonstrate and to hand the prime minister a protest letter in his office. Moved by her daring call these dignified, bourgeois women in their jewels, furs and terribly smart clothes went out two by two and walked in a peaceful demonstration to the prime minister's office. The streets were suddenly flooded with men who were understandably curious to see this unique demonstration. They pointed at us and whispered to each other, saying: "This is the wife of so and so and that is the daughter of so and so," etc. When we reached our destination we handed a letter of protest to the prime minister and sent a telegram to the same effect to the League of Nations, the predecessor of the United Nations. The women were all veiled, but some of them had on very thin veils which matched their clothes and defeated their ostensible purpose by making them look all the more attractive. The veil, in fact, continued to get thinner and thinner until a very few women lifted it off their faces completely; but that did not happen until about 1940.

'During the French occupation there was no university at all in Syria. We only had a medical and a law college, both of which had no women students at all. In 1939, a Syrian woman registered in the law college but only attended for four days and then left. Two years after that I registered in the law college and was actually the first Syrian woman to graduate from Damascus University. Needless to say, I had a hard time at the college but I was determined not to give in. Students and teachers (all male, of course) were harassing me, pestering me all the time and hoping to succeed in forcing me to leave. They particularly hated me because I took the veil off before going to university. One lecturer actually asked me to put the veil on during his lectures and to choose whether or not to take it off afterwards. I said I wouldn't be that hypocritical; I had taken the veil off because I didn't believe in it and I was not going to put it on again against my convictions. At that time the women in Damascus who went out without the veil could be counted on the fingers of one hand. All teachers were showing their vehement disapproval of my presence by failing me in oral exams, but I used to pass the written exams without any problem. My colleagues also tried their best to make me feel odd, but I had the strong support of my family.

'Four years later, in 1945, I graduated with a law degree. Once I was a graduate, however, there was no place which wanted to employ me. Wherever I went I was told there was no job for a law degree graduate. I couldn't even get a teaching job because there was nothing in the curriculum relating to law. Finally I met the President of Syria, Mr Shekri Al Kouatli, who advised me to go into teaching because it was a respectable profession for a woman. He rang the Ministry of Education and they assigned me to a particular school. When I received my first salary I discovered that I was employed on the basis of my secondary school certificate without my law degree being taken into account.

'I wonder whether our men nowadays don't think the same way,' Makboula Shalaq continued. 'What men say publicly in their lectures and meetings in connection with women's liberation is in most cases quite different from what they actually practise at home with their sisters or wives. A Syrian author whose writings I came to admire a lot once said to me he wouldn't marry an educated woman; he would marry a 14-year-old girl who served him, looked after him properly and didn't dare discuss things with him. And he did just that. I once asked him how he talked or communicated with her. He answered: ''I spend ten hours a day reading and writing and enjoy a silly chat with her for an hour or two.''

'On the whole, however, women's situation now is totally different from the way it was then. Women now go to school, to university and get the job they are qualified for. What women in Syria have achieved in the last 40 years is indeed incredible. We achieved independence in 1945; in 1946 the university opened its colleges to men and women equally. Women immediately jumped at this golden opportunity and registered in all colleges. Since then, women have time and again proved themselves to be more intelligent than men, and in effect men have had to change their traditional outlook on women. Now, Syrian women are not only doctors, engineers and MPs but also parachutists, army trainees and officers. I don't think we should be complacent, however; we should still fight for the further betterment of our position in society, yet I don't find room for complaint. For we have really come quite a long way since my early days and we are still travelling.'

'Do you think that women's economic independence was accompanied by their social independence and as a result they are happier now?'

'No, I don't think they are happier because they are exhausted. They are working a double day. They go out to work to contribute to the family budget, but at the same time they have to cook, clean, wash and look after their husbands and children. I think they are suffering from a new division of labour. They go out to work to be somebody but no allowances have been made for them in the areas of traditional work. To give you just one example: there is a world of difference between the way my grandmother lived and the way I live, but I still cook the same kinds of food she used to cook. Although a dramatic change has happened to our lives we haven't developed our diet a single step; we haven't developed our cuisine. Damascene cooking is designed for leisurely housewives who spend long hours preparing the most complicated meals to impress and please the family's bread winner. All our dishes are so complicated and so time consuming they have become a heavy burden on the working mother. One of the first things that the working woman needs is to free herself from this old slavery by breaking into a simple, easy kind of cookery. We also need good, efficient and cheap restaurants where the working mother can meet her husband and children to have their main daily meal and where she can relax and enjoy her food instead of rushing home to put the potatoes or the meat on. We should also develop our taste, particularly men's taste, in designing and furnishing houses. We should use easy-care furniture which doesn't take hours to dust and clean. I resent spending so many precious hours a day dusting chairs and shelves and wiping floors. This summer I had many relatives coming to stay with us and, as you know, on such occasions you have to cook all the very best food you can. I had to abandon my desk for about two months to do what I neither believe in nor enjoy. A problem which most creative women have to face is that they are hardly, if ever, taken seriously. Even if you are a Tolstoy working on your master-piece you are not excused from the social duty of cooking *kebab* and *doulma* for your guests, whereas anything, even writing a letter, will excuse a man from a social duty.

'To me this means that women are still regarded first and foremost as cooks and cleaners and only secondarily as creative workers. Hence we have to re-educate men about women and explain their role and rights so that they start to share the housework and treat us as equals. We are partly to blame, too. As women we don't support each other; we don't vote exclusively for a woman MP and we don't trust a woman doctor; we would still rather trust a male doctor. We spend our best years in the kitchen and yet when we have an important feast we hire a man rather than a woman chef. We have to believe in our sex before we expect others to believe in us. I think once we achieve this women will start to enjoy their jobs and their homes a lot more than they do now and will certainly be much more creative. What the government will have to spend on restaurants, nurseries and other social services will be made up for by the increase in productivity which will certainly jump dramatically, especially when we remember that women constitute half the working population in the country.

'The nub of the problem lies in the fact that a man tries to subject a woman to his will because he is afraid of her, of her intelligence and her ability which might be more than he can take. Otherwise how can you understand an intelligent, creative man choosing to marry a woman who is practically a servant and breeder instead of searching for a true companion? In our society I have noticed that once the man believes that his wife is a real companion he starts to fear that she will soon be superior. Many women friends of mine – both married and unmarried – complain about the lack of any real intellectual stimulus from their male companions. I am not saying that all women are better than all men; what I am saying is that women have the potential to develop and to be more inventive and creative than men. But we need to give ourselves a helping hand.

'I think you have to see Thorea Hafez,' Makboula Shalaq concluded. 'To me she is a heroine. She is a great fighter for women and she lived through all the bitter-sweet battles for equal rights and emancipation.'

In the taxi, on our way to meet Thorea, Makboula recited her latest poem to me which was about the startling heroism of the Southern Lebanese women. I was attentive, listening with admiration to this interesting poem, when I saw Makboula's expression change and become very serious. She suddenly made an effort to meet the driver's eye in the mirror and said to him: 'Would you please turn that radio down a bit.' He lowered it very slightly, which evidently did not please her. 'Could you lower it a little more, or better still turn it off, please, because we want to hear each other speak.' As soon as she got out of the taxi, she turned to me, saying, 'I felt like using stronger terms with him, but I didn't want to be rude in front of you. The moment I started reciting my poem to you he put the radio up so that he couldn't hear us. He perhaps found it absurd that two women in the back of *his* taxi should talk about poetry and literature rather than about cooking and cleaning. These men make me so angry. Once they see a woman's ability surpasses theirs they feel embarrassed, confused or even threatened. You didn't see his face in the mirror. I did. He was shocked. He just wanted us to go away, to vanish somehow.

For how could we, women, talk about something which he, a man, does not understand?'

The door opened to an elderly but active woman who was still in her nightdress. Thorea Hafez looked quite embarrassed and addressed herself to Makboula saying, 'Oh dear, I forgot all about the appointment. You should have rung again to remind me. You know I tend to forget a lot nowadays.'

'Don't be fussy,' Makboula said jokingly, 'Bouthaina is like my daughter. You may go and get changed now; it is quite all right.'

'Please do,' I said. Makboula then invited me into a small room furnished with old-fashioned furniture – embroidered curtains and carved wooden chairs. It had a cold air about it which unused places usually have. But the lovely Arabic coffee which was instantly served, the telephone ringing and the constant hiss of passing cars took away the cold feel and breathed life into the place.

A high-spirited atmosphere animated the room as soon as Thorea, completely unassuming and spontaneous as she was, entered, already talking to Makboula as if she was resuming a conversation which she had been forced to leave only half finished. 'You know, Makboula, we seem to be living again in the times of *Yaeish* [long live] so and so and *Yaskot* [down with] so and so.' While handing me another cup of that lovely coffee she looked me in the eyes saying, 'There is a story to this *Yaeish* and *Yaskot* and I am going to tell it to you straight away.

'During the revolution a male friend of mine came to me and said, "We want you to go out on a women's demonstration in support of our comrades who were exiled by the French enemy to Erwad Island." Men couldn't go out on a demonstration then, because we had the emergency law according to which any public gathering which exceeded three men was liable to arrest. I said, "But what excuse can we find for going on a demonstration?"

' "I don't know," he answered. "You have to find one." About four days later the French government put the price of bread up by one *kierish* (half a penny) per kilo. I thought, great, this is a good reason to start action against the government. I called my sister-in-law, her two sisters and two of my neighbours and said: "We are going to go out on a demonstration."

'They said: "What is that? What are we supposed to do?" I said: "When I say *Yaeish* so and so you all answer in one voice *Yaeish*,

Yaeish, and when I say *Yaskot* so and so, you all repeat *Wili, yaskot* [Oh, down with] . . . ''

'On the day we were about seven women whom I led to the market-place near Al Mirji (the central square in Damascus) shouting *"Yaeish"* and *"Yaskot"*. In the marketplace I stood on an over-turned, empty wooden container and started addressing people around me as well as passers-by thus: "Why are you still asleep while the French enemy is trampling on us every day, putting the price of bread up so that we starve to death? How are the poor going to feed their children? The French enemy has arrested our best citizens and is torturing them in their prisons. Awake, awake. Fight for your rights, for your pride, for your dignity and future. *Yaskot* the French enemy. *Yaeish* our sincere and honourable fighters who are locked away in their prisons.'' I was talking for about 20 minutes, during which time over a hundred women joined us. So I went down to lead a proper demonstration in the direction of the government building. At the city centre I saw the car of the Syrian High Commissioner and immed-iately ordered the demonstrators to block his way and force him to stop. He got out of his car and asked what the trouble was. I told him to be ashamed of himself; he served the French enemy against his own countrymen and people. He had even agreed to the rise in the price of bread so that the poor and needy in his country would starve. He said we should go back home and there would be no rise in the price of bread. He went home and we carried on.

'Near the government building a policeman came up to me, held my hands up (I was wearing white gloves), and said in a very loud voice: "Look at this prostitute. Do you think she is likely to starve? This rich bitch?'' My sister-in-law ran to him and started hitting him and a few other women hurriedly carried me across the demonstrators to a nearby, prearranged hiding place. The police tried very hard to find me but they couldn't. Next day the government withdrew its deci-sion to put up the price of bread and in a few days' time it released the prisoners who were the prime reason for our demonstration. So you see it is useful sometimes to shout *Yaeish* and *Yaskot*.

'If you are looking for a more organised life story I shall try for your sake, although I don't like organised stories and I don't think I can manage one. I am proud to say that I am the daughter of Amin Lotfi Al Hafez who was hanged by the Turkish High Commissioner in Beirut in 1916 for his political activities in connection with Syria's independence from Turkey. He was one of the first group of martyrs which this country provided in the first half of this century. Two years after my father's death my mother got married to Mr Mustafa Al Shihabi, whose brother had been hanged with my father. I was brought up to love my Arab people and a longing to see an independent Syria was running in my blood. In 1928 I went out on my first women's demonstration demanding free elections, although at that time we were still under French occupation.

'I seem to have a voice which invites a good response from the crowd. So from all sides around Al Mirji people started flooding the place, primarily because a woman was giving a speech – which was unheard of then. I was too young to comprehend the complexities of politics. But I remember shopkeepers showering us with perfumes and sweets as a sign of support and respect. Suddenly a voice sounded in the distance: "Disperse! They are going to shoot you!" The voice was that of our candidate, Fawzi Al Ghazi, for whom we were campaigning in the election. It turned out that the French were sending a military force to attack our women; their reputation had already been established as merciless aggressors. Some of us went into hiding in the nearby houses and others just managed to get away.

'After that first demonstration of 1928 I started to be active in my school. I used to write and challenge the French directors and their policies. The French enemy tried to eliminate our day of martyrs from the school calendar because it was an occasion when conferences and demonstrations were held to discuss national issues, so we used to celebrate it in our society, Montada Sukeina Al Adabi [a literary women's society established by Thorea Hafez].

'I had an aim in life. I clung to it, fought for it, and sure enough I reached it. My aim was to see women in my country free and equal citizens, and here they are both free and equal. We used to fight for nurseries for children; now every factory, every school and every job centre has a nursery. We used to ask for women's right to go out to work, for equal pay and equal opportunity. Women have got all that now. It is true that things happened only very gradually but at least they did happen. First women won the right to vote but not to stand as candidates, and there was another condition that only women who completed their primary education could vote. This condition didn't apply to male voters. We put forward conditions in support of candidates. We announced that we wouldn't vote for candidates who were puppets of a foreign power and we wouldn't elect anyone who didn't support women's rights. Our list, I mean the list of candidates, even conservative ones, had to publicly state that they were not against women's emancipation. Saying things was not enough; we used to ask them to put their statements in writing and sign them so that when they became MPs they couldn't support any anti-women legislation.

'It is a truism to say that every time the French government wanted to do something nasty to our country and people it incited the men of religion with ill feelings towards women, so that Al Shieokh (Muslim religious leaders) would go out on demonstrations against women and would throw eggs, tomatoes and even acid on female passers-by. The excuses they fabricated for such acts were ludicrous. Sometimes they would attack a woman because she had had her hair cut, or because she was wearing light socks instead of black or blue ones, or because she had been to the cinema.

'In 1943, I was getting fed up with both Al Shieokh and the hypocrisy of wearing the veil. So I arranged a demonstration of about a hundred women and led them to Al Mirji in order to take off the veil, both officially and publicly. I stood there and gave a speech in which I averred that the veil we wore was never mentioned in God's holy book or by the Prophet Mohammed. At the same time, there have always been renowned women public figures: poets, novelists, fighters and national heroines, and I cited many names which proved my statement such as Khola Bent Al Azwar, Ghazali Al Harroria, etc. So as our religion doesn't ask us to veil ourselves and expects us to show our faces and be men's equals we now take the veil off. At once, all the hundred women lifted their veils. University students and young people cheered us and lent us their wholehearted support, while the men of religion immediately set about punitive action against us. They tried to burn my house; they even considered and planned killing me, but there were many young men who volunteered to guard my house for quite a long time. Even so, these "religious men" passing me on their bicycles or in their cars used to throw eggs, tomatoes or even stones at me. Yet, the process which we started in that demonstration was irreversible and more women were taking the veil off by the day.'

'Did women's lot change dramatically after Syria's independence from France in 1945?'

'No. Immediately after independence things were left where they were and only very gradually began to change. For example, we didn't have a woman MP until 1958, the date of our union with Egypt. And, even then, women MPs were appointed to their jobs; they were not necessarily the women who got the largest number of votes. I, for example, got twice as many votes as anybody else and yet I was not nominated an MP because, as the prime minister at the time put it, my voice was too loud! How right he was! My voice has always been loud, especially in condemning wrong things. I am so glad that I always spoke my mind out loudly, and that nothing on earth was able to shut me up.

'I love our president Hafez Assad and believe that we, as women, are very lucky to have him. For the first time ever he has given Syrian women a great chance to be really equal citizens. We now have a woman minister and thirteen women MPs. Our universities and polytechnics are full of women. We have five universities instead of just one as previously, a fact that has made all citizens in the country feel equal instead of looking with envy at the Damascenes. Although I don't get out a lot I feel from the group of people I live with that everyone genuinely believes that women are equal to men and all the men I know act and behave accordingly. There are, of course, some men who still believe that women are inferior to men, but those must surely be in the minority. I don't believe there is any discrimination against women in Syria. We have equal pay, equal opportunities and equal rights in every field. Look at these women parachutists, army officers, lawyers, doctors and engineers. Women are everywhere they would like to be. I never dreamt I would live long enough to see all this.'

'So you don't believe Syrian women have to fight any more battles?'

'They only have to fight men's reactionary and torpid mentality through work, as the government actively fought religious sectarianism and narrow regionalism. The Women's Union has adopted and propagated policies which have helped women to prove themselves and establish their values on a national level. Personal initiative is also important. We have to have full confidence in our ways of doing things, that is of doing things in the female way, and in the female way of thinking. As soon as we believe in ourselves people will start believing in us. Once I gave a lecture about superstition and cited evidence from the Koran and the teachings of the Prophet Mohammed against it. An enlightened Shiekh rang me up and thanked me for this wonderful lecture, asking for more of the same. I told him that instead of thanking me he and his colleagues should give similar lectures in the mosques. After two days he phoned me, asking me to listen to the Friday sermon, broadcast on the radio. I never used to listen to the Friday sermons, but on that Friday I did and heard a wonderful sermon against black magic and superstition. My husband and I couldn't stop the tears running down our cheeks because we were so touched by what was said. So you see, if we have enough courage to speak our minds men may very well learn from us and follow our example.'

'Do you believe that there are no limits to women's development and progress?'

'Only the limits stated in our religion which we can't go beyond. I have a friend who is so liberal with his wife that she bosses him around all the time. Yet he doesn't allow her to receive a strange man in his absence. Although they no longer make love – they are too old for that, he argues – it is against his religion to allow a strange man into his house when he is not there. This is what his religion dictates; the prophet Mohammed is supposed to have said that whenever a man and a woman are left alone Satan will surely be a third person present.'

That startled me. 'This is what a Shiekh might say,' I addressed her a bit sharply, 'but not a fighter, liberator and revolutionary like yourself. She should know that a woman may work, fight and meet men without being seduced by them.'

Thorea replied: 'A woman has to put up with a lot of things. It is an inescapable fact that however liberated and enlightened men may become they will always be interested in women sexually. Even in the West a woman doesn't receive a man in her husband's absence.'

'I don't think this is true,' I replied. 'I lived in Britain for quite a few years and saw women receiving male visitors whether or not their husbands were there.'

'In Britain,' Thorea almost shouted at me this time, 'the Anglican church has accepted homosexual relationships; it is inconceivable that we could accept this in Syria. There is no reason why we should do what the European woman does. We are quite different from her in religion, beliefs and traditions.'

There was no way I could have defended the right of homosexuals to have the relationships they wanted. Most of my interviewees consider homosexuality to be the ultimate crime, an inexcusable evil for which no punishment is severe enough. Yet a homosexual English friend of mine who visited Damascus in 1980 said to me that homosexuality was more rife in Damascus than in London. Deeming it mad to take exception to what Thorea said on this topic I picked up another point on which I disagreed with her.

'May I say,' I started quite calmly in an effort to avoid any heated argument which might erupt, 'that you seem to me to be too complacent about the position of Syrian women. They are not as happy or as fulfilled as you wish to imagine. I had the chance to listen to some disconcerting accounts of their agonising experiences. Quite a few women confided that they wouldn't stay with their husbands for the rest of their lives if they could only get divorces and keep their children. They also stay with their husbands because, when they are divorced, women hardly, if ever, get an allowance from their husbands. Many of these women are hardly living but just putting up with life – and a nasty one at that – for the sake of their children.'

'Why don't they divorce?' Thorea asked, baffled by what she had heard. 'Our law gives a woman the right to divorce if she has decided to reserve that right and has had it written on her marriage certificate.'

'But 99 per cent of women in our country don't know about this law. I certainly didn't know about it when I got married in 1981.'

'Well, you have to tell them in schools, universities and public lectures,' she added. 'I think our law is fair to women. It allows them to nurse their children until the girls are nine and the boys are seven years old. At this age children are very difficult to manage and a man might be more capable of handling them than a woman.'

About half way through our conversation a friend of Thorea who was a lawyer came in and sat listening very quietly, although I made explicit efforts to invite her to participate in the conversation. Now that we were talking about a topic with which she was familiar she decided to make one or two qualifying statements. She started to talk in a very gentle voice which was only just audible.

'A major problem for women is that men are allowed to travel abroad for long periods without securing a financial livelihood for their wives and children. Some of them go to Europe, get married to European women, and never come back at all. In Lebanon the wife has the right to hold her husband's passport until he has made definite arrangements to support her and her children during the time of his absence. We need to issue and implement such a law in Syria. Another legal area in which women are not treated fairly is the area of Punitive Law. In the case of adultery, for example, the woman is punished, sometimes with death, while the man is left unscathed. The Koran says that a man and a woman who commit adultery should be whipped 70 times in public. What usually happens in all Arab countries is that the woman is killed without even knowing who her partner was. The only law in Syria that is biased against women is the Punitive Law, and the Women's Union is trying its best now to change it. If *Al Shieokh* would understand the Koran properly and apply it correctly we would have no problem whatsoever.'

'I think you're right,' I replied. Although there are some statements in the Koran which claim that women are not to be considered absolute equals to men, their actual position in the Koranic and Islamic text is in fact much better than the situation for women prevailing in most Arab countries. All Arab countries are ostensibly governed by *Sharia* (Islamic law), but all laws relating to women are male chauvinist oriented versions of Islamic texts. However, to move on to my next question.

'What do you think of the Muslim Brotherhood as far as women are concerned?' I asked Thorea Hafez.

'The Muslim Brotherhood is a reactionary political movement, not a religious movement. In fact it is against Islam. It tried to do what the French occupation failed to do. During the French occupation the reactionaries were against women who had their hair cut, put a light veil on, or even wore pale socks. They wanted women to wear *Al Izar* (a very strict veil). There are many Arab women who still wear *Al Izar*. In brief, the Muslim Brotherhood planned to deprive women of all the characteristics which make them thinking human beings and to drive them into becoming unthinking dolls and servants.

'Neither the Muslim Brotherhood nor any power on earth, however, can deprive women of something they themselves don't want to be deprived of. Give me two women who believe in an idea; the two will in no time become four and the four eight and the eight a hundred.'

As if inspired by Thorea Hafez's enthusiastic account of an unusual past, Makboula, in the back seat of the taxi on our way home, started to recall and briefly relate to me, in a voice that betrayed a deeply buried agony, the dreams she had once dared to entertain and the bitter reality that had dashed them, seemingly only for a while.

'Immediately after my graduation everyone was eager to know what I planned to do now that I had fought a fierce battle and won. But having got married and having had children almost straight away I found it impossible to be both a successful professional woman and have a peaceful family life. When things became unbearable I decided to shelve my plans for a career and concentrate on bringing up my children for a while. The longer I stayed at home, however, the more difficult it seemed to me to go out and catch up. My time at home, though, was not totally wasted. I was reading extensively and developed literary interests. I started writing and publishing poetry, short stories and critical essays. Yet I was all the time aware that my mind was working at ten per cent capacity, which was a very painful and frustrating feeling at times. Years passed by in a huge, turbulent sea where life is experienced rather than observed. I read, wrote, published and fought most feminist battles, but didn't have that striking career which at one time I had glimpsed through the eyes of my imagination. Still, I am optimistic. Now that my children are old enough to look after themselves I can sit for eight hours a day behind a desk. This is a new life for me, though it has come at the late age of 64. I am in a great rush because I want to make up for the long lost years before it is too late.'

A year hence, Makboula was giving public lectures, poetry readings and participating in almost every cultural activity that took place in Damascus. I had the good fortune to attend quite a few of her short-story and poetry readings; the last time I saw her was after a short-story reading by another Syrian writer, Fadel Al Sebaai. I walked past her on the stairs as we were going out. With her small, full and dynamic figure, she quickly embraced me, gave me a nice hug and a kiss on the cheek.

'Come to the short-story reading I am giving here in four weeks' time,' she said. 'Excuse me now. I have to rush to see the poet Hind Haroun . . . she has come all the way from Latakia to attend this meeting.'

Makboula Shalaq bade me good night and ran up towards the door. That was the last time I saw her. Two weeks after this I was shocked to read her obituary in our national newspaper; she had died after a very brief and simple illness. No wonder she had been in such a rush for the last year or so, as if she had known there was no time left and was doing her best to catch up. The uncompleted novel and the unwritten poetry and stories must all remain unwritten. How true and how perceptive Tillie Olsen's *Silences* is of women's lives and experiences. Women are either forced to live and die in total silence, or they find a way to say a few scattered things about what they could and would love to say at length. They keep waiting for the big opportunity, the big chance, to say what they want to say and write what they want to write. Such a chance might still be looming on the horizon when death kidnaps its victim and leaves no trace of many potentially creative and talented minds.

Only a year or two ago I read in the weekly *Guardian* that Sweden and Japan had their first women ministers. Although an event of historical value for some people, here in the Middle East it is regarded with a tinge of irony: what have these women been up to until now in such advanced countries? Syria has had a woman minister since the early 1970s and 13 women MPs. So also is the case in Egypt, Iraq, Tunisia and Algeria. In fact, Egypt and Iraq had their first women ministers as early as the late 1950s. Furthermore, the law of equal pay has been enforced here since the early 1970s, whereas according to a recent report a woman's wage in Britain is only 64 per cent of that of her male counterpart. It is ironic that in a country in which a woman's right to choose a husband is not yet generally acknowledged she should enjoy absolute economic equality and a leading political position, whereas in Europe, where personal freedom triumphs, we find women's political and economic opportunities lagging far behind those of Syria.

Wafa Sunien, whom I came to know as a postgraduate student at Damascus University and who is, like myself, the mother of two girls, is a member of the executive bureau of the Syrian National Students' Union and an MP. Though quite young for the posts she holds, she has a reputation not only for efficiency but also for excellence in all that she does. She is a quiet, low-key but distinctly intelligent speaker. The intermittent words she utters might well tempt members of her audience to try to find words for her, but when she comes out with fresh, short and concise sentences you are always glad not to have done this, for her words are carefully and appropriately chosen and are always to the point. She is impressive. Like all true feminists she always has time for sisters who like to see her, talk to her or even seek her advice. She spoke to me for some time.

'I am from a conservative borough in Latakia (a Syrian port city on the Mediterranean coast) where all the good old habits are held in high esteem. Our borough, the Siliabi, was known all over the country for its rigid conservatism. My father, a barber, and my mother, a dressmaker, had twelve children, nine girls and three boys. I was their second child, preceded only by my eldest brother. At that time it was acceptable for rich women to acquire their education wherever they liked, but no such right was granted to poor and working-class women – except in very special circumstances when the parents were ready to challenge bad habits and deeply entrenched taboos. I was lucky to have parents who encouraged me to continue my education, despite all the social and financial difficulties. Members of my father's extended family, however, stood firmly against my education, and my own classmates, children from poor families who got used to being classified as unintelligent and inevitably early school leavers, found it funny that I should be determined to continue my education. But my mother lent me her wholehearted support. Social pressure and family problems which aimed to thwart me and eventually hinder my progress were an incentive for me not to falter in my quest for a better educational standard. Because of the suffocating atmosphere which tried to smother everything new or progressive I was desperate to find a window on the world. So at 15 I enrolled with the Youth Union and Students' Union. It was in the Youth Union that my political awareness was formed. Our male colleagues were extremely well behaved and self-disciplined; they never said hello to us. They were terribly concerned that everyone should have a positive opinion of this new generation of women which challenged old habits and outworn traditions. In retrospect I can see this was very important.

'As women we were almost too conscious of our presence in the public eye and every step we took, every word we uttered had to be carefully measured and weighed in advance. Thus, in a very short time we started gaining people's respect, admiration and, occasionally, envy. There was a price to pay, of course. We had to look more reserved in our clothes and appearance than ordinary women. Two years hence I became a member of the Baath party, although it was quite unusual for women to become party members. Although my political affiliations and my intellectual ambitions were unorthodox, my appearance and the way I dressed remained well in line with acceptable traditions.

'My grades qualified me to register in an engineering college but my father wouldn't agree to this because according to him women could be either nurses or teachers but not engineers. So I had to compromise and enrol in the mathematics department, which still sounded quite radical to neighbours, friends and acquaintances. This was because most Arab films with which our people were familiar presented the university in a very bad light. The university was shown to be a storehouse for social problems, immoral relations and misdirected Westernised habits. On the other hand, people had a mistaken belief that to go to university was very expensive and that only the very rich could afford it. They were amazed to find out that it hardly costs anything at all to attend.

'Although there were four hundred men and only one woman (me) in my college unit, I was undaunted. I played my role the best I could and was one of the most active members in my college. Other women were encouraged by my example to become unionist and party members which pleased me immensely. Then I became the college committee's secretary, an experience which gave my self-confidence a boost and reflected positively on the image of women at the university. I was subsequently elected as the deputy head of the Students' Union Administrative Bureau and was the first woman to be in this high executive position for about ten years. Despite the pressures of study and work I was always there and got letters of acknowledgment and thanks for my good performance.

'In the late 1970s I stood bravely against the Muslim Brothers and spoke loudly against their crimes. Because of its old-fashioned design and winding alleyways, our borough became an ideal hideout for them. They could jump from one roof to another and cross into a different street within minutes, which made it quite easy for them to outwit the authorities. Most of my colleagues despaired and left the borough, but I stayed on for two whole months trying to find ways and means of discovering them. I depended on my very young brothers and sisters to inform me about their movements, so the Muslim Brothers had no doubt that everyone was watching them. Once a complete plan of their movements had been perfected I gave orders to attack their centre, and I seem to have chosen the right moment. We arrested most of them but the very few who fled tried to avenge themselves by blowing up my father's shop. Fortunately my father had just gone out to buy some cigarettes thus very narrowly escaping instant death.

'After the Muslim Brotherhood incidents we had our election. In this election the president urged women seriously to participate in the executive bureau in Damascus. I was the only woman who had spent a whole elective session in a high executive post in the Union. So, I suppose I was an obvious choice for the executive bureau in Damascus. That was in 1980 and our next general election was to be held in two months' time.

'Traditionally, the membership of parliament had been confined to two rich families in our borough but since President Assad's takeover in 1970 he has tried his utmost to encourage women and working-class people to enter the political arena and people were then taken on merit rather than because of their family's name. People were moved and excited when they found I had enrolled as candidate, because I was the first woman and the first working-class person to dare to do so. They were excited to know that the same possibility was open to their own children. Thus, men and women, young and old, came out to vote for me. The incredible support I got surpassed anything I dared even imagine. I won the seat with an overwhelming majority. On that day I was convinced that our people have no prejudice against women; they just need an example, an encouragement, someone to tell them not to be afraid to be what they are and to speak out their minds. The ground is fertile, I thought, to achieve true equality between men and women. I still think so and I believe we are making fast steps in that direction.'

'As you are working mostly with men, do you feel that your colleagues treat you as a female or as a job-mate?'

'Generally speaking, our men have treated women as sex objects since they were born; if the woman is serious and strong they describe her as manly. At the beginning I found things extremely hard and seriously considered leaving the job. A friend of mine only stayed for two months because she couldn't stand an atmosphere which was so overwhelmingly male. After all these years, however, I think the solution is simple. We have to avoid trying to excite men by the way we talk, walk or dress. When you dress simply and talk seriously with your colleagues they can't help but take you seriously. If, however, you come to work wearing the latest fashions, the latest hairstyle and putting a mask of colours on your face, you can't blame your colleagues for treating you as a "female" because this is what you are asking for.

'What I believe is basically wrong with the movement for women's emancipation in Syria is that the Women's Union is not managing to get any message across to women in general. Representatives from the Women's Union go to far-off villages to talk about the constitution of the Union or about sewing. What have women who work in the field all day got to do with the constitution or with sewing? They all take their dresses to a dressmaker, and most of them don't have any time to try them on before they are finished. We need to address women in the language they understand. The Women's Union does everything but that. We have to speak to women about issues which concern them most; otherwise they won't listen. We have to get them interested and involved if we want to change them. Therefore our starting point should be the kind of life women live rather than the theory we hold. The Women's Union has to get down to earth and speak to women in their own language. It is an awful shame that the Union in our country is not doing justice to the president's championship of our cause.'

'What is the solution?'

'The solution is to encourage the young, educated women who are very enthusiastic about feminist issues to invade the Women's Union. It needs new blood and we've got the blood; it is just a matter of transfusing it to the main body. The crux of the problem lies in the fact that most Syrian women are years ahead of their Union. Thus the Union no longer represents the reality of Syrian women, and does not speak of their ambitions and aspirations. Furthermore, I think it has become an obstacle in the way of our progress, not because of its constitution but because of the people who are running it. The Women's Union was established for a certain purpose – to get women out to work. This aim should have been reached by now, but if the Union continues to function in the way it is functioning now we will need another 50 years to reach such a simple goal.'

One of the strongholds of male authority that has been successfully undermined by women in Syria is polygamy. Though still permissible from the religious and legal points of view, and also still rife in other Arab countries such as the Gulf States and Saudi Arabia, polygamy has become obsolete here. Even without any legislative measures being brought in against polygamy, women in Syria have already succeeded in almost abolishing it, both socially and economically. The irony is that for the older generation of women, and particularly rural women, polygamy seems to have been the nucleus of female solidarity and support against the male master. While telling me her life story, Um Mohamad always referred to her husband's other wife as *Rafekiti* (my friend and companion), and never mentioned her without clear indications of true love and genuine affection.

Um Mohamad, the mother of a friend of mine, Amal, is a quiet, serene woman with an almost majestic air about her. I was first introduced to her in a room full of young men and women, where she happened to be the only elderly person (she had just passed her 60th birthday). Yet in no time she became the centre of everyone's attention. At one point in the evening she let her photographic memory reproduce with amazing accuracy accounts of women's lives in the 1940s and 1950s, and everyone felt as though they were in the company of a social historian. Shrewdly oscillating between serious history and humorous evening chat she grabbed everyone's attention. She related true stories in a folk-tale style which I found fascinating. The theme of her story was *zena* (sexual relations outside marriage) and how the killing of a woman started a war of attrition between two families which ended in their total annihilation.

Before leaving I expressed my wish to listen to a full account of her life story. 'You are welcome to do so,' she whispered to me, 'but we have to choose a time when my son Mohamad is not around because he doesn't like me saying a bad word about his father, which, as you will hear, is inevitable in such an account. Although he has been a witness to his father's horrid treatment of me he still adores and feels proud of him.'

The day finally arrived when Um Mohamad, her daughter Amal, Amal's sister-in-law, Leila, and myself had the flat to ourselves. The atmosphere was unusually amicable and relaxed partly, perhaps, due to the absence of men, and partly because we were very conscious of the fact that we all wanted to listen to each other and share each other's experiences. After lunch we started a round-the-table conversation in which Um Mohamad was the first speaker.

'I am illiterate; I never went to school, because in my days there were none. What all villages had during the French occupation was a Shiekh who taught the Koran to a few interested boys; no girls were invited to join in. After independence the Syrian government started opening schools in towns as well as villages. Our village had its first school, then, and its first teacher had just finished his primary education.'

'How did your family treat you as a girl?'

'I don't feel I grew up in my family's home. I remember leaving it as a child, for I was married off at the age of 12 so I hardly have any memories of my childhood days. What happened was that my sister-in-law said she would like me to marry her brother. My family didn't like the idea, and suddenly fearing that she might convince me I should marry her brother in spite of their wishes they hurriedly married me off to the first man who came along. When this unknown man asked for my hand I flatly refused, not because I knew then what marriage was all about but because I didn't want to leave my mother and father and go away with this strange man to a strange place. My father beat me and forced me to go away with this total stranger. When I reached his house I found I had two mothers-in-law and couldn't possibly live with them all. So in less than two months' time I went back to my family who by then realised the irreparable harm they had done me. They welcomed me back home and my father had to pay a lot of gold to get me out of this marriage.

'During this time our neighbour, a very rich farmer, became interested in me. He was already married but claimed that his wife didn't understand him. My father promptly agreed to our getting married, because our neighbour offered to pay all the gold my father had had to pay to divorce me from my first husband. Soon afterwards we were married, and ever since my wedding day (that was 48 years ago) I've been going through absolute hell.

'He was very difficult right from the beginning but I was in a difficult position. I had already divorced once, and if I were to ask for another divorce people might start to gossip about me. The very least they would say was that she couldn't live with just one man; she had to try lots of different men all the time. So I decided to put up with my lot, which was an awful one. I had to work all day, every day of my life; whether I was pregnant or had just given birth didn't make any difference whatsoever. I had to feed the sheep, milk them, make the cheese and butter and all other dairy products. I also had to grow cotton, vegetables, vines, melons, look after fruit trees, reap the crops and do every kind of farming work you could imagine. The same applied to his other wife too.

'For the first three months of my marriage his first wife and I treated each other as enemies. Once we started talking to each other, however, we got on really well. We worked together, ate together, looked after our children jointly, and really enjoyed each other's company. I decided that instead of leaving my husband and getting married to another man who might turn out to be just as bad I would do better to live my life amicably with this woman. In her turn, she used to say to me: "You and I are in the same boat; neither of us is to blame for the other's lot. We are both doomed to live with this horrid man so we'd better help each other and look after each other."

'At that stage we completely forgot about him. He was outside our lives. He had no idea about what we felt, said or did, neither was he interested in knowing. He treated us equally in the sense that he never gave either of us any money to buy clothes or food, either for us or for our children. We used to work all the year through but never had the right to touch a grain of wheat. As for him he never saw the farm except at harvest time, when he would sell all the wheat and barley but would never give either of us or even his own children a penny. *Rafekiti* and I had to breed hens, sell eggs, cheese, grapes, etc. to buy provisions. We didn't have to buy much in the way of food because we produced most of it – wheat, vegetables, fruits and all dairy products – but we still needed to buy clothes, cooking oil, sugar, soap, gasoline and so on. The only way we could manage was to hide a kilo of wheat or cotton which we would later exchange for a piece of soap or a kilo of sugar. It was very hard, extremely hard, because we had to manage with so little while we had to work from dawn to dusk. I didn't want to have children because every newcomer made my life more difficult but we had never heard of contraceptives at that time. I was glad to get away with only five children (four girls and one boy) when everyone else seemed to have ten or more. I used to breastfeed for two-and-a-half years, and so managed to have a child only once every three or four years. Besides, over 20 years ago, my husband took the unilateral decision not to go to bed with me, which was quite a relief.

'Real trouble started in the early 1950s when we had very little rain and no crops to speak of. The sheep had either to die or be sold; nothing was left at home and my husband still wouldn't give us a thing. It was during these years that *Rafekiti* decided to leave home and live separately with her children. I tried my best not to let her go but couldn't stop her. It was awful to lose her but I was glad to see how well she managed with her children and how happy they all were. Encouraged by her experience I thought of following her example, but couldn't because my children were still young – and when my daughters matured I was frightened of the gossip. My only son refused to come with us, and by so doing destroyed my plans to leave home because my daughters and I couldn't possibly live in a house without a male guardian. The only choice left for me was to work day and night to feed my children and pay for their education.'

'Did you ever ask your husband why he didn't look after his own children and pay for their upkeep?'

'I never managed to say more than four words to him at a time, because by the time I reached the fourth word he would have already started beating me. He used to beat me almost every day. Whatever I said or did I seemed to invite a violent reaction from him.'

'Did he treat his other wife in the same way?'

'Yes. Whenever either of us made a mistake he used to beat both of us. So he was equally hateful to us both. In the Koran it says he should be generous and loving. He was the exact opposite of that.'

'Did your friend have a legal right to take her children with her?'

'She didn't ask the law nor did she divorce her husband; she just left. He neither asked her where she was going, nor did he try to keep the children or even see them. When she eventually took him to court she won her case and the court ordered him to pay her a monthly sum of money, but despite incessant attempts by the court to make him pay he never actually did. As for me I felt totally lost without *Rafekiti* and my life became a lot more difficult, for I was held responsible for everything that might go wrong in the house.'

'What did your family and neighbours think of your ordeal?'

'I had no family by then; my parents and only brother had already died. As for my neighbours, they didn't show great support for me. They used to look down on me for selling cotton and wheat to the local shops so that I could get some of my daily needs. Because we were reputed to be so rich no one would believe that I didn't have enough money to spend on my children. One of my neighbours once saw me exchanging some cotton in the shop for a piece of soap. She turned to me and said: "What is wrong with you? You have almost impoverished your husband. Why are you trying to dissipate his fortune and drain his wealth?" I told her to shut up. "Had you seen me buying lipsticks or perfumes you would have had the right to say such a thing, but as you see me buying a piece of soap for my children the least thing you can do is shut up.'' '

Amal, Um Mohamad's daughter, at this point qualified what her mother had previously said. 'My father is kind but his brothers and sisters who used to hate my mother pushed him to treat her badly. My mother was the only woman to come from outside their family; they always had inter-family marriages and they resented my mother because she was not one of the family. They strongly believed in family or even tribal relationships; they were rich and conservative.'

Her mother added, 'But his resentment extended to his own children. I still remember when my eldest daughter became seriously ill I had to carry her on my back and walk to town. In town I spent the night on the pavement in order to see the doctor the next day, yet when we arrived back home he never asked where I had been or how the little one was. He was busy then chasing girls around. He even started selling the land to buy precious presents for those who offered him sex. To him, family and children were a burden which he forgot about and he spent his time chasing women and leading a promiscuous, debauched life.'

'Did you ever think of making love to your friend?'

'We didn't think of making love to each other, but we did all the same. On a cold wintry night he was away chasing one of the Bedouin women he wanted to fornicate with. *Rafekiti* knocked at my door and said: "As the children are all in bed, come to my room and let us spend the evening together." As it was very cold we sat in bed trying to keep ourselves warm. As usual, we felt close and intimate. Our legs touched, we hugged and we kissed each other, and suddenly our hearts started beating fast. We started panting, feeling all the warm blood in the world thrust into our veins. Neither of us knew what was happening to us but when we parted we were both feeling more satisfied than we had ever been before. Living with ten children and a husband in two rooms made it almost impossible for us to repeat this exciting experience, but after that night we did a lot of hugging, kissing and playing and on the odd occasion we managed to spend some nights together before my friend's sad departure.'

'Now that you are 60, do you regret not divorcing him?'

'For sure I do. Had I divorced him my life would have been a thousand times better. I didn't want to divorce him because, as a divorcee, I would have had to put up with gossip and all kinds of social pressure.

People would have started to watch the streets leading to my street and count the men passing in them. I wanted to be separated from him, because separation is more socially acceptable than divorce. If you are separated you are understood to have said you don't want to get married again, but if you are a divorcee it is reckoned you are fishing for another, nicer man and people want to find out, before you do, who this other man is.'

'Did you have a say in your daughters' marriages?'

'No. My husband would decide and my opinion didn't count at all. Once the girl and her father agreed that was it. No one came to consult me.'

'My sisters,' Amal added, 'got married to the men they liked and they were going to do that whether or not my father agreed. If you were able to listen to my father talking you would never believe he was the same person you've just heard about. Socially, he was able to keep a good image of himself with everyone around him. You know, like all men; when you talk to them you think they are great, fair and progressive but once you look into the way they treat their sisters, daughters and wives you know exactly the kind of people they really are.'

Addressing myself to Amal I asked: 'Now that you've heard your mother's account of her life, how do you compare your life with hers?'

'Personally, I didn't experience what my mother has just told you. I was too young; the only thing I knew was that my parents didn't have a good relationship. However, I had my first shock in life when, like my mother, I was forced into an arranged marriage at the age of 12. Strangely enough, this time it was my mother who used the little authority she had to decide my fate. She desperately wanted to relieve me from the dire circumstances I was living in at home and to secure my future by marrying me off to a rich relative of hers. My mother was wholeheartedly for this marriage and played a decisive role in forcing it upon me. I was beaten, almost tortured – my brother tried to strangle me – but to no avail. Their last resort was to carry me off in my pyjamas and throw me into a strange home and a dreadful wedlock. Having been forced to be with this man I immediately hated the sight of him; I couldn't look at him. When all his attempts to win me over had failed he started beating me and treating me like a servant. When my father paid his first visit to me (about two months after my marriage) I insisted on going home with him and never went back to my husband again.

'As a divorced woman I was expected to shut myself in and wait for a second husband to knock on my door, yet for me it was going back to school which was the panacea that repaired the damage wrought by this disastrous marriage. Immense family and other social pressures were exerted to blur my vision of a better future but I was undaunted. I went back to school as a regular pupil because my age allowed that; there was nothing to prove I had been married except the social recognition of the fact. Yet persistent gossip and incessant social pressure made every day a painful event for me. When social pressure became too much to bear and the vexations of life preyed too severely on my mind I tried to commit suicide by throwing myself off the three-storey school building. Even the freedom which death confers on us was denied me, as I was alive with a broken back and limbs. In retrospect I can see that my suicide attempt was a stark cry for pity and sympathy; I so much wanted to be noticed by people around me who seemed to me so impassive, so insensitive to the way I felt and thought. Fortunately I succeeded in doing just that. My family, particularly my mother, tried their best to make up for their senseless treatment of me, and my brother began to understand my problems and supported me against social gossip. As a person I emerged from the experience both stronger and more positive. Just over a year later I got my baccalaureate, registered as a law student at the university and moved to Damascus, leaving my society and all that it thought of me behind.

'At the university I met Nasar (my present husband) and we had a lovely relationship. I decided to marry him, notwithstanding what family or society might think because when I had been in dead trouble neither family nor society had stretched out a helping hand to me.'

'What do you blame for your ordeal: our laws or our society?'

'The law is illiberal and society not sympathetic. Our society is full of superstitious ideas presented in new forms and under new guises in the name of progress. Even men who speak using progressive political terminology turn out to be most reactionary once they are faced with a problem concerning their wives and their sisters. It is fashionable now among men to talk about women's emancipation, but a simple test would prove that those who believe in emancipation are really very few. I feel the most central problem of our lives in the

Arab world is the problem of what seems to be and what actually is; of our public and personal lives.'

'As a law student do you believe that the law is one thing and the practice another? Or do you think that the law hasn't succeeded yet in mastering the strong social traditions but is bound to do so soon?'

'Our study is mostly theoretical. No effort has been made to relate our law to the social reality. For example, according to the law, when a man divorces his wife he has to pay her the full, unpaid dowry, provide her with a home for her children, and pay her money. But if the woman gets a divorce she gets nothing of all that. Most men don't want a divorce, but they put their wives through hell until they ask for a divorce – irrespective of what they might or might not get. It is a society governed by men, in which everything, including the law, is put to the service of men. All our judges are men and most of them are not in the least sympathetic to women's causes; they try to find ways round the law and they often succeed. I feel that those people who make these laws have deliberately left loopholes to be manipulated by men to their advantage.'

'Do you believe that Islamic laws are good for women?'

'They are better than what we actually have in practice; they at least treat women as sane, independent individuals with equal rights. Islamic laws give women more rights than they actually have in most Muslim countries. It is only in Syria, Algeria and South Yemen that women's full social, economic and political rights are acknowledged. In this respect, the Syrian law, for example, leaves no room for misinterpretation. "The government ensures for a woman all the chances which allow her to participate fully and completely in the economic, educational, social and political life, and it tries to lift all the barriers which prevent her development and participation in building the socialist, progressive society." Here it is interesting to note that Syrian law, which is partly inspired by socialist, progressive ideology, is much closer to *al Shari* than laws in conservative Muslim countries which consider themselves to be the guardians of Islam.'

Amal continued to talk. 'There is a real dichotomy between Arab men's political and social attitudes. You find so many of the educated, progressive men in the Arab world the most reactionary socially, particularly in their attitudes to women. But women are marching on; they are paying no heed to reactionary, chauvinistic policies; they have enough confidence now to choose and stand by their choice.

Even so, what we need in the Arab world, more than anything else, is the female equivalent of Galileo who, through her personal experience, would undermine the biased, prevailing conceptions. The Arab world is exceptionally poor in pioneering, personal experiences. That is why we want brave women who can challenge and reject the reactionary mentality. Arab women still don't dare to express themselves, even in writing. We hardly ever find in the Arab world writing in which women freely and spontaneously express themselves; hence the almost total lack of women's autobiography. When you find something which is close to a female autobiography you find discussions of social and political issues rather than personal ones, whereas an Arab man's autobiography is usually a chronicle of his personal experiences, including his sexual relationships with his wife and mistresses. Thus, personal experience is very difficult for Arab women to write about but it is a necessary requirement which Arab women have to achieve. Despite all the literature available on women's emancipation there is a total ignorance of the daily reality in which Arab women have to live.'

Directing myself to 20-year-old Leila, Amal's sister-in-law, a second-year student at the English department of Damascus University, I asked her whether she still partly suffered from the social pressures which Amal and her mother were subjected to. 'Not only partly but mostly,' the terribly thin, visibly nervous and sensitive Leila answered with a sarcastic, even bitter, expression on her face. 'My family is part of this society which, however liberated and progressive it might think itself, still has a long way to go as far as women's liberation and true equality are concerned. Amal has just given a bright picture of women's position in rural areas; in towns women are still in a much worse position than that which she has described. I am the only girl in a family of five sons, which deeply believes in male supremacy. I was treated badly by everyone, particularly by my mother. My mother herself had a very difficult time; she eloped with my father to Beirut where they had to work as servants in different homes. She was completely cut off from her social milieu, and neither family nor friends showed the slightest degree of sympathy for her. So when she had me she must have resented the fact that as a girl I was likely to suffer her experiences, which she hated to recall or even think about. That is why, I believe, she always loved my brothers and was very laid back about them, whereas she couldn't achieve anything more than a nervous, erratic relationship with me. When my father treats me well she gets terribly upset and warns him against spoiling me. She has hardly ever talked to me, and has never made an effort to explain things to me. I had no sister and was not allowed either to visit or be visited by any girlfriend of mine. So I lived in total isolation. Although I sympathise with my mother because she suffered a lot I can't see what satisfaction she could get from inflicting the same suffering on me.'

'Do you think that was her intention then?'

'I don't think she was malicious or did unkind things deliberately, but as a human being she needed outlets and there was no one around her on whom she could exercise authority except me. Even regarding the question of marriage, she tried to force me into an arranged marriage which she herself had rebelled against over 30 years ago. She often stipulated to my brothers that they should marry women of their choice, regardless of religion or nationality, while expecting me to marry our next-door neighbour who was her choice for me.

'My other problem,' Leila continued, 'was that my family was living in Harasta, a very strict and backward suburb of Damascus. Although we came from a different religious sect to that of most inhabitants of Harasta (we are Alawites while the majority who live in Harasta are Sunni Muslims), and despite the fact that our sect's attitude to women is more liberal and progressive, my family had to observe all the social rules which were enforced by the local inhabitants. Among these rules was that from the age of seven girls were not expected to play with boys. I still remember the day when I was a pre-school child and was playing with my brother in a pool we had in the courtyard. I was seen hitting him by our neighbour, who took the matter extremely seriously and asked my mother how she allowed her daughter to hit her son; when she got older she might hit her brothers or even try to rebel against her husband. Another time I was playing with my brother in the same pool when another neighbour of ours came in and exclaimed: "Oh, my God, how can you let them see each other naked!" In that area girls had to put the Islamic veil on from the age of seven. I resisted until I was 12. I was the first in my class and everyone, including my teachers, thought that I was a mess because I didn't cover my hair. At the age of 12 I had to put it on because social and family pressures became unbearable. My friends who were with me at school got married at the age of 12; now each of them has four or five children. In that area parents send their daughters to school only until they know how to read and write and then they marry them off. Very, very few girls manage to reach university level. So my position, bad as it was, was one thousand times better than that of my friends.

'At least my family didn't stand in the way of my education, which was something. But when I went to university they wouldn't let me study what I wanted to. I always wanted to do English, but as all my brothers are doctors and engineers my family forced me to register in the department of mechanical and electrical engineers. I, however, was determined not to continue in the field. So I failed the first year and did not sit for the exam in the second year. By that time I was strong and mature enough to go ahead and change to English without letting my family know. When I told them later they stopped my allowance. So I left home, went to live at the university campus and started looking for a job. When they saw that I was not going to give in they started to support me again. The main problem, I believe, was that they were paying my way. Had I been economically independent I would have gone ahead and done exactly what I chose. Therefore I see economic independence as the first crucial step for women's emancipation.'

'Do you feel ready now to stand by your convictions and fight your family if they tried to impose something such as an arranged marriage on you?'

'Of course! I learnt my lesson. I don't think either family or society can really stop us from doing what we want to do if we are determined enough. When I read a book, sit for an exam, or even as I talk to you now, I feel myself to be a sensible, independent, fairly intelligent individual. But when my parents discuss any issue with me, especially marriage, I feel I am being deliberately regarded in a belittling light, and this turns me into a dull, slow, feeble-minded individual. I think most Syrian women suffer from this dilemma; the discrepancy between what they feel they are and what they are taken to be.

'It seems to me that the root of the problem lies in the fact that most men in our society believe that however educated women may become they remain "women" and this connotes being weak, emotional, and perhaps even obtuse. Even educated, politically progressive men who spend hours talking about women's emancipation, get married to docile, obedient girls of 13 and 14. The gap is really between theory and practice, between what men say and what they actually do. Therefore what we need before anything else in the Arab world is a consciousness-raising movement to liberate both men and women from their oppression.'

Back at the university hostel where I was living at the time, the disconcerting sight of a helpless mother trying extremely hard to manage four children attracted my attention and commanded my sympathy. This woman was always breathless because she had to climb over 30 steep stairs with one baby in a sling, two young children holding her hands, and her eldest daughter walking in front of them.

Her husband, a lecturer at the university, always went out unaccompanied. Whenever I saw him he was wearing a smart, well-pressed suit, a shirt and a tie. It is strange, I often thought, that he doesn't help her with the children, not even as far as taking them down these difficult stairs.

Gradually the woman and I started to get our children – I only had one girl then – to play together and during this time we would talk about family affairs and life in general.

I was intrigued to hear her full life story. She herself was keen to talk to me. An extremely isolated woman, she saw nobody except her husband and children 'and now you'. I soon noticed that she didn't like seeing or talking to me when her husband was around because, as she explained later, he didn't like her to talk to anyone except him. So we became like two discreet lovers, waiting for her husband's absence to meet and talk. One day she knocked on my door at about ten o'clock in the evening and said: 'My children are in bed and my husband is away. Would you like to come and have a cup of coffee with me?'

'Yes,' I answered immediately, jumping at the opportunity of talking and, more importantly, listening to her, hoping to unravel that mystery which I could sense in her life.

The coffee was ready. She lit a cigarette, let out a deep sigh and immediately started her tale at the beginning.

'Since early childhood my life has consisted of both constant attempts to flee unhappiness and deliberate efforts not to succumb to it but to survive it. I lost my father when I was only a little girl. Unfortunately for me I was the only child to survive my parents' unhappy marriage, which was truncated by my father's early death.

My mother always felt bitter and angry with my father and she never made an effort to release her anger. Her misfortune, she often complains, started on her wedding day. Just before going to bed she was shocked to see my father taking out false teeth and putting them in a glass. She nearly went out of her mind. Of course she knew that he was older than she was, but not that old. He was a very rich relative of hers and this was an excellent credential for my grandfather who never hesitated to marry his daughters off to rich suitors.

'Emerging from an unhappy, chaotic marriage, and being still young and lively, my mother wanted to make up for the lost days. So she got married again, but unfortunately for her this marriage was not a success. The man was 20 years her junior and the marriage was kept a secret from everyone close to them, including myself. It was only by chance that I found out about it. One day I had to come back from school to fetch something I had forgotten and was shocked to find my mother lying in bed with a strange man. She explained that he was her husband but that ugly picture put me off her for quite a while.

'My true predicament started when my relatives decided that my mother was a morally unfit woman to bring me up and that it was incorrect for me to live in the same flat with my mother's husband. According to the law my mother couldn't keep me because she had got married and my relatives had priority over her in bringing me up. It was agreed that I should be taken to my uncle's home, where I had to live in austere and adverse circumstances. For one thing I never had enough to eat. I used to steal a piece of bread or a biscuit and eat it when everyone else was asleep. I shall never forget the day when I managed to have an egg for breakfast. But just before finishing it I heard the footsteps of my uncle's wife approaching. So I quickly put the rest of the egg and its shell into my pocket, forgot about it and went to school. On our way to the classroom a friend of mind quite casually put her hand in my pocket and suddenly screamed "Oh, my goodness! What is this?" The humiliation I felt at that moment was indescribable.

'With similar bitterness I recall the first time I had my period. Obviously I had no clue about what was happening to me and the spectre of what my uncle's wife might do to me if she found out terrorised my inmost thoughts. Just as I expected, once she saw me changing she started beating and abusing me till I had a haunting foreboding of what I might have done. My brain started to wonder whether

I had really committed a crime and whether my own blood wasn't perhaps a clear condemnation of my own foul play.

'During the time I spent at my uncle's I made two suicide attempts and started behaving like a freak. I distinctly remember signalling to our neighbour's son in a desperate attempt to attract his attention and, perhaps, sympathy. As usual, my uncle's wife was the first one to notice me doing this and she threatened to tell my uncle. On that day I tried to commit suicide because I was so terrified of what my uncle might do to me. After that incident my uncle took careful measures to keep his son out of my way because, he said, he was frightened that I might seduce him. It was only recently that I learnt what the word "seduce" meant. Even so, his fears were so real to him that he decided to take me back to my mother.

'My mother's marriage had finished but she had already got herself into another marital relationship. It was a great relief to find that this time she had picked on a decent man. Despite his extreme kindness to me I could never call him "papa". This was in spite of the fact that I never had a good image of my own father, basically because my mother never loved him and, by all accounts, was not happy with him. When this third husband of hers died my mother started having an illicit affair with his nephew which I found extremely embarrassing. We became the stock joke of the neighbourhood, with everyone gossiping about my mother having a boyfriend. She was the one who had committed the sin, but I was the one sent to purgatory. At least this is how I felt. In fact, I felt I was subjected daily to a severe public trial until I could take no more and decided to flee my mother's home to my aunt's. There again, I was an unwelcome guest and constant pressure was exerted on me to go back home. In the end I had to succumb to this, although home was sheer hell for me. Finally, and fortunately, my mother realised that this young man was only interested in her money, so she decided to leave him which was a relief.

'But she didn't keep quiet for long. She soon started having a relationship with a cousin of hers who was married and had seven children. Suddenly he started paying us daily visits; he started doing the shopping for us and eating with us and the gossip started eating into my brain cells. I hated all men by then and felt that I never wanted to hear of something called sex. Even today I still have a block in my mind against sexual desire and sexual satisfaction. I've only ever heard of something called a climax but I've never experienced it.

Perhaps I never had a normally developed sexuality. Sex, as far as I am concerned, is a marital duty which I perform for my husband, just as I cook for him and iron his shirts.

'Now I understand, of course, that my mother committed no crime; all she did was to live her life the way she liked, but this, as you know, is an unpardonable sin in our countries.

'My other problem was that my mother used to adore me in her own way, but she had a domineering character which made me feel inferior to her. She used to kiss and caress me in front of my friends, which I used to find very embarrassing. On the whole, my life at home was very far from satisfactory. As a result I made up my mind to leave home with the first man who asked for my hand. That man was my present husband.

'I was first introduced to my husband by my aunt when I was 17 years old. He was working with her on the same magazine in which he published poetry and literary essays. When he proposed to me my family nearly went berserk, because he and I came from widely different and even conflicting religious sects – and I believe if my father had been alive he might have killed me. All that I knew then was that I wanted to leave home at any price and that when people got married they usually left their parents' homes. Yet, despite my insistent pleas nothing happened at that time because my uncles and aunts stopped anything from taking place.'

'Didn't you find it painful to compare the attitude of your uncles and aunts to you when you went to them as a homeless orphan and they left you starving, and their attitude to you when you became an eligible wife; how they warranted themselves the right to interfere in the most crucial and the most personal decision you are likely to take in your whole life?'

'But this is what extended families are all about, isn't it? They would prohibit, beat and even kill, but they would never offer love, affection or even help. To most Arab women extended families mean one thing: extra male authority. I can think of many women who have been prevented from marrying men of their choice or from following up a certain career or profession because a cousin or a father's or mother's cousin didn't approve of their decision. Women are even killed by their cousins if they are thought to defile the family's honour, but we have yet to hear of a woman whose life has been saved, happiness achieved or even chances improved by a cousin.

Thus, extended families guarantee a tighter grip and exert efficient male domination over women.

'Within a short while, my future husband left the country to pursue his postgraduate study abroad. In my turn, I got my baccalaureate and registered in the English department of Damascus University. I lived a luxurious life then, having as much money as I cared to spend, I went out, travelled around and experienced life to the full.

'I was in my second year at the university when the same man surfaced in my life again. He proposed to me and, predictably, my family produced a duplicate of their former objections, but this time I was not going to listen, and neither was I as easy to control. Believe me, I still didn't have the slightest feeling for him. The only thing I liked about him was that he came from a poor family which meant that we had to struggle for a living. I so badly wanted to fight for my life instead of having everything offered on a silver plate. I could even say I never liked the way he looked, dressed, spoke or behaved. Yet, despite all this I ended up by getting engaged to him – how and why I still wonder sometimes. None of my family attended the engagement except my mother and my aunt, and the only thing he bought me was the engagement ring because he was penniless which, judging by my psychology then, must have pleased me.

'Shortly after our engagement he went abroad again to resume his studies after he had made specific arrangements for me to follow him. In no time I was a bride on a plane, wrapped all in white, the symbol of happiness, while my veins experienced neither love nor even affection for the man for whom I was crossing countries and leaving home and university to meet as a husband. Although I was certainly glad to leave home I did not want to reach my destination.

'I took a taxi to the Syrian Embassy where I learnt that my fiancé had for some mysterious reason just flown to Syria the previous day. I booked the next plane back home and there I found him waiting for me with a big, rather sarcastic smile on his face. When I saw him at the airport I wondered why I was getting married to this man.

'After officially, but not actually, getting married we went to live with my mother. The few weeks we spent there were horrid. I had no feelings for him and he obviously had none for me, together with the fact that he was passing through a difficult psychological state bordering on lunacy. He was masturbating all the time, and despite his desperate attempts he couldn't make love to me. After two weeks of trying and failing he accused me of not being a virgin, which was a lie.

'My mother and I were shaken by the prospect of a social scandal. So we went to a gynaecologist who confirmed that I was a virgin and, using a pair of scissors, he cut my virginity in front of my would-be husband. The doctor looked at him and said he was to drink a bottle of whisky before he went to bed with his wife. I got a medical report from the doctor saying that I was a virgin which saved my honour and the honour of the family.'

'You are aware, of course,' I interrupted her, 'that what "honour" here means is precisely the preservation of a girl's virginity for her prospective husband and her abstinence from any sexual relationship before marriage – and this applies only to women. This is the prevailing definition here not only of a woman's honour but the honour of her family.'

'You are right,' she said. 'But can you say such a thing outside this locked room or in any other society? What you've just said, simple and true as it is, would be taken as a disparagement of Arab morality and Islamic religion, because it would be taken by most men to be an ominous sign of female consciousness-raising which threatens men's absolute dominance over our sexuality and lives even.

'Using some devious means,' she went on, 'he managed to get himself a grant to go to Europe to do some research in his field. In Europe he seemed to develop a hatred against me, making battering me a daily exercise for his muscles. Life then became horrific, with spasms of pain and unspoken suffering smouldering beneath the surface. His biting oppression of me engendered a nagging suspicion in him that I might try to poison him – perhaps this is what he would have done had he been in my place. So he stopped eating my food. The reason why I didn't try to leave was that he made it clear to me that if I left him he wouldn't give me my daughter. When my agony reached a stage in which I started to falter between life and death I said to myself: "To hell with my daughter, I want to save my life." So I bought myself an air ticket and said to him he could keep his daughter but that wouldn't stop me from going home. When he saw my unshaken determination he put our daughter in front of me and started crying and kissing my hands and feet, begging me to stay and promising never to treat me badly again. Neighbours and friends pressed me to give him a last chance, so I did.

'After this incident he stopped battering and abusing me, which was a relief, but he by no means became a good husband. He still won't trust me enough to eat the food I cook and won't allow me to write letters to my mother or ask after her. I am her only child and yet when we came to Damascus on holiday he wouldn't let me talk to her on the phone. He even doesn't like to hear my children speaking with my accent. As for the extended family of uncles and aunts, they are complete strangers to me now; I am not allowed to say hello to any of them, although I receive all members of his family and give them a warm welcome in my house. His excuse for that is that he doesn't want his children to learn anything from my family's dishonourable values. I resent the fact that I treat him so well and respect him and yet he doesn't bother to treat my mother decently. But I know that had I not submitted to his will our marriage couldn't have lasted until now. I am now the person he wants; there is hardly anything left of me.'

With the conclusion of her life story, Salma broke into a hysterical fit of crying. She hugged me passionately, rested her head on my shoulder and said in a smouldering voice, 'My life has atrophied through disuse; I've been deprived of the appetite to live; I would be content to have you as my neighbour for the rest of my life, but even that won't be possible. In two months' time we will be moving to my husband's home town, where I shall perish into nothingness. I want to sense life, I want to feel that I am alive, just as I can feel your warm, affectionate body right now.' She was still holding me tightly with her head heavily resting on my shoulder when this sudden spurt of anger and passion turned into the heavy breathing of someone who has fallen into deep sleep. I put her in her bed, closed the door of her flat and walked the few steps which separated her flat from mine.

Back in my flat, my husband and little girl were enjoying a deep, peaceful sleep. The tangled, exhausting conflict which had waged within Salma had by now been transmitted to me and succeeded in awakening other, perhaps less severe but certainly no less agonising examples of male tyranny. Although I've been the subject of envy from neighbours and relatives for my helpful and very understanding husband, my life with him, I thought as I lay down in my bed, is not without its agonising moments. My husband would take our, then only, daughter to her nursery school, help with the shopping, cleaning and cooking. However, if I put the food on the table a few degrees cooler or hotter than he wanted, we would have a row. It was just by chance that I discovered how deeply terrified of him I must have been when, in the middle of a lecture on the Romantic poets attended by a multitude of students, I suddenly stopped as if struck by lightning; the words jammed in my mouth, my colour must have changed and, judging by the way I felt, my heart must have almost stopped as well. It was already twelve o'clock and I had forgotten to take the meat out of the freezer when I left home that morning. The problem was not, of course, that I would have nothing to eat – that was the least important part; my real quandary was what I was going to say to my husband now that he had yet more proof of my 'incompetence', 'carelessness' and 'unorganised mind'.

I have only recently understood why I feel more peaceful when I am cleaning, ironing or cooking than I do when I am reading or writing, though incomparably I prefer the latter two activities: I once caught myself thinking how happy my husband is when he finds me working like a 'normal woman' at home. Over 45 years after Virginia Woolf's death, we women are still the prisoners of the stereotyped 'normality' moulded for us by men. Salma's story raised many questions in my head about my own life. So often I come out of the university feeling proud of the way I have explained Shelley's 'Ode to the West Wind' or Arthur Miller's *The Crucible*, yet on my way home the high, professional spirit starts to shrink within me until, by the time I open the door of my flat, I feel as though I'm a bad cook and, to some extent, a bit of a failure as a housewife. The difference between Salma and me, I concluded, was that she was trying to live with the fact of being classified the less intelligent, the less competent and certainly the less equal, while I was trying to fight and defeat such classification whenever and wherever I encountered it. This fight is fought by women all over the world, as all women still have to prove themselves every day, sometimes every hour.

Notes

1. The Women's Union is a public organisation, an offshoot of the Baath Arab Socialist Party, which is the governing party in Syria. It represents women, defends them, fights for their rights and puts up quite a few women MPs. Most women in Syria, however, do not see the Union as either radical or feminist.
2. In Syria a women's society is a women's group which is set up to plan women's affairs, defend their rights and speak in their names.

2. Lebanon: Women Embattled

Lebanon, the country that has borne the brunt of Israeli aggression over the past decade, is at once the smallest Arab country and the most divided. The French, during their period of mandate after World War I, divided Lebanon from Syria, set up an administration and education system in the French language, and devised a constitution for 'independence' in 1946 that guaranteed the major government offices to the Maronite Christians, who have ruled the country ever since, though their numerical ascendancy is based on a census some fifty years old. The Shiite Muslims are the largest single community, though they remain the poorest; the Sunni Muslims, who represent the mainstream throughout the rest of the Arab world, are a minority in Lebanon, like the Druze, a third Muslim sect. The last two groups had strong connections with the Palestine Liberation Organisation before its departure from the Lebanon. The Shiites on the other hand have been the principal victims of the Israeli-Palestinian fighting, and Amal emerged as their political and military arm, originally to protect the Shiite community; after the 1982 Israeli invasion smaller resistance groups such as Hezbullah and Jihad have sprung up with strong Iranian connections. In 1982 the Phalange, representing the Maronites, actually sided with the invading Israeli army, while Amal and the other Muslim groups fought what they saw as a war of liberation against an occupying force.

Before the war, Lebanese women, citizens of a uniquely cosmopolitan country, had won a considerable degree of emancipation, and Lebanon was already the sole Arab country with an independent women's organisation not affiliated to a political party. Then came the fighting, and it was of course the women, and their children, who found themselves the first casualties. The total of women and children killed in the south of Lebanon far exceeded the number of men killed.

Women's issues became issues of war, resistance and liberation. And in the southern battlefields it was the women's policy of 'non-departure' – refusing to leave the land whatever the cost – that played a crucial role in encouraging resistance to the invasion and eventually forcing Israel to withdraw in 1985.

So the voices in this chapter are the voices of women embattled, living through tragedy and loss at the same time as committing themselves utterly to the struggle. They are the voices of amazons, viragos, as much as of mothers and sisters and wives.

Women Embattled

Segregation of male and female passengers is still *de rigueur* for most Arab drivers. The driver of the five-seater car with whom I travelled to Beirut had to show his 'respect' for the women travelling with him by squeezing them into the back seat, away from the men. So he signalled to the man accompanying me to sit next to him in the front seat and asked me to join two women in the back seat. I opened the door, looked in and said, 'There is no room for me.'

'No, no, plenty of room,' said one of the women who had two boys on her knees and a third on her lap. She stretched her neck round the children in a concentrated effort to see me, and pulled the two children nearer to their brother, who by now was climbing up her neck and nearly suffocating her. One of the children had a piece of bread in his hand and the other a dirty sweet, while the third was content to chew his mother's breast and steal wicked looks at those around him. The mother wiped the first child's mouth and the second's hand and stroked the third on the cheek, clearly anxious to show that she was managing.

Once we left Damascus the car started moving along a winding road surrounded by beautiful mountains. It was a typically sunny Mediterranean morning and I was in a cheerful mood, in love with the sun, the mountains and the delightful breeze gently massaging my face. As I was wondering how the French had dared to set up the border between Syria and Lebanon, two countries which extend over the same land, have the same people, the same language, the same history and the same culture, a sleepy child bounced against my stomach. Being five months pregnant, I put my hand on my belly to try to protect it from an accidental blow. The frequent bends somehow helped to pull the child's head towards me until it rested on my breast. I turned to the mother who was still smiling half triumphantly and said: 'Excuse me, please, I happen to be pregnant at the moment.'

'You are not the only one,' she answered sharply. 'I am six months pregnant, too.'

That really shocked me. Her three children ranged between the ages of one and four and here she was expecting a fourth in three months' time.

'Are these three your children?' I asked, wanting to dismiss the awful thought.

'They are God's children,' she answered briskly. 'I am only fulfilling God's will on this earth.'

'But how could you be breastfeeding your baby while you are pregnant?' I asked, stunned at what I saw and heard.

'I will continue to breastfeed him until his brother arrives,' she answered deadpan. 'This is what I did with all of them.'

Her tone was a bit unfriendly, I thought. I turned to her with a questioning look in my eyes. The triumphant smile still had not left her. She was wearing a black nylon dress and looked quite healthy and well nourished. Despite her unfriendly tone I felt I liked her and decided to ask another question.

'Isn't it hard for you to look after these three young children, especially as you are pregnant at the moment?'

'No, it isn't. It is my job and I have to do it.'

'I know, but I mean, wouldn't it have been a better idea if you had delayed getting pregnant until your youngest became a little bit more independent?'

'I can't delay getting pregnant. The key of the womb is not in my hands – it is in God's hands. He opens and closes it whenever he likes. I have a friend who had one child ten years ago and could not get pregnant a second time. She consulted the top gynaecologists in the world and still couldn't get pregnant – so why should I complain about being pregnant?'

'I didn't say that you should complain, but just organise your pregnancies in a way which allows you enough time to look after your children properly without killing yourself.'

'*I am* looking after them properly. God creates them and he takes care of them.'

'Are you saying that you refuse to use contraceptives?'

'Of course I do. Why should I use contraceptives? These children are God's gift and it is a flagrant attack on his wisdom to refuse his gift.'

'Do you work?'

'No.'

'What does your husband do?'

'He works as a clerk in a publishing house.'

'How much does he get?'

'One thousand liras a month.' (About £100.)

'Is that enough for you all?'

'It is. We manage. So long as there is a God we are not going to starve.'

While I was wondering whether it would ever be possible to reach this woman, who had obviously decided that I was an atheist and started to give me a lecture on Islam, I heard the driver pointing out the devastating effects of the long and bloody war in Lebanon.

Suddenly, my friend shrieked in horror, saying, 'Look, look, just look! Could these be the once beautiful Allieh mountains?'

I saw houses on both sides of the road either abandoned, burnt or pulled down. About 15 minutes later we entered a subdued town on which the marks of the war were only too apparent.

'This is Borj Al Barajneh,' said my companion, looking at me. We were in the middle of a narrow, busy but somehow pleasant street which looked very much like a Sunday market in which people bought and sold everything from fruits and vegetables to sheets and mattresses. We got out of the car and entered a *shawrma* sandwich place, where I was the object of much curiosity. Women do not usually appear in such cheap places, but allowances are always made for foreigners. I was too hungry to care, and in a few minutes devoured a *shawrma* sandwich and drank a cooling glass of thinned yoghurt.

We started walking in narrow, dirty alleyways which told of extreme poverty and prolonged deprivation. In the middle of these alleyways stood a small, old, unimpressive building which I was told was the Amal's headquarters. Working here, I thought, the leadership of Amal could not be too far removed from the living conditions of its membership.

On entering the centre, one immediately senses a homely and modest atmosphere. I went to the information desk and told the man there that I would like to interview a woman member of Amal. He left his desk and went upstairs. About ten minutes later, a woman in green Islamic dress (*Al Shari*)[1] with matching green scarf and eyes came down the stairs. Her confident steps and the bright gleam in her eyes told of an unmistakable self-awareness of her position as a political woman. She hurried towards me, warmly shook hands and said: 'Why are you standing here? Come up please,' and hurried towards the stairs to show me the way.

We started to talk about Lebanon and Syria, about the war and about Islam. Being very conscious of the need to use my time effectively I explained to Zeinab (for this was her name) the reason for my visit and the nature of my book. I also told her of my wish to hear how she had become a member of the Amal political movement.

Looking at me with friendly eyes, she began her tale.

'I came from quite a strict working-class family. We live in a conservative area and a conservative society and my family is no exception to this. My parents tried to impose on us – that is, me and my sisters, for I have five sisters and one brother – the same kind of life which they themselves had lived. My father was totally under the influence of his family, but my mother had a much more open mind, particularly as regards our education. She managed to send us all to school. I and my elder sister managed to get our baccalaureates, but my younger sisters only managed to finish their preparatory schooling. In 1978 I did a typing course as a means of getting a job; I wasn't wearing *Al Shari* then. In 1979 I got my baccalaureate and have been working since then.'

'Why did you decide to wear *Al Shari*?'

'My parents didn't force me to pray but they forced me to cover my hair and wear *Isharb*[2]. So it was not really religious but a social habit. I used to argue with them that if they wanted me to be a real Muslim they should ask me to pray rather than just cover my hair. Like most people they were conservative but didn't understand Islam. Later, I wore *Al Shari* from choice. I was at school, and it was then I first got to know women from the Amal movement. I liked them and could see that the way they dressed was very suitable for women who wanted to take full social responsibility in all fields. As you can see, our dress is comfortable, practical and smart. That is why all women in Amal wear it. When I compare the way I used to dress before joining Amal with the way I dress now I find myself so much better off. For one thing, this dress guarantees me free movement and peace of mind. I climb stairs, get into cars and sit in meetings without having to worry about the way I move and sit or about the decency of my dress. For another thing, men no longer follow me in the streets uttering obscene words and dirty jokes. All Arab men respect women who wear *Al Shari*. This is why I feel this dress strengthens my character and confirms my independence.'

'How did your parents react to your joining a political movement such as Amal?'

'At the beginning I didn't tell them. I worked in the movement for two years without letting them know. At first, they were really frightened that I might join the movement, but they seem to have undergone a total change of heart during the war. They used to worry only about us, their family, and had no idea about the problems which most Muslims were facing in Lebanon. I hate to speak of Muslims and Christians – I am a Lebanese citizen first and foremost – but we are forced to talk in these terms. Now, my parents understand a lot more about the country and its problems and they appreciate the national role of Amal. During the war Amal played a crucial role in feeding, sheltering and protecting our people. The Shiites are over 50 per cent of the population, but they hardly have any rights at all. The State has so far managed to ignore us, but no government which wants to survive can afford to do that any longer. We have at least to be participants, if not an equal party, in decision making and running our country. What is interesting is that my father, who used to be the only supreme authority in the house, never takes any decision now concerning the family without consulting me first. Sometimes I stay out till eleven o'clock at night and when I come back they give me dinner without ever asking where I have been. For they know that I must have been working somewhere. I feel that they have an utter and complete confidence in me now. Women in the Amal movement have proved their ability to play a responsible role in their country's affairs and most people acknowledge that.'

'Was this change in the way women were generally perceived accompanied by any legislative or practical social change?'

'No. Nothing has changed. But the Lebanese law is quite democratic. The law was not an obstacle to our emancipation. The real obstacle was the attitude of the family and society as a whole. As this is changing, however, I don't think there should be any residual problem.'

'Is your political struggle within Amal accompanied by another aspect of the struggle for women's rights and emancipation?'

'I think my character, as it is now, was formed in the movement. I now lecture to women groups in the movement who ask me why we don't train them to carry arms. I say our arms are our thoughts and words. We have first to understand where we are and where we stand before we carry arms. If we have to carry arms, then of course, we will; otherwise our role is primarily social and educational. When the men were out fighting we were explaining to families and neighbours what was going on. We taught them how to face grave situations bravely. We offered them various services and ran special courses for mothers to teach them how to cope with the war situation. We also taught them religion and the place of women in Islam. Thus I can say that there is a comprehensive, educational movement, aiming at a fundamental reform in women's character and present position in society. There is a rebirth of the fundamental character of women within Amal, which is here to last. I don't think there is any danger that Lebanese women might go back to what they were before the emergence of Amal.

'Throughout Islamic history women were excellent fighters, warriors and army leaders. In some battles the men used to shave their heads completely to distinguish themselves from women fighters. In one battle in which the Muslims were short of supplies the women had the ingenious idea of riding horses and causing dust storms to mislead the enemy into believing that they were getting more supplies. The Prophet Mohammed found women braver and more reliable warriors than men. And for us, we aspire to be true Muslims; to emulate our female ancestors. The head of our women's organisation[3] in Amal never goes home from early morning till late evening. Her time is divided between meetings, lectures and other services. I once asked how she managed at home, and was told that her husband cooks, cleans and looks after their six children. He is a member of Amal, too, so he is very aware of the complexity of her work. It is quite normal for men in Amal to marry women who devote all their time to the movement. We never imagined that our men would reach this stage of understanding women's position – even in a hundred years' time – but here you are!'

The taxi I took drove through overcrowded, dusty alleyways where you could not tell the streets from the pavement. People were sitting in front of their shops drinking small cups of Turkish coffee. The children were everywhere: on the pavement, in the streets and between cars. They looked a bit shabby and dirty but very healthy. Although we passed about five checkpoints in about ten minutes' drive I was not in the least disturbed; people were smiling, joking and very friendly, even when they held guns. Zeinab asked the driver to stop in front of an unremarkable building which had nothing to distinguish it from any other poor building in deprived West Beirut. Inside, the office was simply furnished and the atmosphere was friendly, even homely. On the table there was a bowl of sweets to which everyone helped themselves, and on the wall there was a huge map of Lebanon and Amal's motto. Women wearing *Al Shari* came in, opened cupboards, put *caffans* in them and took black flags out. (A *caffan* is a white cloth in which a dead Muslim is wrapped.)

'They are preparing for *Ashora*, which is tomorrow,' said Zeinab noticing my curiosity. *Ashora* is the day when Imam Al Hussein, the Shiite's historical leader, was killed over twelve hundred years ago. On this day, Shiite Muslims all over the world go out on sad marches wearing mourning clothes and *caffans* and striking themselves, sometimes violently on the chest and head as an expression of sadness on the one hand, and on the other, readiness to sacrifice themselves for their murdered leader. The head of the women's organisation was holding a meeting next door. After about ten minutes, during which I tried to relax over a nice cup of coffee, a slim, middle-aged figure in a pale grey *shari* made even paler by a thin and evidently tired face, emerged.

'This is Um Mohamad Biadoun,'[4] Zeinab said.

We shook hands, exchanged greetings and before sitting down Um Mohamad Biadoun supported her back with both hands, muttering: 'This back pain is killing me; I've been sitting on these awful chairs for ten hours.'

'I am sorry to give you some extra work to do,' I felt obliged to say.

'No, no, not at all; it is my pleasure. In fact, I must thank you for coming all the way from Syria to find out about Lebanese women.'

Once she started talking I forgot most of the questions I had intended to ask and allowed myself the pleasure of just listening to her story.

'I am a Southern woman. I was born and brought up in Tyre. When

I finished my primary school there was no secondary school to go to. This was the first setback I had to face as a Southern woman. I had been doing extremely well at school and couldn't see why my schooling had to be brought to such an early and unnatural halt. I begged my father to send me to Sidon or to Beirut, but he was quite conservative and didn't approve of sending a girl on her own to another town away from her family. I was deeply hurt, wondering all the time why other girls who were much less intelligent than me should have the chance to continue their education while I was denied such a right. My younger sisters had to face the same fate. Once we finished the class available in the local school we had to sit at home as if doomed to a low educational level; that is, the level which the local school had provided. I was terribly unhappy and stopped eating. My father sympathised with me and showed his willingness to help by bringing me books and a teacher to teach me at home. I passed both my preparatory and secondary school examinations. I intended to continue my university studies but couldn't because I got married at the age of 16.

'I don't think I really wanted to get married, I thought deeply about the kind of life I wanted to live and seriously tried to do something about it. I was determined not to be a housewife spending my time cooking, cleaning and chatting to neighbours. But my family and brothers wanted me to marry, so I did. Of course, I had a say. Had I refused they wouldn't have forced me, but when I saw that they were all in favour of the marriage, I agreed to it. I was not in love or anything like that but we all had to get married some time or other. That is why I didn't mind getting married then. And, thank God, it has been a very happy marriage, full of understanding and love. The man I'm married to and I have the same ideas, principles and ambitions.

'In 1956, two years after our marriage, Samahat Al Imam Al Sadre[5] paid his first visit to Lebanon. My father was the secretary of the ''Charity and Beneficiary Society'' and had the honour to be host to Al Imam Al Sadre. So we were some of the first people to see him and respond to his call. I felt very close to him because he showed deep concern for the tragic conditions of the Southern people and started to point the way for us.

'There was another incident which also had a lasting effect on me. When my brother got married, he and his wife went to spend their honeymoon in Bhamdoun (a beautiful mountain resort on the outskirts of Beirut). I was ten years old then. They decided to take me with them. I had never been further than Tyre in my life. When we reached the mountains, I saw colourful lights, paved streets and beautiful houses. I couldn't believe my eyes and thought that perhaps we had entered another country. I asked my brother what the country was. He said that it was Lebanon; we were in Beirut travelling to Bhamdoun. When we reached Barouque and saw pleasant restaurants and cafés on the river banks I thought I was in Eden. I really did. Because this is how God describes Eden in the Koran. I started trembling, held my brother's hand and said that we read in the Koran that we would see all this in the afterlife, in Paradise. Was it possible that we were already there? But how could we be there and not have died? Looking at me with tearful eyes, my brother kissed me and said: "No, we are not in Paradise; this is all Lebanon and we are still alive."

'This shows you the incredible difference that existed at that time between South and North Lebanon. Following that incident I wanted to work day and night for the South. I desperately wanted to help all Southerners to improve their lot. We were living in darkness, in caves, in incredibly backward conditions. We used to wait until midnight to have electricity for two hours – and our town was the capital of the South.

'When Imam Al Sadre came to the South in the late 1950s he started to give lectures to both men and women in mosques and streets; he talked to people in their houses and on the street. He was so modest, humble, and open to all people, with an amazing gift for listening to both old and young. We found in him a father, teacher and saviour. He taught us how to face our terrible conditions and fight injustice. He told us that we only had to want to change our lives and we would be able to change them. You have only to want to be something and you will be that thing; you will be whatever you decide to be. If you want to stay in darkness you will stay in darkness, and if you decide to press ahead and be part of a civilised nation you will be such a person. We used to complain about the government and say that it was unfair. He used to answer: "You are being unfair to yourselves, because you have at least to try to fight injustice." I always felt that our traditional life and women's confinement to the home didn't generate anything but injustice and a stupid acquiescence towards it. So when Imam Al Sadre said you have only yourselves to blame we started to raise our voices; as women we started forming groups in which women were educated and encouraged to rebel against their unfair conditions.

'Thus the role which Southern women played during the Lebanese war was no surprise. We had been preparing them for it for over two decades. When Imam Al Sadre came I had two children and he explained to us the story in the Koran about the wife of Imran, the mother of the Virgin Mary. He said: "Before Jesus was born God prepared for him a good, strong and enlightened mother who could cope with pregnancy, childbirth and child rearing on her own, who could face her people and undertake the huge responsibility which God placed on her. No one could have brought up the Virgin Mary in such a way except a good and responsible mother. That mother was the wife of Imran."[6]

'Al Imam always stressed the importance of the mother's role in bringing up virtuous individuals. He often maintained that the Virgin Mary must have been an exceptionally strong and confident character to be able to mother Jesus and bring him up without the help of a father.[7] She formed the character of Jesus, the prophet and teacher of humanity.

'When I first got married I had a deep conflict within. I desperately wanted to do something to help all Southern women out of the misery which was engulfing them, and yet I found myself married, with babies and children to look after. I was not in the least convinced that I should spend my life looking after my home and family; I wanted to do something with my life, something worth doing. So when I heard Imam Al Sadre's account of the wife of Imran I started to imitate her in promising my children to God. When my son, Adib, (the one who was killed in the Lebanese war) was born, I promised him to God. Although I had six other children, Adib was very special to me. From early childhood he distinguished himself at home, at school and with friends. I always thank God for accepting from me the best of what he had given me. My son wasn't killed in the first battle. He lived through four years of war, and every time he came back from a battle with slight wounds in his hands and legs I used to clean them for him and he used to cry because some of his friends had died as martyrs and yet he was still alive. Every time before he went off to a battle he would come to ask me to pray for him that God might accept him as a martyr. He used to ask me: "Why doesn't God accept me from you?" and I used to answer, "Perhaps you still have a role to play." Finally, God answered our prayers and received him.

'My heart was cut in two. That particular night there was a very heated battle. Before he left my son kissed my hands and asked me to pray for him that God might accept him as a martyr. I did. He got into the army vehicle, looked back at me, smiled and left. Although I used to say goodbye to him every night, that night was very different. His eyes were saying to me that this was for the last time. I felt I was not going to see him again. It was a decisive battle; we didn't sleep all night. In the morning I prepared breakfast for those returning from the battle. All his friends came, but Adib didn't show up. I asked them one by one where he was; they said he was in an advanced position and might take a while to arrive. I started to prepare lunch, and still Adib hadn't turned up. Rumours started circulating that Adib might have been held hostage by the Israelis or that he might have been wounded and moved to hospital. I knew, however. I asked them not to play with my feelings. Adib had been killed.

'I tried to give first aid to a friend of his who was with him in the same group. I couldn't save him. He had deep wounds, lost most of his blood and died in my arms. I sent my daughter to his mother to tell her that her son and mine were two bridegrooms and that I was giving a party in their honour. All through the war I had been consoling mothers of the dead young men and giving them sound lectures about duty, honour and sacrifice, and today it was my turn. What should I say? Should I say I didn't mean what I said to the mothers? It is so very hard to lose one's child; to accept that one can never see him again. I felt terribly weak and was trying to resist with all the strength I could manage my body's urge to collapse. For a few minutes, all the theories I believed in turned into dust: I just wanted to see my son, to hold him, to embrace him and look him in the eyes. I wanted to feel his warm blood running through his veins; I wanted to feel his heart beat, to kiss his eyes and see that lovely smile again bidding me goodbye. Yet I had no choice but to pull myself together. He had made me promise not to cry or wear black if he had the honour to become a martyr. I never wore black and never shed a tear over him. Instead, I congratulated him and celebrated his death. When my husband and family started crying I stopped them and reminded them that Adib didn't accept that. "The party is in his honour," I said, "and we have to observe his wishes." The only thing I said was "*Mabrouk*" (Congratulations). God granted me patience and strength and I always thank him. Every time I see a dignified girl walking with her head high I say thank God. My son died but those women kept their honour and dignity. Thank God we didn't have a similar massacre to that of Sabra and Shatila. There was a plan that night to attack our area and do there what they did in Sabra and Shatila but the brave martyrs pre-empted this plan and defended us.

'Women play a decisive role in bringing up their children to be reliable and responsible citizens. Immediately after my son's death, my youngest brother came and said *"Mabrouk"* to him; "I promise you I will not lay down my arms." My younger son had deep wounds in his thigh and had to stay one whole year in hospital. When the Lebanese army entered West Beirut during the civil war they crushed his bones. Yet, once he was able to stand up, he prayed, carried his arms and went out to join his group. He refused to absent himself from any battle. The Shiites in Lebanon decided either to live digni-fied lives or not live at all. Our women are fighting the Israeli occu-pation with sticks, stones and boiling oil. They are standing unarmed in front of Israeli armed vehicles. You must have heard of Yassar Mroui, the brave woman who carried out 12 operations before the Israelis managed to kill her. Other women were pouring boiling oil on Israeli soldiers and were answering their shots with stones and sticks. All Southern women urged their children to join the Lebanese resist-ance and give their blood for the liberation of the land. Here, it is no longer the habit of women to mourn their dead children; instead they celebrate their death and hand their guns on to their younger brother or sister.

'There is a new type of marriage emerging in which partners seem to have rejected the traditional division of labour. Here, the woman spends the whole day working, the man does not complain. If there is no food in the house he either goes out and buys something ready-cooked, or he and his wife start cooking together. Men are becoming more and more aware of the huge burdens which women have to shoulder. I say to my husband and children: it is your right that I should spend more time with you; that I should bake you cakes and serve you tea, etc. But this right is something extra, it is not a neces-sity without which you can't survive. I have seven children. I say to them that if one of them got a fever or dangerous illness I would leave the rest and spend the whole time with the sick child, and that they would then have to manage without tea and cakes; they would have to understand that there is an emergency at home. I would say that this is what would happen if something were to happen to one of them.

What, then, about all the terrible things happening to our nation? All Lebanese women have announced a state of emergency in their homes because they have realised that our dignity, humanity and even existence are at stake. How could I celebrate my son's graduation from school when there are thousands of children crying in the streets wanting to go to school? I like to go home at one o'clock to prepare lunch for my family, but sometimes I have a widow, an emigrant or an orphan with a pressing problem to solve. Should I leave them and go home to cook lunch for my children? I don't, of course. My children can eat cheese or boiled eggs; there are other people who are starving. The important thing, I believe, is to make your husband and children feel that your cause is theirs; that they have to support you in your work which is both your right and your duty.

'One of my sons argues that if I want him to become a doctor or an engineer I have to provide the right atmosphere for him at home. I say I am ready to support him to perform very well in his studies but also ask him what he thinks he is going to do once he graduates. Won't he be denied 90 per cent of job opportunities because he belongs to a certain religious sect? As a Shiite you are immediately classified as a second-class citizen. There were no schools for us. We opened schools and universities. Now, a Shiite has to establish his or her right as an equal citizen. This is our problem in Lebanon. We suffer from a terrible sectarian political system. In the Arab world there are not all that many people starving or wanting a shirt to put on their backs, but there are many without dignity and without any rights. Hence, my job as a mother is not only to feed my children and to ensure they become physically strong, but I also have to teach them sociology, politics and religion; I have to inform them about moral and intellectual issues. No one suffers for long from a deficiency in vitamin B or from a dirty shirt, but there are millions of people suffering from slavery and from a lack of dignity. Now, Arab women are taking on the role of re-educating men who get their priorities wrong. Women in Lebanon have become precursors of a different lifestyle; they are ushering in a new vision of the future. Take any Lebanese woman and say to her that the American Navy is moving near Beirut. I am sure she would laugh and say, "So what?" We are no longer afraid of anything. We have rejected humiliation once and for all. We have discovered a deeper and more interesting meaning to our life. When women get married now, they have it written in their marriage contract that they reserve the right to continue their education and to go out to work, and this is quite legal in Islam.'

'Was this change in women's political position accompanied by a change in their social position, particularly concerning the laws of marriage and divorce?'

'Of course, it was; for the social is often linked with the political. People's thoughts direct their actions. I'll give you one example. In the past, people used to point at divorced women and say "poor things"; they used to pity them and look down on them because girls were brought up to think of a successful marriage as the be all and end all of life. Once they were married, women would put up with absolutely anything rather than be divorced; they would endure the most appalling relationships because of the threat of divorce.[8] Now things are changing. Marriage is no longer the centre around which women's lives revolve. Suppose a woman got married and couldn't reach an understanding with her husband and got a divorce, so what? What is the big problem? Divorce is legal and Islamic. If the woman has no freedom and no dignity in her married life she would be better off without it. Islam is very explicit about the rules of divorce and, in fact, favours divorce to permanent conflict and miserable family life which holds no hope, either for the couple or their children. Women cannot fight social or political tyranny if they remain slaves at home. They cannot reform their society unless they reform themselves first and become free and independent individuals. There are women whose self-reform was preceded by their involvement with social work, but they found their lives quite difficult because when there are men who have lived 20 years of their lives according to a certain style, it is difficult to convince them to change. This is why I always maintain that our children are going to be much better off than we are. They started on the right basis; they are freer and more independent individuals, and therefore they are better equipped to do their social and political work properly.'

'It is a historical fact that Arab women perform brilliantly in emergencies, but that once the emergency is called off they are forced back to their domestic, traditional role. What, in your opinion, guarantees that the Lebanese women won't lose this advanced position reached during the war once the war is over?'

'Yes, we do feel we are living through an emergency. And once the reasons for this emergency are removed we would go back to live normal lives. So many women now are working at three times the pace they should. Therefore we all look forward to the day when social justice is achieved and we can go back to live quiet lives again. But this does not mean going back to our domestic roles or to confinement in the home. We are asking for a balance between our social, personal and domestic duties. Now, I am responsible for a whole district which needs a lot of work, but sometimes I stop and say I have a duty towards my husband and children. I have to maintain a balance between my work and my family. Even the Prophets, who had tremendous responsibilities, had their personal lives to look after, as they had secluded times with their God. I don't think there is any danger of going backwards. During wartime we have duties and during peace time we have even more difficult duties. We have educational courses, training courses and social groups to run and through all these we hope that women's lot will improve permanently. Now women are aiming to enter the next election for the Politbureau of our movement.'

'As a consequence of the appearance of the Muslim Brotherhood[9] in both Algeria and Egypt, for example, women are becoming more reserved and withdrawn whereas religious revival in Lebanon seems to be helping women to be more active and outgoing. How do you explain the essential difference between these two ostensibly religious phenomena?'

'I can't say that religion asks women to leave their study or their work and stay at home. The Prophet Mohammed said: "Acquiring knowledge is the duty of each man and woman Muslim." As for the Islamic dress, if I want to understand it as a call to stay at home there will be no need for it. For I don't wear it with my husband and children. I wear it when I need to go out and mix with other men. This is what it is for, this is its primary function. Basically, Islamic dress is holy. If we are Muslims it is a religious law to wear *Al Shari*. There are frank and clear texts in the Koran about it, and the Prophet Mohammed spoke about it as well. If you want my personal opinion, I would say that even if Islam didn't ask me to wear *Al Shari* I would have worn it anyway. I don't like to be treated as a female body. My body is for the secluded time I spend with my husband. We all know that if we lift our sleeves up a bit men are going to concentrate on our hands rather than on what we say. I don't want that. I want to be able to feel a proper human being rather than just a sexual entity. I want my brain rather than my body to speak for me. In society, I want to behave normally and move freely. *Al Hijab*[10] helps me to do that. But *Al Hijab* is not only a matter of clothing; it is exemplified in voice and movement, too. For example, if you see a woman neighbour first thing in the morning, you might say: "Good morning, how are you, etc.", but if you see her husband you might soften your voice a bit and speak in a slightly different accent. This manner of speaking is prohibited in Islam with the injunction, "Don't deceive in speech." *Al Hijab* both protects the family and protects women from being viewed as sexual objects. Indeed, *Al Hijab* is first and foremost to protect the rights of women.

'God trusted woman with the most sacred responsibility; the upbringing of a new generation. "The woman is like the Koran; both are entrusted with the responsibility of making men." It is a fact that women are more courageous and more reliable at a time of crisis than men. I can give you many examples in support of this statement. Here, in Lebanon, the Lebanese army invaded our homes many times and arrested our men. In one of the attacks on our parish it called all the inhabitants of the building – men, women and children – to go outside. It was midnight and everyone went down in their nightdresses and pyjamas. Men and women, old and young, all had to kneel down and put their hands up. Guns were pointed at our heads. None of the men dared say a word, while the women started speaking against this barbaric behaviour. You could hear women addressing the officers: "You are our army, the Lebanese army, and you dare do this to us! We went on demonstrations to bring you here to protect us, and you are here to insult, attack and humiliate us. What sort of crime have we committed to deserve this treatment? We brought our children up to love their country and army, and you are coming here to show us to be liars in front of them. Why don't you fight Saad Haddad[11] and Israel, or is that a bit too difficult for you?"

'In another incident the army stormed a school in front of my house. I looked out of the window and a soldier shouted: "Shut your window," and started firing in the air to frighten me. I said I wouldn't shut it, looked down and saw them kicking young children downstairs. The men didn't dare move. I put my gown on and started to go down. My husband and brother tried to stop me, but couldn't. The soldiers started firing towards me. I opened my arms to them and said that they were welcome. They were our army and they must have been proud of themselves to shoot us. If they were men they would have protected us from the Israelis but they were cowards, coming to shoot Lebanese citizens here. A soldier pushed me to go inside. I said to him: "I won't go in and we won't keep silent; we shall answer you, soon." '

'During the war, only the Muslim women involved themselves with all national and local issues, whereas Christian women seem to have kept themselves apart from what was happening. Why do you think that was?'

'Compared with Muslim women, Christian women are privileged. As citizens they have more rights and their problems are less pressing than those of Muslim women. As for us, we didn't have schools, we couldn't go to university, we couldn't get jobs, etc . . . So we had a cause to fight for. Compared to this, Christian women were born in Paradise – what did they have to fight for? This is what I believe. They have all the schools, jobs and positions. They also have the support of all countries in the West. Many Western countries speak in their name, but none speaks in our name. As citizens of the same country, we believe that Lebanon should be for the Muslims as well as the Christians. This has created a problem and a cause for us; any one who has a cause has to fight for it. Christian women had no cause, so they didn't have to fight.'

'Lebanon is the only Arab country which has many women's organisations. Do you think this is a positive phenomenon which is enhancing women's struggle for emancipation?'

'In our situation one organisation is not enough. We need as many organisations as we can possibly get. Most women's organisations here have played an honourable role in helping people on the social level. Perhaps they could have done more, but on the whole I find it a healthy phenomenon that instead of spending their time doing mundane, futile jobs, women have started to live the problems, hopes and ambitions of their society through these organisations. There are some purely social societies which bear no relation to any political party, and there are some groups which are offshoots of political parties. Our union belongs to the latter group; we are part of the Amal movement. Our main task is to fight for women's rights and try to help women, but our policy is that of Amal. Our aim is to achieve justice for all the oppressed. When our movement started it was called the "Movement of the Oppressed". We aim to lift oppression and achieve social justice and equality without any discrimination on the basis of sex, religion, race or class. We are trying to help all the oppressed, both socially and politically.'

Mrs Fatima Fawaz, the deputy head of the Southern Woman's House Society, is one of those intelligent women who fully understand the important role of the press in disseminating information about the welfare work she is doing, and therefore at every stage of her work she pays attention to press coverage. Mrs Fawaz, a young mother of two boys, was more trendy and Westernised than most of the women I met in West Beirut. Although a member of the Amal movement (and an important one at that), she did not wear either *Al Shari* or *Al Hijab*. Her flat was quite well furnished, and she was keen to show me that she had the latest gadgets. It was in her flat that I first saw a cordless telephone when she came towards the reception hall, speaking on a phone attached to no wire! She was very friendly and welcoming. Zeinab and I arrived at her flat at about six o'clock in the evening and were told that she was expecting visitors around eight o'clock so we had better get on with the interview straight away. Even before we had a chance to start, however, some other unexpected guests arrived and we had to go to her bedroom to talk briefly to her in private.

'The Southern Woman's House Society,' she said, 'is a society of Southern women who are anxious to offer their services to the occupied South. We started in 1981, and the first thing we thought of doing was to open nurseries and kindergartens for the children of working mothers here. We started contacting societies and individuals until someone volunteered to give us a piece of land to build on. The land was in Toul, near Al Nabitieh. Three young engineers also volunteered to supervise the building. We started collecting money for the centre, but on 6 February 1982 the Lebanese army bombarded West Beirut, hoping to destroy Amal rather than come to terms with the organisation. As a result, thousands of people became homeless. We had to shelve our plan for building the centre and started trying to house and feed thousands of people who overnight had become refugees in their own town.

'We contacted big businessmen who owned tower blocks of empty flats, got the keys for hundreds of flats, and started calling people over loudspeakers to come to us. They responded. We opened five buildings which had over 150 flats and started to place one family in each room. There were too many people; we couldn't house one tenth of the homeless. The flats had absolutely no furniture; there were no chairs, no beds, nothing in them. But first we wanted to feed people. Each woman tried to do things in her own way. I rang the Red Cross and asked for food for all these hungry families. The Red Cross answered my call and it took us a few days to register the names of all these people, make proper statistics and distribute what information we had about them. Then we discovered that there was no medicine, milk, or nappies for babies. So we contacted the Save the Children Fund and asked them to supply us with these things. They did and we bought some of these items from our own funds. After 6 February some of the refugees went back to their homes and things got a bit quieter. It was time for some political activity. We held a press conference in which we announced the beginning of our society and at the same press conference we announced that we were going to occupy *'Dar Al-Fatwa'* (the house of legislation) in support of women in the South. Mothers of kidnapped children and wives of kidnapped husbands joined us and the occupation turned into a big demonstration. After all this we thought of giving the orphans a treat. We invited all the children to a huge party in Borj Al Barajneh, and distributed clothes, presents and sweets. On Mother's Day we invited all the mothers to a big party, auctioned the food and devoted the funds to the single mothers. Then we made silver medals with our society's name and offered them to patients in hospitals. Throughout all this time we were collecting information about women fighters in the South. There are women who go to the South and collect information and provide us with pictures and stories of women fighters there. Some women in the South plan operations, hide the fighters and secure an escape route for them. We wanted these women to feel our support for them, so we started going down to the South despite all the humiliations and difficulties we faced in getting there. I suggested going on women's demonstrations in the South. I contacted Mr Nabbih Berri and Mr Walid Jumblatt and asked their opinion. They said it was a good idea, but that we might be risking our lives; the Israelis might shoot us.

'Despite all the warnings from different political figures and organisations we decided to go ahead with our plan. We announced it in the newspapers and on radio and television. On the day we specified for our demonstration we travelled in cars to Pieter, at the border with the occupied South, where we left our cars and started walking towards the Israelis. The Red Cross there warned us that the Israelis intended to shoot. We said we didn't care and went ahead. When we advanced towards the Israelis they retreated and started taking the barbed wire back. Many women had loudspeakers and you could hear them shouting at the Israeli soldiers: "This is our land, get off it; this is our beloved South, we will never let you rest on it."

'We put our Lebanese flags up and started throwing stones at the Israeli soldiers. It was an emotional sight. The women were very enthusiastic and we were all prepared to die and embrace the land which we love. The Israelis didn't open fire on us and the demonstration was a great success. Now we are planning a sit-in in the United Nations' building in New York. We want to raise our voice against the Israeli occupation so that all women in the world will hear us and, I am sure, support us. We want the whole world to know what our people, particularly women, in the South are suffering; we want to expose the crimes which the Israelis have committed against innocent citizens. We have films, leaflets and literature for the world to see and read, and I am sure that most women will support us.'

'Is your society affiliated to any political party?'

'No. It has no political identity. It is the society of the Southern women. All our members are from the South; they belong to all religious sects: Christian, Druze and Muslim. If other people from other parts of Lebanon would like to help us they are welcome, but all our activities are concerned with the South because the South has always suffered both from the neglect of the State and the continuous and barbarous Israeli attacks, although if you consider the land geographically, the South has the richest soil and its people are the best.'

'Do you feel that this new political role which the Lebanese women played during the war has changed the traditional outlook of women as the weaker sex?'

'For sure. Women are working harder than men. Take me, for example. I teach all morning; in the afternoon I am active in my women's society; and in the evening I have my children and husband to whom I also have a duty. Our men understand and appreciate our new responsibilities. Had they not supported us we would have had family conflicts and we wouldn't have been able to perform so well in our social work. However, they are very encouraging to us in this new role of ours which we started playing in the life of our country.

Most educated men have now accepted women as their equals. Even if you consider the question from a religious point of view, you find that Islam has called every man and woman who is able to work to do so for the benefit of his or her society. It is irreligious for both man and woman to stay at home if they can offer something useful to their society. Islam never prevented women from playing their full role in society. During the life of the Prophet Mohammed we had the best women poets, fighters and activists in various social and political fields. As far as the teachings of Islam are concerned, women should never be confined to housework, cooking and bringing up children as some Muslims claim nowadays. I feel if Islam were to be properly applied women would reach their full rights and achieve absolute equality with men. Although I don't wear the Islamic dress I feel it helps a woman to carry out her role. Look at nuns; the way they dress is very similar to the way Muslim women dress, yet no one has ever suggested that the way they dress hinders their work – and they work very hard. I feel there is something decent and self-respecting in the ways we dress but don't feel it necessary to wear *Al Shari*. A mature woman has a stronger presence if she dresses nicely and decently. Here in Lebanon I feel that the war has had a positive effect on women's struggle for emancipation. It has marked a new dawn in the life of the Lebanese woman. She has become more confident and more efficient, but at the expense of her nerves and rest. A huge number of women have had nervous breakdowns. Tranquillisers were sold out in pharmacies all over the country. There was a general state of exhaustion. When you have to double or treble your working hours over a long period, naturally you collapse.'

'What do you think about the future of the Lebanese woman?'

'Lebanon has always been an open country. We are influenced by the Western style of life. So I don't think there is any fear that the Lebanese woman might go back on her achievements. The role she is playing in the current emergency will continue, perhaps in other forms, once the emergency is over. For the decisive role which the Lebanese woman has played during the war has engendered a new vision of the role she might always play in the life of her country in the future. I certainly don't think there is any danger that the Lebanese woman might face the same fate which the Algerian woman had to face after the independence of Algeria. It is true that the Algerian woman fought, carried arms and played a crucial role in the war for independence, but she didn't enjoy the same awareness and under-standing of the nature of her role which the Lebanese woman now enjoys.

Mrs Randa Berri was not a political woman but the wife of the leader of the Amal movement, Mr Nabih Berri. Being pregnant, Mrs Berri looked quite pale and tired but nonetheless showed a genuine willing-ness to talk to me, and even allowed me to choose between conducting the interview in Arabic or in English, which is unusual because the second language in Lebanon is French rather than English. She was clearly an intelligent, well-spoken woman.

The first thing I wanted to know from her was whether she belonged to any women's society in Lebanon. 'No, I don't,' she said, 'because this would need time and I have to be in touch with all the societies. But we now have a plan to build a big centre for the handicapped and the maimed. Conditions after the war forced us very seriously to think of something for the handicapped, so we started the Lebanese Society for Looking After the Handicapped of which I am president. I have the four founding members of doctors and nurses with me. We started with small centres, hoping to be able to build the big centre soon. The small centres only offer medical care, while the big centre is expected to offer medical care, career training, leisure facilities, etc. but even this is not going to be enough, especially in West Beirut where the war has left us with a huge number of injured people. At first I wanted to open this centre in the South. In the South alone we had 7,000 handicapped in 1982. But the difficult situation in the South and the difficulty of getting in and out, particularly for me, forced me to change my mind. In this society we have men and women mem-bers; I don't spare anyone who can help, especially as our great need is not for building and equipment but for manpower.'

'How did your role as a working woman develop and change during the war?'

'I have always been against the theory that women should stay at home, though I believe, of course, that every woman has a duty towards her home and children. The woman who decides to partici-pate in social life and work has to make more sacrifices than the woman who opts to stay at home. But you forget about the sacrifices when you really want to do something with your life and to play a positive role in your society. When I left school I started working in my father's publishing house, Dar Al Andolos. After my father's death, my elder sister took charge of the business and I started to help her. After getting married and becoming active in the social field, however, I was no longer able to work regular hours with my sister. Eventually I stopped working in the literary field and devoted all my time to social work. I strongly believe that women who stay at home and content themselves with looking at glittering dishes and producing delicious meals are throwing their lives away. In Lebanon, more than in any other Arab country, women have great freedom to do the job they are qualified to do. You notice today, for example, women in the Amal movement might appear to a passing onlooker to be conservative, Muslim women. Quite the contrary; you may find them better givers than other women. I tend to favour the role of the Muslim woman because Islam asks Muslim women not to spare any effort in serving their society. So the Muslim woman goes out to work with a clear conscience because she is fulfilling an Islamic duty. Islam, more than any other religion, acknowledges the social value of women's work – because if you are able to manage a family you are likely to be able to manage a much larger social unit. What distinguishes Islam from every other religion is that it contains a complete system for both religion and State. Despite the length of time which has elapsed since the Koran was written, there is hardly any contemporary question to which you don't find a reference in it. This is why I find that the woman who understands her religion and the Koran well is necessarily a good giver.'

'But the present role of the Muslim woman in Lebanon was unknown before the war, surely?'

'On the contrary. Perhaps the war made it known to the world press; perhaps the number of women working in social work has increased. For example before the war two or three centres only were enough for the handicapped who were deformed either by birth or as a result of road accidents, whereas during the war we had more people injured in one day than we would have had in three or four years of peace time. So naturally we needed more people, and more women turned up. Women were always working in social work in Lebanon, but their number has increased dramatically during the war. Even now, the press has not done the Muslim woman justice. She works day and night but no one seems to hear of her. As you know, in Islam we are warned against propagating the good work we do; the real

Muslim is the one who "doesn't let his left hand know of what his right hand has given". It is the duty of each man and woman Muslim to serve his or her society and this should be done without a feeling that anybody is being done a favour. There was a certain number of women working at grassroots level, but the war required more – and more women – who came along. Naturally, the larger number made a stronger impact on the world's press. When there is an understanding built on Islamic principles between partners the woman finds no problem in going out and doing all the work she wants to do. Take me, for example. My husband, Nabih Berri, is the leader of Amal, and with all his work he has no objection whatsoever to me doing twenty-four hours a day of social work. On the contrary, he encourages me, enthuses me and sometimes, when he finds me tired, comforts me and says: "God will help because you are helping the needy". I am sure I couldn't stand all my duties if it were not for his understanding and support. In fact, I found myself very happy when I started treating my husband according to true Islamic principles and I could see from those around me that people who follow the rules of Islam in their family and social life are much happier and much better off than those who don't (and regretfully they are the majority). I treat my husband as my religion has asked me to do, and he does the same. There is no doubt that men are "the protectors and maintainers of women"[12], but I know my limits and I don't have to go beyond them to clash with my husband. Thus I live happily. I have no objection to my husband's work, though sometimes he doesn't sleep and doesn't rest at all which upsets me. Still, I don't show any objection to his work because I might prevent him from serving people who really need him and that would make me feel guilty. According to my Islamic education and understanding I should share his burden rather than try to stop him helping others. From my personal experience I find that Islamic principles are good for a happy family life.'

'What do you think is the difference between the experience of Lebanese women and that of Algerian women?'

'I believe that the political system and situation of women in Lebanon is different from that which obtains in Algeria. During the Algerian revolution there were no societies for women and even now there is only one which is supervised and directed by the political party there. In Lebanon at the moment we have a great number of independent organisations for women which, together with the social services, are spreading new information about women's rights and emancipation. As well as enlightening people these women are gaining experience, and I believe in the political action which results from experience rather than from education and academic knowledge. Politics is not an easy job. There are very few women in the Middle East now who would really like to pursue a political career. As for me I never want to be in a leading political position because I know that I wouldn't be good at it. On the whole I think that the situation in Lebanon now is quite different from that in Algeria during the revolution. Time and again the Lebanese women have proved their determination to play an active role in the life of their country. Women played an honourable role during the civil war and the Israeli invasion of the South. Even women who lost husbands, children and sometimes homes, came out on the streets to help the hungry, the orphaned and the old. Most women left their homes and children and went out to offer whatever help they could. These determined women will not give up what they have achieved; they certainly won't go back on these achievements.'

'Was this great role which the Lebanese women played during the war an extra burden which she had to shoulder, or did she manage to shake off some of her traditional duties at home?'

'The change started when women began to go out to work, a stage which preceded their total involvement with social work during the war. But in all cases, going out to work required further sacrifices from women. It might well have caused some chaos in their homes but they were determined to carry on. They had dual responsibilities and they certainly got exhausted. I am not sure how willing the men were to understand their wives' position and to help at home or with the children; most Arab men refuse to help at home. Moreover, the man has his rights, too. Just as the woman has the right to go out to work, he has the right to see his wife and enjoy her company. We shouldn't aim at a life where the man comes in and the woman goes out. Family life should be lived and enjoyed by both partners. In this case everything depends on the woman and how dynamic she can be. For example, as my husband is not here this week I am trying to see all those I would like to see because I am anxious that when he is here I should spend more time with him at home. If he comes back from his office to find that I have opened another office here, how can he get any rest? In my opinion no educated man objects to his wife going out and exercising her full social right, provided she doesn't neglect her husband and house.'

'As the wife of the leader of the Amal movement what is your opinion on the position of the Lebanese woman in general – her role, achievement and future?'

'There is no doubt that woman's role in society should be acknowledged gratefully, but it also needs further encouragement. We have many intelligent and capable women, but we need a lot more. Sometimes family responsibilities or other circumstances prevent women from giving as much as they can. This is why we need every woman to be involved; we need all women to give as much as they possibly can because we need a lot of help. If I want to speak about the South and the poverty-stricken areas it is not much to ask for 70 or even 100 societies for women to come about. There is horrifying misery and intense wretchedness in the South; we need consciousness-raising movements. Our people in the South suffer a great deal, though they are just as capable as people here or anywhere else in the world. Even today there is about one school for every 50 villages. This is why I would like our women to go there, see the kind of life people are living and try to help. Educated women, I believe, are best qualified to do such social work; they are much better at it than men.'

Meeting Nadia Nouihid in Beirut was a real treat for me. When I rang her she had already packed and was about to set off for the weekend. 'If you arrive within half an hour,' she said on the phone, 'we shall sit and talk; if you don't I'll take it that you are not coming and will be free to leave.' There was no way I wanted to miss the chance of meeting the author of *Candles*, an elegantly feminist book, and most beautifully written, about the genuine problems of Arab women. Apart from *Candles* she has also published hundreds of articles in various Lebanese papers and journals. She was also working on a 'Who's Who' type of book for Lebanese women called *Examples from History*.

Nadia Nouihid started talking in a beautiful literary language and with a voice which mesmerised me, particularly as I knew that the speaker was in her mid-fifties and that she had raised a family of six children, all of whom were university graduates. I knew beforehand that she was the head of the Druze Welfare Society, so I decided my first question would be about this society. Her story was as follows.

'I was in Venezuela and came to Beirut, to Al Msietbi borough which was a poor one. The Druze Welfare Society was already established, with its centre in an elementary school. So it was at a modest level, you might say. I joined the Society and started discussing a plan for improving it with other members. Shortly afterwards we started a health centre in the area, opened preparatory and secondary schools, and a training centre for women who either don't want to or can't continue their education. As you know, education in Lebanon is not free – in fact it is quite expensive – and therefore a great number of women can't afford to continue their education. We teach at least 120 women a year to be dressmakers and we run other training courses for typing, drawing, knitting, needlework, etc. . . . I believe in the Chinese proverb which says, "Teach the poor how to fish instead of giving him a fish," because you can feed him once or twice but not every time.

'In our society the number of women members has exceeded the number of men and has surpassed them in achievement. There are more than twelve women on each of the health, education, finance and propaganda committees. We have over 500 women members to only about 20 men and there are about 2,000 honorary members. These honorary members are not very active. They only meet once a year and pay their contributions to the Society. But the members who are really active and do most of the work are women. Through carrying out various jobs women have proved themselves to be more patient and efficient than men. That is why I would like the Lebanese State to give women the chance to participate in the political life of the country especially after we have proved that we are at least as good, if not better, than the men. We are not given the chance to play a political role in the life of our country because men are very selfish. They always say women can't do this, that and the other, although women have time and again proved themselves better than men in whatever jobs they have undertaken. A woman who manages a family successfully is surely able to run a bigger social institution. The woman who gives her society successful children is often able to be an MP. We have many MPs and even government employees who never say a word and whose voice or opinion we never hear. If women took their place they would surely do far better.

'Men will never let women in if women don't force their way in. To do that, women should help each other; they shouldn't allow envy and jealousy to spoil their support for each other. We should help and vote for each other. As we have the right to vote we should vote for good, capable women, but unfortunately we still lack solidarity with each other. We all say we want to see women reaching high positions, but we don't do anything about it. It is about time we started taking definite steps towards that. First of all a woman should help her sisters. Whenever there is a capable woman candidate all women should vote for her. Why should they vote for a man if there is a woman just as good, unless they feel inferior and can't believe that a woman could be as good as a man? We have to support all women who are trying to reach key posts in our country.

'Today women are just as well educated as men, if not better educated, and I can see that we have many women who are better than our ministers and MPs. Yet we still don't have a single woman MP. We once had Mrs Munera Al Bostani who inherited her father's seat in Parliament, but she didn't stay long and was not very impressive. Perhaps she was the wrong person to be the first woman MP. But we have many other Lebanese women who are much better qualified for such a job. We have at least 15 women who are ready and able to occupy ministerial and parliamentary posts. The Lebanese women should press the State to change its attitude towards women. For example, during this war the Lebanese women played a glorious role in helping the homeless, the hungry and the orphans; why shouldn't they have a say in deciding their own future and in helping themselves? We are trusted with giving birth to children, bringing them up and making them men, but not with taking any decision concerning their lives. Quite the contrary; they decide our lives. We create life and they control it. If you want to know about the civilisation of a nation you have only to ask about the role of women in it. Ignorant women bring up slaves while educated and enlightened women bring up educated and healthy members of society. This is why it is our responsibility to bring up our children, boys and girls, in the same way. We always bring up boys to be heads of families; for girls we have only warnings: "Don't do this." "This will harm your reputation." "This is socially unacceptable." And so on. This way we make her feel inferior. Whereas we have only encouragement for the boy: "You are a man; you have to do this and should be able to do that," etc. If we give girls equal freedom and bring them up in the same way we bring boys up, they will surely be just as good in every field.

'Freedom can be interpreted in many ways, but the freedom which we should give women is the freedom to know, to understand and to behave as a free and independent character. In Lebanon, now, women should participate in decision-making. The Women's Council which represents all societies of women in the country, should press for the political participation and representation of women. I strongly believe that if all women's societies united and worked together through the Women's Council women would soon reach key political positions in the country. In the past women tried to do this through the Women's Council but they didn't succeed because people didn't have enough understanding of women's important role, but the attempt in itself was a good thing. Even women voters, then, did not give them enough support. Women voters usually vote for what their fathers, brothers and husbands vote for. In most cases they have not reached a stage where they can hold an independent opinion and defend it. You know the problems of election. Some people buy votes; candidates exert various influences on the voters to vote for them. All these things are symptoms of backwardness of which we should be ashamed. I hope things will be different for our children's generation.'

'What do you think of the women's societies which appeared during the war? Do you think they stressed the traditional role of women – teaching, nursing, etc. Or do you think they signalled a new beginning in the life of the Lebanese woman?'

'It was not a new beginning at all because throughout our history whenever there is any problem in the Arab world you find women rushing in to do all they can to help, and they always perform marvellously well. There is nothing new in that. I have always maintained that our role should not be only to teach, nurse and help at moments of crisis. We should play an active role in deciding the fate of our country. We need a different political system in which women are allowed to play a fundamental role. Women should not only treat the wounded and feed the hungry. Our mothers and grandmothers used to do this efficiently without having our education. Moreover, men may decide the wrong policy for the country. Perhaps if we had three or four women ministers in the Government Lebanon might have been saved this bloody civil war. Because by nature women are not bloodthirsty; they fear bad things happening to their children. That is why I much prefer to have women politicians and I can't wait to see them at the centre of the political arena. Women nowadays are not sitting at home consoling the homeless and offering first aid to the wounded; they are facing the Israelis and fighting bravely to liberate their land. They are challenging the system which ignores them. The Southern woman has become the pride of Lebanon.

'The Lebanese woman also has to economise to help her cause. We have been asking all Lebanese and other Arab women to help the South; every pound is needed in our battle with the Israelis. As Lebanese women we want to be heard and we are sure that all women who love their children and their countries will sympathise with us. The trouble is that what counts nowadays is the media rather than the truth. The Israelis have all the American and Western media at their disposal, whereas we have no access to either. That is why they have more supporters in the West. As for the Americans they might have a lot of human knowledge but they don't have a clue about the Lebanese, the Palestinian or Arab problems in general. They finance Israeli attacks on us but they have no idea about the Lebanese–Israeli conflict. Israel portrays the Lebanese as ignorant, primitive people and they believe that. And the problem with the Americans is that once they learn something about something they can't learn to think of it in a different way. They must be the most gullible people on earth. I believe people have to think about what they hear, but the Americans don't think about what Israel tells them; they always take what is said to be the ultimate truth.'

'How do you think the role of the Lebanese woman has changed during the war?'

'Before the war most women's societies aimed to help the poor, the needy and the handicapped, while during the war they took on a more national role. They started calling upon men to go out to fight and defend their country. In these societies women were taught how to inspire their husbands and children with enthusiasm to face the Israeli enemy and protect their homes and land. Women's conceptions of themselves also changed during the war. They became more aware of their abilities and the role they could play in their country's life. Their concerns were no longer only to feed their children and keep their homes tidy; they wanted to fight; they wanted to prove to the Israelis that they were not going to have an easy task bombing and shelling Lebanon whenever they felt like it. During the war I found women to be more challenging than men. They were perhaps discovering for the first time not only how much they love Lebanon but also how much they could do when they need to. So you could say that the wai has helped to show women's ability and potential. I didn't see one woman moaning or complaining; they were all full of enthusiasm and determination. I looked at them and said to myself, "Oh my God, where were all these brilliant creatures previously? In their homes spending ten hours a day cleaning floors and washing dishes? What a terrible waste!" The war gave me to believe that women are more courageous, resolute and determined than men.'

'There are many Arab women who share your view that women's abilities surpass those of men and yet they are always kept in a subordinate position in life. Why do you think that is?'

'Men always say about women that their passion rather than their minds directs them. Men like women to be weaker than themselves. Once I was asked if I believed that a man is the head of the family. I said surely. Even if he is weak the woman should help him to feel strong, because women like strong men. Let the man be the head of the family, but the woman has to be a strong neck which knows how to move and direct this head! No woman should accept the position of being a man's shadow; she should be his companion and friend. Why should I feel less than a man? I am his mother, wife and daughter and I might be a better citizen than he, so why can't I be his equal? Both man and woman should respect each other, consult each other and ask for each other's opinion. It is not a woman's duty to say "yes" to whatever her man says in order to be described as a good, obedient woman. Such an act would be done in ignorance rather than obedience. The more we raise our voices and let our opinions be known the more men respect us, rather than just take us for granted. Our women in the East suffer from the fact that if a woman fails or makes a mistake all women are blamed and pointed at. A bad or ignorant woman is always taken as invincible proof that all women are weak and ignorant. The same thing does not apply to men. A man who blunders in one way or another is singled out as a bad individual, but his experience is never taken to touch on other men's reputations. This is an Eastern mentality. In the West people don't blame all women for what one of them does. We keep saying to our women: "Don't do this and don't do that." "This is *aib* (socially shameful) and that is *haram* (religiously prohibited)", until we give them a complex about almost everything. People don't seem to think that what used to be *aib* is no longer *aib*. As Easterners we give too much importance to social opinion and as women are taken to be the honour of the family, the source of its pride or shame[13] they end up paying the price. But I must add that most of our educated men have outgrown the traditional regard for women as sex, decor or beauty. When you go out to work among men and you appear and dress respectably and you take your job seriously they can't help respecting you. We can say that the educated, well-informed woman is quite appreciated by our men.'

'What do you think of Lebanese law? Do you think it treats a woman as a man's equal?'

'Some sects have unfair legislation regarding women, but on the whole Lebanese laws do not discriminate between men and women. Take, for example, the Muslim section, I think the Koran is fair to women. What we have to make sure of, though, is that the Islamic laws echo the Koran. It has to be said that in the Koran a woman is not quite equal to a man but still most of her rights are spelt out. She is even allowed to trade and to have her personal property, independent of family and husband. As for the Christians in Lebanon, women have exactly the same rights as men. The Christian woman inherits an equal share with her brother, whereas the Muslim woman inherits only half of what her brother does.

'Still, I believe that what needs to be changed in the Arab world is not the laws and legislation; rather it is men's attitudes to women. It is true that the laws are not perfect, but it is also true that people's attitudes lag far behind these laws. I blame Arab women for not making more effort to change people's convictions and opinions. The Arab woman should bring men up the right way. She should teach them to respect their mothers, sisters, etc. She has to make her son feel that he is equal to his sister, no more or less. Why should the boy get a better deal? Why should he be treated any differently from the girl? They used to teach boys and leave girls without education because the boys used to go out to work and earn a living for the family. Nowadays the woman also goes out to work and earns a living for her family, so where is the difference? Now there is even more stress on women's education because women are going to bring up the next generation. In my opinion we have to respect ourselves, to think well of ourselves to force men to think well of us and respect us. My son now tells me where he is going in the same way as my daughter does. I am not going to prevent either of them from going out, but I expect to be told where they are going to be and they both tell me in the same way. There is no law which can change a man's attitude to a woman if she herself can't do that. We give birth to men, we bring them up, we make them what they are – why can't we give them the right attitudes to women? If we don't do that for ourselves, no one is going to do it for us.

'There are some women who try to win their husbands' affection or sympathy by behaving in a childlike fashion and asking their husbands' opinion about everything, either big or small. This will keep them in a subservient position and reinforce the traditionally inherited image of them as the weaker sex. There is a difference between consultation and discussion on the one hand and blind obedience on the other. For example, I wanted to go in a women's delegation to a sit-in in the United Nations' building in New York. I didn't say to my husband, "Would you please let me go, darling! Do you love me? Would you allow me to go?" No such nonsense! I said to him: "Did you know that the House of the Southern Woman is sending a delegation to the UN and that they have asked me to go? What do you think?" He said "Well, we can discuss it." So we did, and I am going, of course. You might consult your neighbour or ask for a friend's opinion, and there is nothing wrong with asking for your husband's opinion, but there is everything wrong with women reducing themselves to mere followers of men instead of being their equals and companions.'

'How do you compare the liberation movement of the Lebanese woman with that of Western women?'

'The Lebanese woman has no reason to envy any woman in the world. I have lived in North and South America and experienced different attitudes to women. I still like women to have their pride, honour and dignity. We have beautiful traditions and we should keep them. Cleanliness in body as well as in the mind is lovely. Women's honour is priceless; if she wins the whole world and loses her honour she won't be in an enviable position. The Western woman has lost her family. I love my family. I would not exchange my family happiness with anything, absolutely anything, in the world. When we sit all together round the table to eat I feel I am the happiest person on earth. Western women miss this precious feeling. I feel that the Western woman is lost. It is true that she has more personal freedom than the Eastern woman and that she is more comfortable; she enjoys leisure and rest times – which we hardly have at all – but I feel we are still happier than Western women. We are happy to be able to give so much to our homes and families. Our life-long sharing of our children's experiences throughout the different stages of their lives is lovely. Also, when your children get married you have grandchildren. I have eight grandchildren and I am interested in their growth and development. There is no happiness to equal this lovely happiness, and this is what the West needs. I don't think there is any woman in the world better than the Lebanese woman. Except for this war we would have been the envy of the world, because Lebanon, in fact, is a happy and civilised country. The Lebanese man is faithful to his wife and she is faithful to him. This is why I don't want the Lebanese woman to imitate any woman in the world. As Gandhi said, "We open our windows to the whole world but we prefer to stay indoors." We have our morality, traditions and ways of thinking and we should try to keep our character rather than be lost in futile attempts at imitation. As Muslims we value the family dearly, and we should continue to do so.'

My aim was to meet Lebanese women from all religious sects and from all social classes so that I would do the Lebanese woman justice. I was debating with myself as to whether or not to cross the line in East Beirut, but I am a Syrian and everyone warned me it would be too big a risk to take. Having heard many differing accounts of the situation on this dividing line I decided to sleep on the idea until the next day.

We spent most of the next day in Zeinab's office dialling phone numbers. She rang almost all the women she knew in West and East Beirut. 'Beirut hasn't been divided for long, you see,' Zeinab made a point of saying, 'and we always had friends on both sides of this hateful line.'

The clock struck 3 p.m. I was in the kitchen making a cup of tea for us both when I heard Zeinab's hurried steps approaching the kitchen. She opened the door and exclaimed in a loud voice: 'Guess what? In one hour's time you have an appointment with a Christian woman who comes from the heart of East Beirut. She is visiting friends in West Beirut, and like you she got stuck here. She can't tell you much about the war situation because at the start of the civil war in 1975 she emigrated with her husband and children to California and has been living there since then, but she will tell you her memories of the position of the Lebanese woman prior to the civil war.'

Mrs Lina was a smart, polite, eloquent and evidently very intelligent woman. Her account of the life she had either experienced or knew about was related in a short-story style.

'I am a Christian Lebanese raised in a Christian family and Christian community in the Lebanese culture which has a different dimension to it from the Arab culture. Before the war, Christians were quite clannish, they wanted to keep their identity, they over-stressed their separatist tendencies. We were sent to Christian schools and were more involved in the Christian community than in the large, Lebanese community. Being a Christian seemed to be something I could identify with, but I also felt Lebanese; I felt Middle Eastern. I felt I shared the problems of other Lebanese women as I grew older. I think whether Christian or Muslim we, as women, were going through the same processes as we grew older.

'I was the second child in my family, eleven years younger than my elder sister, so I felt as if I was an only child getting the full attention of parents and grandparents. For a long time we had an extended family of aunts and grandmothers living with us. That was something positive for my parents. Of course, there are disadvantages: the conflicts in-laws always have, for example, but it was helpful to have so many people to help in bringing up the children. Children in my generation, however, did not grow up very freely because the society was not so much orientated towards childcare. We had to conform, to follow the adult's lifestyle. We had to be in the background; it was the adults' system we had to adjust to. While they were visiting each other we had to keep quiet and be "good girls". We were raised to be "good girls" from the very beginning; toilet-trained very early, with constant orders to behave ourselves, there was not much room for play and fun. On the other hand, the thing I very much appreciated in my childhood was the community feeling we had; people living together, taking care of each others' children, babysitting for each other. So there was a support system in the neighbourhood and that in itself prevented feelings of isolation and alienation that a lot of women in the modern world face. I feel that I had a lot of love in my childhood; from my family, my immediate family, the extended family, the friends of the family and the neighbours, and I think that gave me a lot of security compared to what children get nowadays. Although children now have a lot more fun and a lot more playtime than we did, we had a lot of adults other than our parents to relate to and to feel comfortable with outside our homes. That was something very positive in my view. We were less anxious about being separated from our parents, whereas children nowadays have only their parents to relate to, and things are very difficult for both the parents and children. We had a lot of children to play with in the neighbourhood, and could relax with their mothers and feel very comfortable in their homes.'

'Was there any question about you being sent to school?'

'No. There was no difficulty whatsoever. As far as my parents were concerned they were very encouraging. There was no question in our community about sending girls to school; it was a matter of course. Not all girls continued their higher education because they were encouraged to get married early. I think that one of the basic values in that society was that by the time the girl was 16 or 17 she was an eligible wife. The school programme was a very heavy one – in fact, overloaded. We learnt three languages: Arabic, English and French. My parents were very encouraging. In fact, my mother even encouraged us to pursue non-traditional professions, such as an artistic profession, which were not very acceptable socially. I used to play the piano. Because the Arabic programme was not very heavy our Arabic was not marvellous. We were taught by French teachers; our papers were corrected by French teachers.

'I went to a mixed school all my school life. Although almost all parents sent their daughters to school, most of them sent them to girls' schools run by nuns, but I was lucky to go to a mixed school where we learnt to deal with boys and relate to them without any problem. Of course, these schools had their problems as well. There were stories of love and attachments at an early age which were something to be looked at as not quite taboo but still something to feel uncomfortable about. People would talk about boyfriends and girlfriends and this would have some side effects on the girl's future life. It was a black mark in her history if she once had a boyfriend. It was safer to stay with a girlfriend, because nobody would talk about you and everyone would accept this. Love relationships happened and people talked about them.

'I had a boyfriend at school when I was 15. When we started spending time together in the playground the teacher asked us to be a bit more careful about seeing each other so often because we might be encouraging others to do the same. That really was a very difficult day for me. I felt as if I was committing a crime and things like this create a lot of bottled up tension in you. I feel that as Arab women we didn't grow up freely; free in our emotions. We were constantly trying to conform, to observe the rules and regulations. That was awful because at that age this relationship was such a beautiful thing for both of us. It was so clean, so romantic and so beautiful that both of us felt a very hard hand had come and struck us, and we didn't know why. It seemed to us natural to love each other; we felt they were trying to make us believe in a false morality which had nothing to do with us. My mother knew about my relationship but did not really mind. There were other boys who came to our house to work with me; we used to study together. So my family accepted the idea that friends came to visit me; boys as well as girls. Maybe the neighbours didn't like it; we used to hear gossip sometimes but that did not stop us. I do appreciate the relative freedom we had. There were both more liberated and more conservative families than mine. I think it had something to do with the religion and social class to which you belonged.

'Among the upper middle classes there was a more liberal outlook, while among the lower classes, the Shiites in particular, there was more conservativism. Most of the Shiites were in the South of Lebanon and in the run-down areas of Beirut, whereas the posh areas were Christian. Whether Christians or Muslims, the children of higher-income parents were more exposed to Western culture and ideology. They had accepted Western values and lived according to them. But for most Lebanese, the sole goal they had for their daughters was marriage. They would start teaching their daughters at quite an early age about cooking, housekeeping, needlework, and so on. I knew a number of girls who used to spend a lot of time in the summer doing needlework for their future homes, future husbands and children. They would start at the age of 14 because they were married by the age of 17 or 18. I spent a lot of time in the summer reading, and I remember that one summer I wanted to work. I think it was not so much the money but the work experience that I was after. I wanted to work in a local bookstore, but my father objected to the idea. He asked me how much money I was going to earn; I told him so much. He said he would pay me that money and that I should stay at home. So he didn't let me work. I would have liked to have worked but it was degrading for men to let their daughters or wives work. They were under a cultural pressure not to let women work. They were raised to believe that a real man is one who can keep his family without letting his wife and children work for money. My mother never worked and if she had had to work I am sure my father would have felt bad that he couldn't have supported his family. These were the 1960s, you see. So I didn't work at all until I graduated from college.

'I went to a Christian school for my primary and secondary education. After that I went to a French university (*école de litre*) to study sociology and that was quite an experience. My Arabic was not so good; I wish it had been better. I regret it now. I don't blame my parents for that, rather the Lebanese system for making it so easy for people to get by without learning Arabic properly. People could even get good positions in the political arena knowing hardly any Arabic at all.

'When we were at college there was a strong emphasis on virginity. The subject was a taboo. I felt that at college girls were living according to double standards; we were all living like that. We had the idea that we should not have sexual relationships with boys, yet we had boyfriends. We went out with them and we did all the petting, cuddling, sleeping naked together, all of that but we couldn't go all the way; we couldn't make love all the way. So there was a kind of artificiality in these relationships because you are not a virgin if you have had ten lovers and have kept your virginity. That is not being a virgin. A lot of women went to doctors; they were not virgins, in fact, and they had their hymens sewn up, patched together so that they could get married. To be a virgin was a prerequisite for marriage. Men could have as many girlfriends as they liked and do with them whatever they liked and nobody could blame them for anything. If a woman had a boyfriend, however, she would always have an adjective before her name, immoral, loose, cheap, or something of that sort, and, of course, no one would want to marry a girl like that. Since it was a very small society girls had to live by these double standards, which was all very confusing and very uncomfortable. You felt guilty because you were made to feel responsible not only for yourself but for your whole family, its reputation and social honour. How would your father look in front of others? How would they see him? You brought a social shame on the family because it was only the woman who was responsible for the honour of the family. If the woman was dishonourable the whole family was dishonourable, and the woman's virginity was the most crucial ingredient to family honour.

'This pressure sometimes led to girls having lesbian relationships.

Stories were circulating of girls who went to girls' schools run by nuns having lesbian relationships. Perhaps because they were never exposed to boys they had their adolescent feelings fixed on girls. I had one girl from my class who was a good friend of mine. She made some approaches to me and I was shocked. This girl is now married and has children. She perhaps projected her feelings on to me because she did not have a boyfriend. She was very poetic, too; she started writing me poems, sending me beautiful letters, but I felt nothing physical towards her. She understood that and we were able to stay friends.'

'How did you compare your situation as a Lebanese woman to that of the Saudi and Kuwaiti women who were with you at the same university?'

'They had it very easy financially. A lot of them came to college to find an eligible partner. So they were not really interested in their studies or in making a career. They were interested in having a nice time until they found a husband and settled down with him, because otherwise they would have been sitting at home doing needlework. So they were pretending to be interested in their studies, but I think in the upper income groups with all the diamonds and the jewellery they got they did not care. As an Arab woman generally you got very confused; you could not get any help or support from your parents; you could not turn to your teacher; you could not turn to anybody. You could only turn to some girlfriends who were also in the same boat like yourself and could not do very much for you.'

'Do you think the upper classes were subject to the same pressures; do you think they really cared about their virginity?'

'I think what happened with them is that they were more exposed to foreigners: Americans, British, French, etc., coming on exchange programmes. Mixing with these students you started to feel that our culture – I mean sexual culture – is very artificial. I know a group of girls who went all the way and did not care. In fact, I was one of them. I was so fed up with the artificiality of the whole thing that I decided to do what I wanted to do, regardless of what might happen to me afterwards. I was very unhappy, feeling very guilty for a long time, and I felt very guilty towards my parents; I felt I had betrayed them and I felt very uncomfortable in my relationship with men later, maybe because I lost my virginity in a relationship which was quite casual. It was not a loving relationship, and this is mostly what I felt guilty about. I did not make love with the boy I loved because we were quite young; maybe we were not ready for the experience; maybe we were both scared. We both wanted it but we did not do it. That relationship had to end because we grew in different directions and we could not continue together. There was all this pressure on me from my parents and from my friends as to what was going to happen to our relationship; it had to end up in marriage or some kind of commitment on his part, and I felt that he was pretty immature; he would have been at that age, and would have found it hard to have made any commitment. I was hoping he would have committed himself and he didn't, and I thought he was very cowardly and was very disappointed. He started avoiding me and got very involved politically. He came from a very well-off family and was carrying out his revolt at that time by joining the Communist party and living poorly and not carrying enough money on him. So he was playing at being poor; he was playing the radical and he probably wanted me to join him but I could not. I couldn't stay out late at night at meetings and activities. We lived very differently. He did not understand my pressures and I could not join him in his ways. We grew apart and I was shattered. Some boys his age were able to feel some responsibility but he could not. Then I knew a Syrian boy who loved me very much and was very nice but he was a Muslim and my mother wanted me to marry a Christian. After that I had a relationship with a Jordanian boy. I was not a virgin at that time and he didn't mind; he really wanted me regardless. I found this quite reassuring. It gave me more confidence and I really respected him for that. Of course, once you are at college people start bugging you about when you are going to get married: ''Isn't it enough the education you've had? You should start a family and raise your children.'' They probably didn't take a girl's education and ambition very seriously, but I certainly did not feel a lot of pressure in my family to get married.

'In the summer of 1972, almost immediately after I broke with my boyfriend, I went to Paris on holiday and there I had my first and last lesbian relationship. Her mother was Lebanese and her father French. It was after the big disaster with my first relationship which made me feel very confused. I didn't know then what to expect from a relationship. We were at a concert and sitting next to each other. She held my hand. I thought it was fairly common for Arabs to be quite physical, and then I understood that she was approaching me in a different way. I was rather deprived of love and affection at that point, so I responded to her and it was quite a pleasant relationship; it was genuine. It was quite an experience for me – not just physically. There was a lot of sharing, talking and understanding. It was not just a matter of sleeping together. So I really enjoyed that time, despite all the conditioning we are subject to in such relationships. It was a pleasant experience, but I didn't want my life to follow in that direction, whereas for her it was for real. She was a lesbian and didn't want to know about men at all. She had an aversion to them, but that was not the case with me. I wanted to have a family, to have children. That is why after a while I felt very suffocated in this relationship, and she felt quite suffocated, too, trying to keep track of everything I did, questioning me as to how I spent my time, calling me all the time, writing letters. Every day I would receive a letter. She was overwhelming me. She was frightened to lose me and I had to take some very hard measures to break from her; I am glad I did.'

Mrs Lina went on about these hard measures and how many times she had either to put the receiver down once she heard her voice or to ask her not to call again – and then would sit and cry her eyes out for most of the night. I started to feel deep sympathy for both women. I would have hated to lose this lovely, intelligent and warm woman, I thought to myself. So her ex-girlfriend was right in feeling anxious and insecure. How cruel we can be sometimes. I found myself asking Mrs Lina whether she knew where she was now. She said no. She didn't want to know. She had changed her address and had asked all her mutual friends not to give the woman her new address. 'But you seem to have made extraordinary efforts to break away from her. Surely this means you were in love with her?'

Here she could not suppress her tears any longer but tried to be brave, then saying: 'I suppose I was. What frightens me is that I might still be in love. In love or not I shall never see her again; I have two children and a very nice husband and I want to keep my family together.'

'How do you compare your relationship with her with your marital relationship with your husband?'

'I cannot generalise about relationships with women or their relationships with me. With this woman I had an intense, loving, caring and relaxed relationship. Also it was more exciting than my relationship with my husband, probably because it was happening most of the time in secret. We had to play everything very carefully. All this added to the excitement of the relationship, just like two people from two different religions meeting and wanting to marry each other. There is always an element of excitement, you know, even if the relationship is between a woman and a man. I feel I can relate to some men very comfortably. Also, there are some women to whom I cannot relate at all. I really don't want to say that women are easier to relate to than men. I have met very sensitive men and I feel that my husband is one such. He is my best friend. I can talk to him about everything. I have his companionship, love, friendship and help in raising the children. Most Arab women don't feel comfortable with men because society hasn't encouraged the relationship between men and women. So you feel more comfortable with your own sex. I feel I understand my own sex better than I understand men but I still think that a relationship with a woman has as many difficulties as a relationship with a man. It has more anxiety, more pressures and more tension, partly because society does not accept it and partly because of the problem of children. The fact remains that there are more lesbians in the Arab world than there are in Europe. These are not open relationships and the women can't speak out. I have been told that it is because the women don't have understanding and supportive husbands that lesbian relationships are encouraged. In many Arab countries husbands leave their wives and go on long business trips and perhaps have affairs with other women, leaving their wives with the children for long periods of time, so the women get involved with each other. A news item which appeared the other day in the papers is very telling of the immense pressure to which lesbians in the Arab world are subjected. The news item was about a bride who found out that her bridegroom was another woman. The woman acting as a bridegroom tried to convince the bride to live with her away from men but the other woman didn't agree. The paper mentioned that the "bridegroom" had eloped from her husband. Although this happened in Egypt I am sure you can find a lot of similar examples in all Arab countries.'

'Do you feel equal with your husband?'

'I don't feel that there is any struggle for power in our household. I feel that I am doing all the domestic work such as cooking, cleaning and taking care of the children because right now I am not working and my husband's time does not allow him to do any housework. Practically this is not possible. That doesn't make me feel bad. When

I first got married I felt a little bit resentful, not of him but of my own situation and I asked myself whether this would be what was going to happen to me all my life; every day doing the same, boring work. I was not used to it. I had been studying and working and this was a totally different reality. I feel that I've got used to it now. Whether this is a good or a bad thing, I don't know, but I don't fight it any more, and I feel I want to take on this role for a while until my children are older and I have more freedom to go back to what I wanted to do. This is what I want to do right now. I am enjoying raising my children and I know this is only temporary and that I have a different life in the future. The role of women is constantly changing. Once my children go to school I'll deal with what I have endeavoured to do in my life. Even if you are working and have a career you still have a duty towards your family and children, but I have the support of my husband in the sense that he understands my pressures. It is not an easy thing to raise children and be at home, because you are more isolated.

'I feel that the Middle Eastern mentality, or the Middle Eastern upbringing, has conditioned us and that it is not so easy to break completely from this conditioning. For instance, when I first got married I really did not want my husband to work in the kitchen. It was not that I didn't like it. I felt it was my role and that I should do it. My mother had done it; every woman I know has done it. Now, even if my husband is willing to help me in one thing or another, I feel it is my duty to think about everything in the house and plan carefully. It is not doing the work that I find most difficult, but the thinking, the constant, nagging feeling that I am responsible for everything, particularly for what goes wrong. Even when I used to go out to work I would be deeply involved with something, and suddenly I would think, "God, I haven't taken the meat out of the freezer. What am I going to do for lunch?" I find this psychological conditioning quite exhausting and I am sure most Arab women feel very much the same. In this sense, going out to work does not liberate the Arab woman so long as she still feels totally responsible for all the housework and raising of the children. Arab women have not managed to shake off the traditional role which their grandmothers used to play or the social outlook on women as housewives; they have only taken on extra responsibilities by going out to work. Mothers, especially working mothers, have so many roles to play and they feel guilty most of the time. If you are working you feel guilty about your family and if you are not working you feel guilty about yourself. Staying at home is another dilemma, too, because you feel so far away from your career and you are most of the time anxious as to whether you will ever manage to go back to it.'

'Do you look with envy at the European or American woman?'

'I don't feel envious of them at all. I feel that we are richer as women than they are, richer inside, because I think that despite all the suppression, oppression and taboos we have had more love in our families than they have had and I think we have learnt more about giving. I think we are better givers than they are. They are more assertive of their personal needs; I think they are more selfish.'

'But don't you think that Arab women need to be more assertive of themselves and a bit more selfish?'

'I think if you want to be that selfish and assertive you should not have children in the first place.

'I feel that my aim in life is to find peace inside myself, fulfilment inside myself, whether I am working or not working, staying at home or not staying at home. In any situation you may feel frustrated; it just depends on what you want from life. Maybe because of this belief I've had I did not end up a frustrated mother staying at home. This is the way the West perceives it, not the way Arab women are looked at. Arab women are glorified for their mothering but the West now glorifies a working mother. In the USA the word "housewife" has a pejorative ring to it. There, even if you are going out doing factory work and earning two dollars a day you would be more glorified than being a mother staying at home with your children. I find that very stupid. I think value is put more on work as such, regardless of what kind of work it is or whether or not the work is fulfilling. It is just the fact that you are going out to work that is important; this seems to have a value in itself. I am not saying that staying at home with the children does not have frustrating aspects but that being torn between work pressures, home pressures, and social pressures also must have frustrating aspects, and I feel there is more to bringing up children than people realise.

'I am aware, of course, that not all women have the choice. Some need to go out to work; they can't afford to stay at home. Their husbands don't earn enough money; they have to work to help the family income. Single parents also have to work. As for me, I feel I would like to go back to work for two reasons. First, for financial security.'

In case, for some reason, my husband couldn't carry on in his job. Anything could happen to him and I feel I should be able to support my children and take care of my family. Second, because I would like to be doing something different as I feel a lot of women invest the best years of their lives bringing up their children, and when the children grow up and leave home the women are left totally depressed and lonely. This is a very big crisis from which many middle-aged mothers suffer. I don't want to end up like that; I would like to plan my life so that when my children become more independent I would not cling to them. I hope that I'll be healthier in that way, and that it will be easier for me to make the transition. I don't feel that these years are depressing years for me; I feel that I have grown up a lot in these years, that I have become richer. Bringing up my children has so far been a very challenging and enriching job; you are searching for answers and for guidelines all the time. Perhaps I feel happier because I have this goal to go back to work and pursue my career. So it might be important for mothers to keep their careers in sight.

'Also, I find it fascinating that your image of yourself is constantly changing: you have the image of yourself as a slim, beautiful wife, then you are pregnant, then nursing, then caring for the children. You are a mother of one and then you are a mother of two. You are a mother of a baby, then of a toddler, a child and a man. So you are constantly adjusting to new roles which keep life very far from being boring. There is another way of looking at it; women have so many things to do throughout all stages of their lives that they hardly have enough time to become creative in their careers. On the other hand, men who are free of child-bearing and caring devote all their time and energy to their professions, and this is why you see so many professional men around and very few women.

'I have not even mentioned the major adjustment which most Arab women have to make to the most ordinary thing in life: sex. Most Arab women live in two totally different worlds before and after marriage. Before marriage they are supposed to be saints, holy virgins who never like to know or hear about sex. If they were to hear anything that touches on the subject they are supposed to shy away and leave the place. Once they are married they are supposed magically to change into sexy wives and wonderful mothers who know all about the ins and outs of family life. We were brought up to think that sex was very dirty. I was not even 12 when I had my first period. My aunt used to say: ''Don't touch yourself; if you ever touch yourself you will get tuberculosis.'' That was really frightening. It was very difficult for me to shake all that off and look at sex as something enjoyable, beautiful and clean. Thousands of Arab women spend their lives with their husbands and breed children without being able to accept sex as a good thing to have, and without ever enjoying it. For many of them it is another role which they have to play; it is something they have to do for their husbands, just like preparing a meal or washing the clothes, and as with these things they are relieved when it is all finished. I find that very sad. The complete absence of sexual education in the Arab world is appalling and women are paying the price for this. It is okay for men to talk about sex and to know everything about it, in fact for men it is considered manly to have a sexual education, but it is shameful for women to have any knowledge about the subject.'

Back in Damascus I was introduced to some Lebanese students studying at Damascus University. They were from Tyre and were Sunni Muslims. They were living on campus and we agreed to meet there at ten o'clock one Friday. One of them started to talk to me – I didn't have to encourage her much. She was indignant and articulate.

'Look at the Arab world; there is not a single Arab country in which you could say that women are free and equal to men. Arab men themselves are not free; how can a man be free who doesn't dare voice his own opinion about a political system, a party, or even an idea, and how can such a man help a woman to be free? So long as Arab men suffer from their own weaknesses they will continue to keep women down. Most Arab men feel frustrated in their jobs and society so they go home and try to prove their manhood by pinning their women down. I strongly believe that so long as there is no democracy in the Arab world neither men nor women can be truly free.

'In theory, all people appreciate the great role which Lebanese women have played during the war, but in their homes all women are still treated as females. Women seem to have got used to this treatment, too; they expect it, accept it, or even sometimes invite it. So there are no grounds for believing that any serious change will occur in the position of women in Lebanon in the foreseeable future. Women's societies and organisations are improving women's lot, but extremely slowly. We need generations of hard work before we can reach a qualitative change. The European woman has managed to have a say in the running of her own life; we are quite a way from that yet. Women, of course, shouldn't wait for men to give them their freedom; they have to fight for it and get it, but for Arab women it is not so easy.'

'What do you think of the position of women as Muslims in Islam?' I asked.

'Taking account of the time during which the Islamic religion appeared, we can say that Islam did women a great service, and as far as women were concerned was ahead of all the social systems which existed at the time. When Islam first appeared in Arabia there were tribes who used to bury the newborn females alive. Islam took a revolutionary stand against that and ensured women their full human and social rights. The problem now is that most Islamic countries do not apply true Islamic laws but a biased and male-orientated version of them. I also think that Islamic laws regarding women need to be brought up to date. For example, it is still legal for a Muslim man to have four wives and his share of inheritance is twice as much as that of his sister. A man's evidence in court is still equal to that of two women. Such discriminatory laws are usually justified on the grounds that women are more emotional and less reasonable creatures than men. I believe that as long as women are locked away at home they are always going to be more emotional and less thoughtful than men. We are all the products of our education and social experiences, and in the Arab world illiteracy still runs high amongst women. What the Arab man fears most is that once his woman achieves her full rights she might create a certain imbalance in the family and his absolute authority might suffer as a result. Most Arab men fear that if women became enlightened and free they might very well rebel against the terrible burden which they have always shouldered and if the men didn't show any willingness to move from their selfish stand the Arab family might come under threat. For the unity and strength of the Arab family have always been sustained by women's sacrifices of their careers, ambitions, leisure and even rest-times.

'Mothers in the Arab world are always elevated to the status of semi-divine creatures and glorified as the pillars of society, but I wonder how Arab men accept half-witted women to run their families. There is a stark contradiction between considering women subservient to men and at the same time leaving to them the significant role of building up the basic social unit, the family.

'What I also resent is Arab men's discrimination against Arab women in comparison with European women they meet. For example, a lot of men who travel abroad get to know European women who have had previous relationships and who are not virgins. Even so, they marry them and treat them very well, but none of these men would ever marry an Arab woman who is not a virgin! Why does an Arab man accept the right of a European woman to have premarital relationships and refuse the Arab woman the same right? I feel very cross about this and would like to see Arab men change their behaviour. I would like them to be brave enough to accept Arab women as equals and companions.'

'How do you compare the position of the Arab woman with that of the European woman?'

'The only thing Arab men mention and stress about the European woman is that she is free sexually. They don't mention other important aspects of her emancipation, such as the social, economic and personal freedom which she enjoys. They deliberately stress the sexual freedom of the European woman in order to give women's liberation a bad name, to present to Arab eyes something which contradicts our Islamic culture, and Arab values. By doing this they hope to scare us from fighting for the big issues which the European woman has achieved, such as the freedom to live an independent life, take an independent decision and pursue her chosen career. Hence, European women are often presented in a bad light on purpose; the aim is to put us off the word "liberation". Yet with all the sexual freedom she has the European woman is more moral and more dignified than the Arab woman. There is more sexual libertinism in the Arab world than there is in Europe but it is all done discreetly. Being more open about sex the Europeans are more moral and more serious about it than us. The secrecy which engulfs our sexual lives subjects women – because they are the ones who are prone to social shame – to all kinds of blackmail and abuse. I am sure every Arab reader knows exactly what I mean. Islamic morality should be embodied in our efforts to humanise and make more moral our sexual activities rather than pretend they don't exist, which of course is not true. So I think we should benefit from the experience of the European woman and try to avoid the mistakes she has made. Our emancipation should be moulded in a way which suits our tradition and cultural heritage. It is not true there is no family feeling in Europe; once again, I believe that Arab men have evolved and propagated the myth that the emancipation of the European woman has led to the destruction of the family as a healthy social unit in an effort to intimidate the Arab populace and frighten them against supporting the women's cause or talking about their emancipation.'

'What is your ambition for the Arab woman?' I asked at last.

'I would love to see her a full person, free and independent, and an equal partner with an equal say in running her country. I want her to reject her domestic, traditional role, to occupy high posts and to participate fully in building a better society and achieving a better future, both for herself and her country.

'I do believe that economic independence is of central importance for social and personal independence. A woman who is dependent on her husband financially is more likely to depend on him socially, intellectually and emotionally. The ideal situation is that in which a woman achieves her economic independence and at the same time remains psychologically and intellectually a man's companion. I don't know why a woman's success leads, in most cases, to a state of emotional inertia in her home, as if a man's love for his woman is intrinsically linked with his ability to protect and provide her with the means of living.'

There was one person who totally depended on me for her living and whom I seemed to have forgotten for the last few enjoyable hours. My month-old baby must be starving now, I suddenly thought, as my eyes fell on my interviewee's watch and was shocked to realise it was 1.30 p.m. already. The thought must have just crossed my mind when I heard heavy knocking at the door. 'It must be someone for me,' I said. And so it was.

My sister rushed in, skipping the usual greetings and said anxiously: 'Your daughter has been screaming her head off.'

'Yes,' I said. 'I must go.' The untidy room which I had left at 10 that morning, my starving baby and the thought that I had nothing ready for lunch interrupted my train of thought about Arab women's emancipation, independence and equality. I had no choice but to excuse myself rapidly from these enthusiastic, interesting women. Having spent the last few hours pursuing my professional interests it was time to try to sort out the chaos at home which is normally created by my absence.

Notes

1. *Al shari* is a knee-high coat and matching trousers which Shiite women wear. *Al Shari* means religious.
2. Any piece of thin material which covers the hair and is knotted under the chin.
3. A women's society or organisation comprises only women members. It normally sets for itself a social, political or economic programme. Many of these societies in the Arab world are off-shoots of political parties such as the general women's unions in Syria, Algeria or Egypt. Very few are independent.
4. 'Um' in Arabic means mother. 'Um Mohamad' is the mother of Mohamad. Once they are married, Arab people, both men and women, take it as an insult to be addressed by their own names. They are normally addressed by the name of their eldest boy. If the first child happens to be a girl, they switch to the boy's name once they have one. So the couple whose eldest son is Hassan, for example, are called 'Um Hassan' (mother) and 'Abo Hassan' (father).
5. The founder of the Amal movement who disappeared while visiting Libya.
6. The female child could not be devoted to Temple service under the Mosaic law as she intended. But she was marked out for a special destiny as a miracle child, to be the mother of the miracle child, Jesus.
7. According to the Koran, the Virgin Mary never got married and Jesus Christ had no father; when the angel told Mary she would give birth to a son named Jesus, she said:

> 'O my Lord!
> How shall I have a son
> when no man hath touched me?'
>
> He said: 'Even so:
> God createth
> What He willeth;
> when He hath decreed
> , a plan, He but saith
> To it, 'Be', and it is!
> Sora III, Al Imran, 47

8. According to Islamic law, if the man says to his wife 'You are divorced' three times she is legally divorced from him. Arab men have coined an easy, threatening phrase *'Alia Talak'* (I would swear to divorce you) which they use as a prefix to every order they issue to their wives. In consequence, many Arab women live under the daily threat of being divorced.

9. Muslim Brotherhood is a reactionary political movement which has a religious cover. It claims to want to restore Islam to what it was during the days of the Prophet Mohammed. It urges all women to leave their studies or jobs, wear the full Islamic dress and stay at home to serve their husbands and children. It was active in Syria between 1976 and 1981 and adopted political assassination as the only means of struggle. Now it is quite active in Algeria and Egypt.

10. *Al Hijab* consists of covering the hair completely and dressing in a decent way which does not show any part of the woman's body except hands, face and feet. *Al shari*, worn mostly by Shiite Muslims, consists of a pair of trousers and knee high coat and, of course, the hair is completely covered. There is also *al mindil*, which is a white piece of material with which women cover their hair, regardless of what they are wearing.

11. Saad Haddad, a Lebanese militia leader who works in support of and fully collaborates with the Israelis.

12. *Al Quran, Sura Nisaa*, section 6, *Iaya* 34. *Nisaa* in Arabic means 'women', about whom there is a whole *sura* (chapter) in the Koran. The *sura* deals with women, orphans, inheritance, marriage and family rights generally. The principles laid down in the *sura* have governed Muslim law and social practice since its inception.

13. The way in which an Arab woman brings shame to her family is by having sexual relationships before marriage or by getting pregnant without being married. The concept of the family honour is strictly related to the sexual behaviour of its females; men have nothing to do with that. An honourable family is a family whose females are sexually restrained and 'well-behaved'.

3 Palestine: Women's Way of Surviving

Palestine has been seen historically as the heart of the Arab world, while at the same time it is a religious centre for Muslims, Christians and Jews. Like Syria, Jordan and the Lebanon, it was ruled for centuries by the Ottoman empire; then, after the First World War, it was mandated to Britain, which ruled the country until 1948.

Ever since the turn of the century Jewish migrants, some of them refugees from pogroms in Eastern Europe and later from Nazi extermination policies, flooded into Palestine, some 'legally', others running the gauntlet of British navy patrols. After the Second World War the newly established United Nations recommended the partition of Palestine to give 55 per cent of the land to the Jewish settlers. But before an agreement could be negotiated, Zionist activists, who had been conducting a guerrilla war against British rule, declared an exclusively Jewish state of Israel.

Thousands – eventually millions – of Arabs were displaced and became refugees. The Palestinians have become a people without a country: they have lived in Jordan, Lebanon, Syria, Egypt, Tunisia. As governments and alliances changed, they have been moved on. Following the 1967 invasion of the West Bank (Jordan), Sinai (Egypt) and the Golan Heights (Syria), the Palestinians of the West Bank and Gaza have been forced to live under Israeli occupation, subject to the Israeli government's policy of establishing fortified Jewish settlements among them (some 120 settlements by 1987). The 1973 war expanded Israeli-dominated territory still further (there is no official map of the borders of what Levi Eshkol called 'Greater Israel'); the 1982 invasion of Lebanon added a portion of South Lebanon, where there were yet more Palestinian refugee camps. Today, some 1.4 million Palestinians live under foreign rule in their own country, while a further 1.5 million have been forced to leave it. Some have been trapped in refugee camps for 40 years or forced to emigrate to other Arab countries, to Europe or the Americas.

Palestine's history of massacres – from the notorious Deir Yassin massacre of 1948, when 254 Palestinians lost their lives, to the continual violent suppression of student demonstrations in 1987 – has led, paradoxically, to an exceptional level of education among contemporary Palestinians, both women and men. From the occupied West Bank and Gaza, and from the refugee camps elsewhere, young people are sent abroad to study, to work and to finance in turn the studies of younger members of the family. Education is perceived as the best hope of escape from subjugation and poverty. Since this policy applies to girls as well as to boys, there are probably more educated Palestinian women than in any other Arab nation. And it is no surprise that student demonstrations at Beir Zeit university or in East Jerusalem, and the uprisings of stone-throwing school pupils in Gaza and the West Bank, increasingly involve girls and women.

Women's Way of Surviving

The first time the name of Palestine took on a concrete connotation in my mind was in 1967. We had already heard on the news that the war had broken out when Israel sent its American-made warplanes to bomb Syria and Egypt. Three people from our village were killed in this war and the bodies of martyrs were awarded heroes' welcomes, particularly by their mothers, who danced and sang them songs glorifying their bravery and sacrifice in defence of their homeland. This was the first time I saw death celebrated rather than lamented and the first time I felt I was an Arab, not just a Syrian. Indeed, my blood boiled when I heard accounts of how the Palestinians on the West Bank and the Gaza Strip, and the Syrians on the Golan Heights were forced to leave their lands, homes and belongings in fear of massacres. Although I felt genuinely sad and angry, I had no idea, then, of the depth of human misery inflicted on Palestinian people and of the fact that Palestinian women had the lioness's share of this suffering.

Twenty years afterwards, Palestinian women refugees expelled from the West Bank and the occupied territories by the Israeli occupation authorities spoke to me in Damascus about the agony they suffered while awaiting the release of their husbands from Israeli gaols, some for more than two decades, and fighting for the foreign enemy for their survival. Their stories reveal the other unknown dimension of the Palestinian tragedy: the extra burden laid on women who had to leave home, books and family every time they just managed to settle down. The loss of home, destruction and war added to the suffering already inflicted on women by traditional male chauvinists.

On her first visit to Damascus in 1987, Mariam, a Palestinian woman from the West Bank, gave me the shock of my life when I saw how like my mother she looked. Though about 20 years younger she had the same round, brown face, and the same long neck proudly towering above her majestic figure. Like my mother, her deep brown eyes seemed to be connected with a silver thread to the relatively large hands which clasped each other every time her eyes revealed emotion. On both sides of her face deep brown hair lay straight and smooth, accentuating the pallor of her long neck. The white scarf which covered the rest of her hair was tied with a knot at the back of her neck and covered her broad back and shoulders. Even the placid, good-tempered smile which accompanied her quiet, yet firm welcome was exactly like my mother's. For a moment I was speechless. I wanted to fill my eyes, mind and soul with this vision of my mother incarnate. I missed my mother so much; I missed every single expression in her face, every movement. I missed her smile, her voice, and most of all I missed her very expressive eyes. I so much wanted to embrace this image of my mother in this woman, to hold her, smell her, to see whether she also had my mother's lovely smell. Suddenly I was in turmoil. My face began to show the intensity of the shock I had received and Mariam became aware that something was wrong.

'How much like my mother you look,' I said quickly to break the already uncomfortable silence.

'Where is your mother?' Mariam asked sadly, rather hesitantly, expecting in all probability that my answer would be 'dead'.

'Living in a small village near Homs,' I replied. Then I put on a brave face and changed the subject, saying: 'Many congratulations on your husband's release. When I heard about you I thought what a great woman you must be to decide to share your husband's political fate. It can't have been an easy decision. Don't you think she is marvellous?' I turned to the husband.

Oh yes, she is,' he answered in an obvious attempt to draw attention to himself. 'It was Mariam's decision to wait. I didn't ask her to.

When I was sentenced to 40 years I told her: "This is a life sentence and you don't have to serve it with me. You are free to get married again and live your life and I am prepared to grant you a divorce immediately." She refused and said: "You sacrificed your life for your country and I will sacrifice my life for you." As it turned out, I got away with serving 25 years; I was recently released in an exchange of hostages and political prisoners between Israel and the PLO. Still, 25 years is not an easy time to wait and in the meantime raise up two daughters. As for me, she was my life-support machine, the only real link connecting me with the enviable free world and everything alive and happy. Voluntarily she bore half my burden and thus she is a worthy candidate for a reward.'

Having come to interview his wife rather than him I was anxious to stop short his lecture on women's emancipation (which all men are keen to give), so I turned to his wife and asked her how many children she had; before she could answer her husband turned to me and said courteously: 'I would love to spend more time talking to you but I'm afraid I have to rush back to my work, so please would you excuse me.'

Once the door was closed behind him Mariam suddenly relaxed, she seemed to take on more shape and fill up more space. She smiled and her eyes brightened, while the palms of her hands started to rub against each other in an effort to squeeze some words out. Her mouth immediately responded to the palms' signal and after uttering a deep sigh she answered my question.

'I've got two girls; yes, just two girls, who were born during the first two years of our marriage. The younger was four days old when her father was arrested.'

'Would you like to have another child now?'

'Yes, I would love to. I'm 40 years old now and I don't have much time ahead of me. So I'd like to have a child straight away. But he doesn't want to. He says he isn't ready for a child now.'

Twenty-five years of waiting, I thought to myself, and he won't comply with her simple and most natural wish to have a child.

A friend of hers who had been with us since my arrival said to me: 'I took her to a gynaecologist yesterday who said there was no reason why she shouldn't get pregnant and asked to see her husband, but her husband refused.'

I suddenly remembered what I had once read about Palestinians in Israeli prisons, that on arrival they all get sterilised. I expressed fear to the two women and Mariam's friend said she thought he had in fact been given infertility drugs and that he knew he could never have any more children, so there would be no reason to go to the doctor. He adored children and it was very unlike him not to want a child.

'I only want him to tell me the truth,' said Mariam. 'If I knew that he couldn't have children I wouldn't care. It would put my mind at rest. I want him to trust me enough to be able to tell me what has happened to him. He might think that if I knew this about him I might not love or respect him as a man. How mistaken he is.' Her red face betrayed a controlled anger, resentment, agony and a deep, quiet pain which I knew she didn't want to reveal to me.

'I know exactly how you feel,' I said, trying to convey the genuine sympathy I felt for her. 'Although I don't have much direct experience of what you have gone through, I do have a mother, older sisters neighbours and relatives. I've watched their lives closely and I have a fairly good idea of what you are talking about. So please trust me and try to give me an honest account of your life story. You are talking to a sister who feels and sympathises with you and whose sole aim is to improve the lot of Arab women.'

Her eyes shied away from me, her lips touched each other gently and carefully and her palms stayed clasped in a long, quiet hug which I guessed expressed approval for what had just been suggested.

'I am from Biet Gin village on the West Bank,' she began. 'My parents were farmers working on the land, growing wheat, barley and olive trees. We used to work and live off what we grew ourselves. We were nine girls and one boy. My father was married to four women to get a boy and he only got one – from my mother. The other three women didn't have children at all, so he divorced them and kept my mother. My mother died at the age of 40 and my father soon after, leaving me as the oldest daughter to bring up my eight sisters and one brother. At the age of 13, shortly before my parents' death, I was married to my husband – a relative of mine.'

'Did you know your husband was a PLO member before getting married to him?'

'No. About two years after our marriage he explained that he was actively involved with the PLO and that he felt guilty about me because anything could happen to him. But what could I do then? I already had one daughter and was pregnant with the second one.

Shortly afterwards he was arrested and sentenced to 40 years' imprisonment.'

'When you first heard about his sentence what did you think of doing?'

'What could I do? I reckoned this was my fate and that I would have to put up with it.'

'Didn't you consider getting a divorce from him and living your own life? Perhaps getting married again?'

'No. Though to be fair to him he did offer me a divorce and stressed time and time again that I didn't have to wait for him and that it was my right to live my own life. I told him that even if I had been married to him just for one day I would never leave him and get married to someone else, given the circumstances. He was my husband and I would stand by him no matter what.'

'Had he been in your position do you think he would have made a similar decision?'

'I don't think so. I waited for him for 25 years, knowing full well that he wouldn't have waited for me for even a year. That doesn't bother me at all. I waited for him because I couldn't have done otherwise; because this is me and has nothing to do with him. I thought then about the decision he would have taken had he been in my place, but even so I couldn't ignore him and his circumstances. I considered how he would have felt if I had left him and married someone else. He might have been shattered. To be honest with you, I didn't love him then for I'd hardly had a chance to get to know him. My decision to share his fate was a form of solidarity and support which I felt I had to grant him, rather than an act of love. I also felt sorry for my daughters and couldn't augment their ordeal by bringing home a stranger who would impose his authority on them. It was enough that they had lost their father, and I decided to devote my life to them to make up for all the lack of love and affection which their father would otherwise have given them. This is something I couldn't have done had I decided to remarry.'

'How often did you see your husband?'

'Sometimes I saw him once a week or once every two weeks, and at other times I didn't see him for nine months at a time.'

'You mean you were not allowed regular visits?'

'No. We were allowed to visit him every week. But the whole family wanted to see him. His immediate family consisted of 30 people, so we started to take turns and I had to wait my turn. Every week there was a fight over who was going to see him. His mother would say to his brothers: "Take his wife; she misses him and wants to see him." When I heard that I used to feel disgusted with them and refuse to go. My husband used to get hurt because I didn't go with his brothers, but he had no idea what I was going through. I hated going with his brothers who always insisted they didn't like walking with a "woman" – as if I were an animal or an insect. So whenever their turn came round I used to say I didn't want to go to avoid being insulted for being a woman.

'Sometimes I wouldn't go because I couldn't afford the car hire. Added to this was the fact that it was an ordeal to reach him. Usually we failed to find a taxi driver who would agree to drive us through the forlorn, dark, muddy and miserable roads. So we had to walk all the way, about four hours' walk. This meant we had to start about two o'clock in the morning to make sure of being there at seven o'clock in the morning, only to see him for a few minutes during which time he could hardly be heard at all. Everyone was shouting, screaming and sometimes wailing to make themselves heard by their relatives outside the double-barred windows. The noise was deafening and the scene quite unnerving. Twenty people, together with their children, had to go together to speak with their relatives. It was chaos. There were many visits when I didn't manage to make him hear a word of what I was trying to say. The visit lasted 20 minutes, after which we had to start back home, braving the rain, hail and snow and feeling more miserable than we had felt when we started our journey towards that high-walled, invincible, loathsome prison. To be honest with you, I don't like re-running the tape of those long difficult years in my mind. I spent most of the time feeling ill, exhausted and miserable, with no impetus even to breathe.

'I spent most of those years in a masochistic, suicidal mood. My daughters cried for most of the time. They never agreed to go to a party or wedding, or any other social occasion. They wouldn't laugh or smile or even talk properly. After agonising efforts I discovered they were ashamed of their father because they thought he was a criminal. When they came of age I was able to make them understand that he was not a criminal but a political prisoner, and that there was nothing to be ashamed of. That on the contrary, they should be proud of him because he had sacrificed his life so that everyone in the village might live in dignity. When they were old enough to understand all this they began to improve their behaviour and started talking, socialising and leading more or less normal lives.'

'What was the most agonising thought for you during your husband's imprisonment?'

'His being in prison. Whenever I went to see him I would come back feeling the whole world was a round ball of utter and absolute darkness which no sun could ever penetrate. After every visit, stories would start circulating of how the prisoners were kicked about, beaten and tortured. When I heard of what he was going through I would feel powerless. My life during those long years of his imprisonment was very much like being in a coma, interrupted by intervals during which I gathered my resources and exercised my will power trying to survive, speak to others and socialise in an effort to make my daughters feel better.'

'How did you manage your lives under the Israeli occupation?'

'To tell the truth, we didn't notice their presence a great deal. Our village was quite far off and we carried on working on the land and living off our crops. We would see an Israeli patrol car only once every week or two. But we would hear and see on the radio and television what the Israelis were doing to people in towns. As for us, what we resented was their expropriation of our land and property whenever they felt like it. They would uproot our olive trees to build high buildings or open new motorways for their cars and they would never ask us if we agreed to this or pay us a penny in compensation. They would lay their hands on any piece of land they fancied and do whatever they liked with it, and none of us would dare say a word. It was painful to see them confiscating what we had tended and cherished for generations.'

'How did you feel when you were told that your husband was released?'

'I didn't believe it. His relatives and everyone in the village were dancing and singing, but I just couldn't believe that he was no longer behind those solid bars which had succeeded in closing up my heart and mind.'

'How do you feel now?'

'In 27 years of marriage I didn't live with him for more than one whole year. So I feel as though I'm newly wed at the late age of 40! In fact, I feel like a freak. My whole life doesn't make sense to me. It doesn't feel right. There is a hollow ring to it.'

'What do women in your village do?'

'Both men and women in my village work on the land. They grow wheat, barley, beans and olive trees and, as is always the case, the women work twice as hard as the men. Women work both at home and in the field; they are much more experienced in growing crops but they have no say either in the home or as regards the handling of the crops. Women in our village wake up at dawn to do all the housework before sunrise, and then go to the fields to do all the necessary digging, planting and irrigation. In the afternoons you often find men gathered in the village café or in someone's house, drinking, using the hubble-bubble and playing backgammon, while the women are still working in the fields.'

'How do you compare the position of Palestinian women on the West Bank with the position of Palestinian women in Syria?'

'Palestinian women in Syria are much better off than us. We seem to have retained all the very old-fashioned bad habits which belittle women. In an attempt to keep our Arab identity the men seem to have frozen our habits, traditions, morals and values. So Arab societies under Israeli occupation preserve both the bad and the good for fear of losing their identity. The result is that they live in limbo, while Palestinian communities in Syria and other Arab countries are much more relaxed and can afford to be more open to change. They develop naturally and are not so terrified to accept new habits, new traditions and new ideas about life. Hence, women outside the occupied territories are much better off than women on the West Bank, who are still subjected to outmoded and outdated ideas.'

Mariam's friend who had served us with coffee and mandarins was listening attentively now and taking a keen interest in what had just been said. 'As a Palestinian born in Syria, what do you have in common with Mariam? What do you feel is so Palestinian about your life?'

'The feeling that my home, my land is occupied,' she answered with a rising anger that coloured her cheeks pink. 'I feel I belong to something far away, something distant. The struggle to restore this home is what unites all Palestinians abroad. We have the same history, the same problems and, most important of all, the same goals and objectives.'

Having found her enthusiastic and interesting I decided to venture another question: 'How do you compare the Palestinian woman with the Syrian woman?'

'At least the Syrian woman doesn't have the Palestinian woman's difficulties. However happy a Palestinian woman might be she will always feel a definite gap in her life, a gap caused by her being away from home, away from her roots and her parents' roots. For these reasons she needs to be more conscious of what is going on around her. She needs to be better educated and more far-sighted. The Syrian woman has less problems because she is more settled; she only has to think of how to improve her standard of living while the Palestinian woman has a cause towards which all her energy, efforts and life are geared. I'm only talking about my personal experience with my immediate Syrian neighbours. They only think of what to wear and where to go. The Palestinian woman also liked clothes and likes to go out but her overriding obsession is with the land. As well as supporting our husbands in their struggle, we as Palestinian women are also constantly searching for the best way to restore our land to its people.'

This woman's trenchant and spirited conversation seemed to have enthused Mariam and encouraged her to be more forthcoming. Not wanting to miss my chance I asked the question which had been very much on my mind for quite a while: 'Were there other women in a similar position to yours in your village?'

'No,' said Mariam. 'My husband was the only one in the whole area to get arrested. Women in my village tried to persuade me to get married again, have children and live my own life, but I never wanted to do that. I knew very well that the strong feelings I had for my husband would never allow me to enjoy anything apart from him. I would have been dishonest with myself had I behaved any differently from the way I did.'

'Did the fact that your husband was the only one to be arrested make you feel more isolated?'

'Not exactly; it made me feel more obliged to support him. As he was the only one in the village to suffer this fate I felt I could never leave him. I felt strongly that I had to stand by him and lend him my unconditional support. It was only when I was visiting the prison that I felt there were other women like myself and that I was not the only woman to suffer this terrible fate. I would meet other women who were in the same boat as myself and in no time we would get talking, something I always found comforting. I used to feel so sorry for my husband, and was convinced that the least I could do was to wait for him and make him feel he mattered a lot to me. When I heard from others about the prisoners' ordeals, how they were locked away in tiny cells and how the Israelis gassed and opened fire on them, I used to feel dreadful.'

'Having two girls with no father to help look after them, did you feel nervous about the way you had to bring them up, or were you happy to let them lead their lives freely?'

'I never intervened in their lives at all and certainly never made them feel they had no father. I tried my best to make up to them what they had lost in love and affection. I always bought them the best clothes, the best food and, generally speaking, gave them a better life than their friends received who had both parents. Now I would like them to choose freely the life they want to live. I've never believed in imposing anything on men, women or children. I have an intrinsic belief in an individual's freedom. As for my daughters, I would like them to get degrees and professions for themselves, or at least jobs before getting married. Every woman must have an independent source of income before thinking of starting a family. What I went through taught me that the worst thing women can do is to rely on their husbands as their sole source of income, because whenever anything happens to these husbands women who do so find themselves in serious trouble.'

'At the age of 40 how do you feel when you look back on your life?'

'I feel very upset when I think that after the horrible life I had to live in the past I can't, even now, live with my husband and daughters peacefully. My daughters are still in the West Bank. They don't have passports and therefore they can't join me and my husband here. So the suffering continues but in another form. I used to feel very depressed and had to fight it down and bury it in my heart, because whenever I complained my relatives would start to whisper: "She's getting restless; she needs a man; she needs to get married." So I would just say I was ill or that I had a headache. Unlike my relatives, the women in the village were great to me. They were extremely helpful and understanding. But when I used to see women dressed up and going out with their husbands and children, I couldn't help feeling sorry for myself. I got married so young and had no idea what life was all about. When I dressed as a bride and my friends started to sing my favourite song, I started crying because I thought it was so nice of them to give me such a lovely dress and sing me a song that I loved. I had no idea why they were treating me so well on that day. Even if I'd been told it was my wedding day, I wouldn't have known what that was supposed to mean.'

As Mariam was trying to recall the memories of her wedding day, another friend of hers came in carrying two children, one on each arm. When we told her what the meeting was about she said there was another Palestinian woman whom I should see. This woman had also waited for her imprisoned husband for seven years. She was educated and a true feminist. She worked in women's and political organisations in the West Bank and was able to live with her two children independently of her own and her husband's families. She started doing needlework and handicrafts and had built a beautiful house awaiting her husband's release. However his release was announced at the same time as his expulsion from the West Bank. He was not even allowed to telephone his wife so she had no idea of his current whereabouts. The difference between her and Mariam was that she was living in a town which enabled her to live on her own, while living in a small village means it is socially impossible for a woman to live on her own. Also she was more active and more aware than Mariam.

Mariam backed up what her friend had said: 'It was impossible to live independently in the village. If a man happened to pass me by and say "Good morning" the whole village would know and would wonder what was behind this very suspicious greeting.'

What was so ironic about this other woman's experience was that when her husband arrived back in Syria he rang his brother-in-law in Jordan who assured him that his sister was no longer interested in him. Her family was furious because she had already spent over two months travelling between the West Bank and Jordan, trying to see him but failing to do so. They got fed up with his lack of attention and in a fit of anger told him to get lost. Without making any effort to see or talk to her he became engaged to a Palestinian girl. Having heard he might be in Syria and having no idea of what her family had said to him on the phone, his wife followed him to Syria with her two children, only to find him already engaged to a girl he had never even met.

Mariam uttered a deep sigh and said: 'You should have seen what she went through during those seven long years. For seven years she was visiting him every single week. She never failed, not even once, to turn up at the prison for visits. Very often she would lose her way in the distant hills and valleys which were totally covered in snow, in total darkness, feeling nothing but freezing cold. Sometimes she had to walk barefoot because her feet would swell to three times their original size which no shoes would fit. I said to my husband: "My God, how could he think of another woman so soon after his release when he knows how much she put up with for his sake? The least thing he could have done was to wait until he had heard from her that she no longer wanted him before getting engaged to another woman." He's now left his fiancée, but I don't know how she can live with him after knowing how little he cared about her. She must be an extremely forgiving woman. He is in Beqaa Valley, and again she only sees him every month or so.' At this point Mariam's husband came back and immediately joined in the conversation by stressing that the woman in question was decent and good precisely because she cared about her husband and children, and was so bent on keeping her family intact despite all the odds.

This is what men always emphasise: women's self-sacrifice, self-denial and benevolence. But what women suffer in the name of all these qualities is always brushed under the carpet.

Another, ostensibly simple, woman left me with the abiding impression that her intuitive sense and deep insight into the position of women in the Palestinian dilemma could hardly be improved upon, even by learned and experienced politicians.

When I arrived, together with a Palestinian friend of mine, to see Um Mahmoud, a Palestinian woman living in Al Mokhaim refugee camp in Damascus, we were told that Um Mahmoud had taken her husband to the optician, that she wouldn't be long and that we were to enter the building. It was neither a flat nor a house; it was what in Arabic we call a *dar*, which consists of quite a spacious courtyard open to the sky, around which there are two or three rooms, a kitchen and bathroom. The courtyard was full of plants and the sun was resting peacefully on the faces of those who were sitting there enjoying a late breakfast.

We had only been sitting down for a few minutes when a fair woman with small blue eyes descended the few steps to the courtyard guiding an elderly, weak man. She was wearing a large white scarf and a light grey summery coat. The piercing look in her eyes gave me the impression of a sturdy and robust woman.

According to an ingrained Arabic habit, poverty never stands in the way of hospitality. No more than ten minutes had passed when the young woman who had been breakfasting in the courtyard entered with a huge tray on which she had laid a perfect Arabic breakfast with eggs, olives, *homus, falafil, zatar, makdous*, jam and tea. I was quite hungry and thought it was very kind of them to offer us something to eat. Over breakfast, my friend told Um Mahmoud what our visit was all about and that I wanted her experiences as a Palestinian woman to write about in my book. Her face brightened.

'I came from a farming family; both my parents were farmers. My mother used to work with my father on the farm and then come back to do all the housework alone. As was often the case with Palestinian families I was married off to my cousin at the age of 14. In those days girls were never asked whom they would like to marry, nor did they expect to be asked. Like most girls I was satisfied that my parents wanted the best for me and that therefore I needn't worry about what was happening to me. At the age of 15 I had my first baby, a boy who only lived for a year, and at 16 I had my second baby boy, Mahmoud, who was killed in the Tal Al Zaatar siege in 1973. Only two months after I had my second baby we fled our homes and lands in fear of our lives and honour from the Israeli atrocities which we had heard about from the inhabitants of other towns and villages. My young baby was in my arms and I was on the farm picking wonderful green olives when two young children came running from the village and said that Sofsafi and Safad had fallen into Israeli hands and that Israeli soldiers were killing Palestinians in both towns and raping Palestinian girls and women. We were terrified they might do the same to us. So we fled to Lebanon in a desperate attempt to keep our men alive and the honour of our women intact.

'We arrived in Bent Jobil in Lebanon where we stayed for about 20 days and then we were moved to Borj Shanal in Tyre where we spent the winter. We moved to Anjah where we spent the summer but couldn't stick the winter because there was a lot of snow and our tents provided us with no real protection. So we moved to Nahr Al Bared refugee camp (near Tripoli) where we stayed for the next five years. After that I followed my family to Al Fashidia camp near Tyre where I stayed for five more years. By that time my children had finished their baccalaureate and wanted to enrol at university. As there was no university at Tyre we had to move to Tal Al Zaatar camp near Beirut for my children to enrol at Beirut University. My eldest son became a member of the Arab Nationalist Party. When the PLO was founded he was one of the first people to join it. He became an unpaid political officer in the PLO. My husband was the only breadwinner, though my children used to help by working during their summer holidays.

'In May 1973, the Lebanese militia started attacking Palestinian camps in Borj Al Barajneh, Tal Zaatar, Sabra and Shatila. At that time my son held quite a responsible post in the PLO. On 8 May his God called him to his company and he responded. That day my youngest, whom you have just seen leaving to go to school, was five days old. My second son carried his dead brother's gun and immediately joined the PLO to take the place of his brother. In no time at all my second son became a military officer who was also killed in the second siege of Tal Zaatar in 1975.'

'How did you feel as a mother who had recently given birth to a girl and heard the news of the death of her eldest son?'

'To be honest with you, losing my first son was much easier than losing my second. My eldest son was wonderfully modest, considerate and very affectionate. Yet when I heard the news of his death God granted me patience. A neighbour of ours came in to say that he had just seen my son wounded at a nearby military post. My sister and I rushed out, running like mad. She was ahead of me. By the time I reached her she had already torn her clothes off. So I started to cover up her bare breast and almost naked body. I tried to find my son but the soldiers there were determined not to let me see him. They were worried about me as I had given birth just five days previously. They held me tight. I said to leave me and let me see him, and I promised not to say a word. So they let me into the room where his dead body lay. I stooped over him, kissed him on both cheeks and said, "My lovely son, I congratulate you." But when they tore me away from him a fire was lit in my heart. They took him, together with all the other martyrs, to the mosque. I followed the soldiers and said I would either die with my son and the other martyrs, or they should let me take him home with me. They said I would die with him at home. When I assured them I would be quiet and sensible and they saw for themselves that I was quite patient, they agreed. They took him home and his body remained with me for three days and three nights before we could bury him. His brothers, sisters and father were fainting over him and I was trying to encourage them and help them to be patient.

For three days dead people littered the streets and no one dared to go out to dig graves until we had established a short-lived truce.

'For two weeks before my second son was killed I hardly had the chance to see him at all. I was living in a fifth-floor flat; he would pass by, ring the doorbell at street level and ask me to look at him from the balcony. I used to feel hurt and would reproach him for not sparing me five minutes. On the day of his death, however, he came home early in the morning and asked me to prepare breakfast for his friends and to cook him rice and chick peas for lunch. We were about a fortnight into the second siege of Tal Zaatar, which was to last for three months. He didn't turn up till about four o'clock in the afternoon. I offered him his lunch but he refused to eat and only had a quick cup of tea before bidding us goodbye. After descending the stairs he looked back at me and said: ''Mother, goodbye, goodnight, I am not coming back'' – and indeed he never came back. I learnt later that only about ten minutes after he left me he was shot dead. They brought him home and I went mad. I embraced his coffin and slept on it the whole night. No one was able to move me from it; I completely lost my senses. I didn't have the patience which I had had when his elder brother was killed. Battles were raging so we couldn't bury him until the following night. We went to the nearest square, dug a small hole in the ground and buried him, hoping to move him to a proper cemetery later on. But we never had a chance to do that. Indeed, we were busy enough worrying about those who were alive and almost forgot about the dead. We had immense problems getting hold of a drink of water or a piece of bread. The only thing that prevented a sweeping famine was the discovery of a lentil store on the outskirts of Al Zaatar. Women broke into the factory and brought lentils which they crushed and baked as tiny loaves of bread. We had no gas or electricity or wood to make fires, so we started taking window frames and wooden doors off houses to make fires and bake our bread on it. We very often braved death to fetch bags of lentils or jugs of water. For every hundred women who went out to fetch water, no more than ten would return. Even so, women still went out trying to bring water back for their babies and children. What else could they do? They couldn't sit back and watch their infants die of thirst, though eventually that did happen. Would you believe that people started opening the drains, taking water from them, boiling and drinking it? I had to do that. That is what happened to us in Tal Zaatar. During the siege we lost all hope in life and dedicated whatever energy was left in us to saving the fighters and the dependants. We were no longer afraid of death and stopped counting our losses. If a mother went out for a jug of water and didn't come back, her daughter would carry another jug and go out searching for water rather than for her mother. If you stayed at home with no food and no water you were definitely going to die and if you went out you might die, so why not risk going out?

'A day before our departure from Tal Zaatar we were told that the Red Cross was negotiating with our enemy to secure us a safe exit. But at about nine o'clock that evening Abo Ammar (Yasser Arafat) sent a military order: *"Daber rasak"* (Find your own way out). Most men started to flee the camp through the mountains. Women cried and wailed, not wanting to leave their husbands, brothers and fathers who decided to tackle their own destinies and leave via the mountainous route. Once they reached half way through the mountains, though, the enemy found them out and shelled them. At least 90 per cent were killed; there were few survivors. I heard from one of the few who made it that when they got desperately thirsty they would put their hands under their penises, pee, and drink their urine. When we left Tal Zaatar the next morning we walked for about two miles on a thick layer of human flesh; we didn't walk on the road; we walked on dead bodies. When we reached Dikwani checkpoint they brought in cars to take us. Every man over 12 years old was torn away from his mother, sister or wife and slaughtered at the checkpoint. So only women and young children went out. Women were also taken away and killed.

'My granddaughter who held a responsible post in the PLO was kidnapped by a masked man as she was trying to find her way to a safe haven. Her colleagues had advised her to take a mountain route, but she said she wanted to help her mother with the children. As she was holding the hands of her younger sisters a masked man pulled her away from them; no one dared to say a word. She was never seen alive again. My niece, Hana, used to work for the Red Cross. She went to ask after her mother but was caught by two armed men who tried to push her to a nearby parked car. She slapped one of them on the face and ran away. The second soldier ran after her and struck her on the back of her head with his revolver. She went round in circles and fell down. The two men carried her to the back of the car and that was the last we saw of her.

'What can I tell you? The stories of Tal Zaatar are too horrible and too painful for anyone to want to recall them. For 90 long days, the bombing and shelling didn't stop. We were never granted a truce to bury our dead or catch a breath. The main water and electricity supplies were in enemy territory and they were cut off the very first day. There was no light in the hospitals to enable doctors to treat the wounded. When we broke into the lentil factory we found huge quantities of candles. We took them, melted them down and put them in small tins which were lit in hospitals when operations were being carried out. Hospitals ran out of medicines and bandages. So women started giving away their white sheets and quilt covers to be used instead.

'During the siege there was an extremely dreadful incident which led to the total annihilation of many families. There were about three thousand people in the largest shelter in the camp. The multi-storey building above it was bombed down by a fierce air strike and all the people in the shelter were boxed in. We urged Arab and international mediators to intervene to allow us just a day's truce to get people out, but there was no response. The shelling was concentrated over the shelter and anyone who tried to get there was killed before reaching his destination. The people in the shelter were mostly women and children. Their painful cries and desperate pleas for help were truly heartbreaking. They stayed alive for about five days and then they all died. Not a single person came out alive. Just imagine your feelings, knowing that your mother or daughter is just across the road alive but that you can't get to her or offer her any help to avoid an imminent death. My young niece spent days and nights crying; her mother was in the shelter. She would wait till midnight when the bombing was less intensive and go near the shelter to hear the voice of the mother asking for help. This was the most tragic situation Palestinian women ever had to live through. Sabra and Shatila received more attention, but the massacres perpetrated by the Israeli-backed Phalangist militia were even more horrible. Women in the camps were haunted by the fear of annihilation rather than by social injustices. They had no time to fight personal battles with their male partners because they were all the time busy defending themselves against external perils.

'One day I was extremely thirsty and didn't have a drop of water at home. At that time no one walked on the streets. People opened windows which connected all the flats of the same street and we used to move from one flat to another through these windows. I opened a window and crawled into my neighbour's flat. Having no energy to talk I held the glass up in my hand and gestured that I wanted a drop of water. My neighbour started to cry while pouring me a little precious drink. When I recovered my energy and asked why he was crying he answered because his two daughters were shot while trying to bring back water and he had had to leave them and carry the water back to the thirsty young children before they died of thirst. Next day my niece who was living with me and whose mother had died in the shelter went out to fetch water but was killed on the way.

'In Damour we were exclusively women since only a handful of men survived. The women were dressed all in black and the houses were all burnt, covered with black soot. The rooms had no windows and no doors, just black walls. For seven years I had to do with plastic sheets on my windows and door, in summer and winter alike. Most women had lost the main breadwinner in their families and were left an average of six to seven children to look after. So they had to go out to work to maintain a bare level of subsistence for their families. In 1982, Israeli planes started flying over us. Paying unwanted visits of bombing and shelling. After every air raid women would go out on the streets to collect their dead children for burial. Usually the women were not at home to keep their children in. Whenever they heard a plane children would go out to see it. The plane would drop its bombs and go back home but the children would never go home. This continued until the Israeli–Lebanese war started properly in 1982 when Israel raided the sports centre in Beirut near Shatila Camp, killing most of the people who happened to be there at the time.

'While living in Damour I heard even more terrifying stories than my own, and my own ordeal started to seem light to me. My neighbour there, Um Mohammed Doukhi, lost her four children, her husband, his five brothers and her two brothers. Only one young child of hers came out alive. On the way he was seriously wounded in the leg and his leg had to be amputated. I want to tell you, too, about Um Adnan who lost her husband and two of her children in Tal Zaatar. She came out with a young boy and two daughters, Firial and Samia. After an Israeli air raid on Damour her young boy (in his teens) went out to help. A time bomb exploded and killed him and some others. Her daughter Samia, who used to work for the Red Cross, got a grant to continue her higher education. She was travelling in a car to

Damascus with another woman and three male students, intending to board a plane to the country she'd been authorised to study in. En route, and before reaching the Syrian border, the Lebanese militia arrested and killed all of them. So out of a family of seven Um Adnan was left with her daughter Firial.

'Most women in Damour had lost their husbands and older children, and the younger ones desperately needed their mothers' help. So women went out to work in the farms or as cooks for the PLO. What could they do? Despite all their tragedies they had to gather their energy, or whatever was left of it, to provide food and shelter for the young dependants. Once your baby or child starts crying for a drink of water or a piece of bread you have to try to get water and bread for her, though you know full well you might never come back. Many women left their young, thirsty babies attempting to get them some water but were killed before they could get anywhere. No mother can watch her children in trouble and sit still. Mothers would rather die than see their children suffer.

'My brother, who was living in Tyre during an Israeli raid, didn't have enough time to reach the shelter with his children. So he started throwing them through the window. He threw in three of them and the fourth was in his arms when a bullet hit his spine and immediately paralysed him. Everyone was in the shelter, and he was soaked in his own blood unable to move. When the air raid was over his eldest daughter found her father in a pool of blood in the courtyard with her youngest brother still in his arms. He was taken to Beirut and after two major operations was able to walk on sticks. Later his daughter received her father's consent (and she was only 15 years old at the time) to marry a 55-year-old man who showed his willingness to look after the whole family, bring up the young children and pay for their education.

'From Damour the Israeli planes chased us to the Beqaa Valley and then to Syria. How can I describe our tragedies? They are indescribable – and we still have a long way to go. I can't see any light at the end of the tunnel. In fact our tunnel doesn't appear to have an end. Patience is a virtue which all Palestinians have to enjoy.'

'Did your view of women change as a result of your experiences?'

'In Tal Zaatar I was able to see how much women could do. Men were fighting, but women had to provide food, water, treat the wounded, bury the dead, and raise the morale of the demoralised. I was convinced, then, that no nation could ever win a war without the help of its women. Women who were trying to help the wounded and couldn't get bandages took their scarves off and used them instead. Islamic law decrees that it is permissible to show your hair if it means saving a life. Most Palestinian women encouraged their children to be PLO members and were very proud of them. My boy who was killed went out to defend us; that's why I congratulated him when he became a martyr. Because if we didn't defend ourselves the enemy would come to us, and then what could we do? Don't we have to resist? How would I feel if the enemy took my daughter and raped her in front of me? I would be far happier if her three brothers were killed and no enemy were able to reach her. If my daughter were raped and my honour defiled I would be disgraced, and my sons' lives would be pointless. It was to save our honour from the Israeli rapists that we left our homes and lands in Palestine. The Israelis understood this and exploited this fact to the full. They told us, speaking through loudspeakers, that either we left our homes or they would kill the men and rape the women. Palestinian men's nightmare was to defend their wives and daughters from the Israeli rapists. Now we can see, of course, that it was all a political ploy, and that we played into the hands of the Israelis, but it is far too late. People, then, were not politically aware; they didn't know what was happening to them. Men, including those in responsible positions, were obsessed with protecting their honour (women) from the Israelis. Even when they fought they fought to protect their women rather than their land; land didn't matter to them at all. It was all a plot meticulously woven by the Israelis who understood the Arab way of thinking and made terrible use of it.'

'All your battles seem to be related to you as a Palestinian; have you never resented male oppression which was vented on you simply because you are a woman?'

'In our faming community back in Palestine, men and women were living happily and working hand in hand. The men couldn't do all the work on the farm so the women went out to help them. Men and women used to go to the field together, work together, come back home together and feel much closer to each other than they do now. At home, women were responsible for doing all the daily chores, looking after the children, feeding the animals, milking the cows and making all the dairy products. They enjoyed doing all that; they certainly didn't resent it. It was as natural to them as the fact that the sun rises in the east and sets in the west. They, of course, had a say in running the home, bringing up the children and selling the crops. All in all, we were much happier then than we are now.'

'What do you think is the answer to your problem as a Palestinian?'

'The answer is for all Arab countries to unite, love each other and stand in one line and one heart against the enemy. The enemy is not the problem, because if we unite we could defeat not only Israel but America as well. America is one country and Israel another – but how many Arab countries do you have? Fifteen or sixteen? I just wish to God that we could start loving and truly supporting each other, and then no enemy, however mighty, would be able to impinge upon our rights.'

After explaining the nature of my work to Liana Badr and assuring her that her name needn't be revealed, she surprised me by saying she would love to keep her full name in my book. 'And I'll tell you straight away why I would like this. In Western Europe and America, the mere word "Palestinian" invites suspicion and I don't want to make things more vague by using symbols. I feel strongly that my experience does not belong to me alone; it is an example of my people's experiences. I have nothing to hide. I have already lost everything I can lose; I have nothing to lose any more. Thus I feel I would like my own experiences to be known, especially by Europeans who rarely, if ever, have the chance to get to know the truth at first hand.

'My parents met in 1948 when my mother was doing voluntary work, helping the victims of the 1948 war, while my father was working as a GP. They fell in love and soon after they first met they were married. My father was also a political activist and an intellectual with a deeply ingrained interest in both science and literature. He wrote books on Einstein and astronomy, and his book *Al Kown al Khalid* (The Eternal Universe) is still the most widely read and circulated reference book on this topic all over the Arab world. My mother, too, was a political activist; she was a very sharp woman with a piercing intelligence and capable of deep insights. (She later became a popular fighter and was to me like a perfect, self-contained world: developed, definite and detailed.) So the atmosphere in our house was both educational and political, and became more so after the first part of Palestine fell into Israeli hands in 1948. There was a price to be paid, of course; the childhood I remember was a long ordeal consisting of my father being in prison for most of the time and my mother out working with women, trying to raise their consciousness about what was taking place in the country and about what was happening to them as women. Along with Salwa Ziadine, my mother organised the first women's demonstration in Jerusalem in 1952, in support of the national guard and to object to the presence of the British army in Palestine. She was also the first Palestinian woman to attend the Maternity and Childhood Conference which was held in Brussels in the early 1950s.

'In 1957 my father was arrested while my mother succeeded in escaping to Syria where she lived as a political refugee. After about three months my sister and I were able to join her in exile. So, since early childhood I lived through difficult circumstances, with my father in and out of prison (much more in than out) and my mother engaged in constant attempts to outwit the reactionary Jordanian government and carry on with her struggle. Added to this there was the frequent loss of home and the inevitable chaos which that caused. My mother lived in Syria for a year, and after the union between Syria and Egypt in 1958 (Syria and Egypt were merged between 1958 and 1961) she was allowed to move to Egypt for a year. In 1959 the Jordanian government issued a general amnesty, so my father was released and my mother allowed back home. This unstable, stormy life taught me at an early age a lesson which my later life endorsed: that any apparent stability for Palestinians is a mirage which vanishes as soon as you get close to it. Through experience I discovered that even the institution of the family isn't real for us, though as an Eastern woman I tried hard to make myself believe in the normality of the family atmosphere in which I grew up.

'Apart from the lack of a congenial family atmosphere there was another experience which left a marked impression on my emotional and personal development. That experience was living in an orphanage in Jerusalem called "Dar Al Tofl Al Arabi" (The house of Arab children) between 1960 and 1963. Those three years opened my eyes to a world outside the world of my family which I anyway found vast; it broadened my horizons and deepened my outlook on things. I believe that my literary talent started to blossom at this school, because it is possible that had I remained within the family my role would have been more limited. At this school I had the chance to sing, write compositions and poetry. Thus I was able to build a private, yet bigger, world than that which my family was able to offer me. I was exposed to a world of human relations, of sharing the poverty, oppression and misery to which all the girls at school were subjected. During these years I learnt to live with people in an emotionally honest way without paying much attention to glittering appearances. Also at that stage I started to read extensively. I used to read four or five books a week. It was a period of true discovery.

'In 1964 my parents took us to live with them in Ariha which I still think of as the best place in the world. Although I was born and brought up in Jerusalem, which I still know so well, I loved Ariha dearly because it was a world where beautiful colourful nature breathed out fragrant, intoxicating smells. Ariha was a world of rich colours which still affect me – even today I like hot, very mixed colours,' Liana said, pointing to a distinctly vibrantly coloured rug on which she was sitting. 'This rich mixture of colours,' she continued, 'which I always like to keep around me, is my way of keeping in touch with that rich, colourful, but, alas, lost world. For me, Jerusalem has always meant the place where I was born and a very civilised place. Jerusalem had an air of peace and purity about it. So I had access to two worlds: Ariha was sensuous, full of colours, smells, fruits, plants and trees, while Jerusalem was spiritual, a world of rocks, Roman buildings and ancient civilisations. Jerusalem teaches people to love each other, simply because they share their humanity. I never knew the meaning of the word "sectarian" until I went to Lebanon. In Jerusalem there is a humanitarian openness which is an essential ingredient of this old and long-lasting civilisation. My best friends in Jerusalem, with whom I shared my best memories, were Christians – to the extent that when Father Christmas arrived I was always with them and he never failed to bring me a present! Moreover, the different religious beliefs used to be seen as very positive because it meant that most neighbours would celebrate the various religious ceremonies on different occasions.'

'Was there a similar loving and forgiving relationship between men and women?'

'No. There was no such spiritual enhancement between men and women because traditions and habits were in men's favour. I first observed this in the relationship between my parents. Although my mother was a school headmistress, a political activist, an educated, intelligent, even gifted woman, she found it almost impossible to make my father treat her as an equal. Although my father loved her and was quite open-minded about women's rights he was inhibited by powerful social ties. Thus, whenever my father got near to accepting my mother as his companion, external influences forced him to take a more traditional and reactionary stance. So much so that my father sometimes started to treat my mother with contempt to prove to his friends that he was still the ''man'' in the family. My mother would, of course, feel hurt by this.

'My mother was deeply aware of her problem as a woman, and she felt responsible for other women as well, even my own relationship with her centred mainly around this issue. When she confided in me and started to tell me about the problems between her and my father I couldn't help taking her side. What tormented her most was that she felt lost between two worlds; the world which she renounced and which would have guaranteed her an easy, comfortable life as the wife of a GP and the revolutionary world in which she had proved herself and which made her want so badly to be recognised as a man's equal and companion – a right she knew she deserved but which was refused her. She was very concerned I should finish my higher education and often advised me against an early marriage. She taught me how to be independent, strong and self-sufficient. So our relationship was an intellectual bond between mother and daughter who persistently felt the oppression of the outside world and who got closer to each other as their battle with that world grew fiercer. I recall with enormous pleasure my mother's friendship and her unconditional support for me. This relationship with my mother helped my evaluative, critical talent to mature particularly regarding a woman's role, position and rights. My mother helped me to break the rules laid down for the traditional Arab female, according to which a girl should spend a lot of time on clothes, jewels and make-up, although she always urged me to be tidy and smart in a simple, most natural way.

'Tragically, she tried to fight women's battles single-handedly. Although she was a stubborn fighter who never took a moment's rest, she eventually fell ill and died at the early age of 37 in a state which was evidently that of a frustrated and disillusioned individual who had lost the will to fight or even the desire to survive. I think she got cancer because she was no longer able to put up a fight. As fighting for women's rights was the pivotal point of her life she had no reason to live once she felt she had reached a dead end. She could neither go back to live a conventional life nor reach self-fulfilment in her struggle as a feminist and political activist. She was disappointed, frustrated and exhausted because she couldn't achieve the equality and recognition she knew she deserved and which she strove so hard to achieve. She died because she was alone. And this is what was so tragic about her experience. Unfortunately, at this time there was no women's movement or revolutionary movement which adopted women's rights seriously.

'When I became a PLO member I quickly reached the conclusion that personal battles were not the answer. One has to work collectively if anything is to be changed. Before going to university I had to fight constant attempts to marry me off at the age of 14. Although my mother was against the idea and my father never tried to force me, I nevertheless felt the pressure from the extended family and from society at large; a pressure that bordered on brainwashing. I found their industrious attempts to persuade me to get married exhausting. At university I felt the gap between me and my family network widen even further. I participated in union, cultural and political activities and lived as an independent individual which was neither expected nor accepted of women at the time. The value of what I did was not to do with the freedom it gave me but in the further significance and impact it made on my immediate society. When I joined the PLO in 1969 I felt that all the personal battles I had fought were now endowed with a social significance, because I was firmly convinced then that personal efforts to emancipate oneself are like hitting one's head against a brick wall.

'The point in favour of the PLO arises with the question: "How can a movement liberate women when the people of Palestine are still scattered in many countries and none of their rights recognised?" One has to admit there is a lack of theoretical discussion of women's issues inside the PLO; on the other hand I don't think it's possible to achieve equality or establish our rights until we live in an independent state, because as long as we are in the lands of others it is very difficult to establish anything, or even to start anything.'

'May I raise an objection to this view?' I intervened. 'As a Syrian citizen I find the Palestinian situation ideal for establishing true equality between men and women. You don't have reactionary laws, institutionalised sexual bias, and fixed sexist morals and traditions to fight against.'

'I used to share your view,' Liana resumed. 'I used to believe in the possibility of shaking up social habits and traditions in a way which would revolutionise women's position. For example, I often thought it would be possible to form a really effective Palestinian women's union with no male guardianship whatsoever. But the Palestinian women's union is in fact just like other women's unions in other Arab countries: a token union set up by a political system which is only too keen to list women's emancipation among its achievements. It started courses for teaching illiterate women, and other courses followed teaching women cooking, knitting and dressmaking which all women's unions in Arab countries do, and which accentuate women's traditional role. Whereas back at home, in the West Bank for example, where Palestinians are fighting on their own land, women literally make up half the resistance and are represented at all levels of the PLO leadership. Half the operations against the Israelis are carried out by women. There is a real popular surge of women's activity at home. I am not trying to justify the PLO's neglect of the woman question, but I conclude that the problem of land is crucial. My experience in Lebanon has taught me that building on other people's land is like building a castle in the air. What the exodus from Beirut meant in real terms was that all the institutions, factories and establishments which we founded with our sweat and blood were destroyed and can never be built again. The same thing could have happened to anything we might have built for women. When you are on other people's land you build on sand. What women are doing in the West Bank is much better than anything the PLO has ever done for women. So, as you see, there are two principal factors which have left the Palestinian woman where she is today: first, men's unwillingness to do anything serious about the woman question, and second, the problem of land. Still, the PLO could at least have legislated in women's favour; it could have spread about new values of equal rights and equal opportunities. The PLO could have been active in igniting a spark among people; it could have established values, traditions and ethics even if there was no possibility of establishing any institutions.

'It has to be said that this delay in facing up to women's rights led to a great loss of women's cadres. We entered the PLO with great hopes, but most women soon found out they were accepted on men's terms only, and that as soon as they started trying seriously to improve women's position, both inside and outside the PLO, the organisation made them feel unwelcome. Women were exhausted working on all fronts, only to find out that their freedom didn't exceed the limitations of working a double day and accepting only half the rights. As a result many women quit.

'Of course this is not to say that there are no distinguished women in the PLO: there are, but their distinction is a result of their sheer personal striving, rather than what the PLO has offered them within the framework of a revolutionary movement. Like all Arab regimes, the PLO has a cautious, perhaps reactionary attitude towards women. Take me, for example: the PLO has opened up many new horizons for me but it didn't actually provide the proper conditions for me to reach these horizons. The PLO has broadened my outlook but has offered me nothing to help me translate all the dreams with which it has inspired me into reality; not even a nursery for my baby. You couldn't do what the PLO helped you to want to do unless you were prepared to do this at the expense of your family life, rest and even health.

'Both as a Palestinian and as a woman I feel that things have always been decided for me. Somehow I feel that I've never had control over even the most personal things in my life. In 1967, for example, I didn't make a personal decision to leave the West Bank. My father told me that we were going for a day or two to Amman and asked me to take some night clothes for my sisters and myself. Despite his deliberate attempts to make the journey to Amman sound like a normal visit I strongly felt that we would never return home again. I wanted to scream, but I couldn't argue with him about whether or not I wanted to go; I was too young to do that – only 15 at the time. There was an atmosphere of defeat and surrender. I wanted to take more things with me because I knew I would never see anything again, but I didn't dare to because if I had done this I would be admitting to myself that there was no coming back. Yet an irresistible urge impelled me to take two precious things: a photo of my dead mother and my pen. My mother was the symbol of my ties with home and with my past history, while my pen was the only means I had of expressing myself and my only hope for a better future. Later on, writing became my only means of restoring and maintaining my humanity.

'In Amman we had no mattresses to sleep on, no change of clothes, not even a radio to hear the news. How stupid to have left our home (though there was heavy Israeli bombardment) which overlooked the beautiful orange plantations and where the blue sky was my ever-present companion. In Amman I felt deprived of home, family, friends, traditions and past, and found myself sleeping on the bare floor. At that point my personal history, both as a Palestinian and as a writer, began. After 1967 I started working with Palestinian women in the camps; it was then that I started to discover the relationship between myself as a person and myself as a nation. As part of this common dream of returning home we discovered our true identity, but there was no coherent policy to push things on further in the right direction.'

'In your writing women do not seem to feature prominently. Why is this?'

'I live in a world which is trying to kidnap my rights. As every one is suffering similar destiny, how can I confine myself to women's position and ignore the rest of my people? I have to see women within the world of Palestinians abroad. If I were living in Palestine, even an Israeli-occupied Palestine, things would be much clearer. I would at least be living in a Palestinian world the features of which I know and am sure of. But living here I feel lost, because I have to live out all the crises of the Arab citizen, and in addition suffer the huge problem of having no home, no land, no job and no rights. However deeply I empathise with the women's issue, I can't give it priority in a society which is rife with social and political problems and whose very identity and existence are in question. In Lebanon, for example, men were not allowed to work; they were locked up in the camps, too scared to go out. Only women went out to do poorly paid jobs. The oppressor here is not the husband but society. In one of my stories I speak of a man who was killed in an Israeli bombardment and I speak of his relationship with his wife and friends. But I can't speak of women's problems as the only issue because there is a more serious problem: the threat of annihilation from the outside world. Even so, I portrayed this beautiful image of the Palestinian woman (the wife) who, despite death and excruciating pain, can still smile, love and bring up her children to be loving, forgiving and optimistic. I show how women cling tenaciously to life and make it not only liveable but wonderful. My role in that story was to open people's eyes to these female merits, to draw people's attention to the inner beauty of the world of women and to their capacity to brave death and create life. The women's problem gives depth to my writings, but I cannot deal with it as if it

were the only major issue in a society which is suffering from everything. If I were living in a society in which women's equality was a
major subject under consideration, I would have made it a major issue
in my writings. When I write about women I always consider them
together with the conditions in which they live. History for Palestinians is a daily ordeal; in recent history our lives have always been
governed by historical circumstances.

'I also like to talk about ordinary women. I don't look for the distinguished or privileged type of woman. So I usually tell the stories of
ordinary, unknown individuals and try to study Palestinian history
through them. I always try to compound the documentary side of life
on which I build my fiction. Because when you examine the lives of
ordinary people you discover through them rich, poetic experiences.
You discover more poetry in life than you do in literature. Ordinary
people have a vast reserve of poetic experiences, and my pen feeds on
this reserve. The more ordinary people I know, the better my writing
becomes. Thus, the types in my stories are like drops of water which,
when seen under a microscope are discovered to contain thousands of
living things.'

'You haven't told me about your personal history.'

'Like most Palestinian girls I got married early in an attempt to
escape family and social oppression. Despite the fact that my family
was quite a distinguished one I was still expected to live a double life;
I might be open, intelligent and independent, but once it came to marriage I was expected to marry a man of my parent's choice rather than
that of my own. Amongst Palestinian communities, early marriage is
the norm; as far as young women are concerned an early marriage is
their only outlet from the traditional Arab family in which unmarried
women have no right to act, speak or even think independently. So
my marriage was in a way a bid for freedom.

'Marriage as such didn't limit my activities, but the consequences
of marriage, namely the children, were the real obstacle. I was solely
responsible for them, which was both good and bad at the same time.
It was good for me because I experienced the world of motherhood,
which in itself is very enriching. It helped me to discover depths of
emotions and feelings I could never have reached without being a
mother. I became more capable of understanding and sympathising
with people. Motherhood taught me to be patient as a writer. The
sleepless nights I spent with my children and the utter standstill to

which they brought every other activity in my life taught me to treat my writing with the same patience, will and persistent care as I treated my children.

'Having children, however, limited the experiences which I could have plunged myself into. For example, I could have had interviews with people and written about the particular atmosphere of a Palestinian base when Palestinians had bases. It was virtually impossible to leave my children and live in a base to discover its nature and atmosphere. The children imposed certain limitations on my experiences and work, but I tried my best to make up for that through my intensive efforts in the world of journalism.

'When I felt I had proved myself as a successful journalist (which was one of the most important intellectual professions in Beirut), and there was nothing new to explore, I went back to university and studied English literature for three years. Being a mother and a wife is certainly limiting and to attempt to be a successful professional at the same time is extremely exhausting. At one point of my life I was a journalist, a university student, a wife, a cook, a cleaner, a mother, a nanny and a writer in the evening (or whatever was left of it). My time was divided by seconds, and I was always worn out. But the way I was brought up (which is the way most women are brought up) helped me to shoulder all these responsibilities and to stomach all the difficulties. There are many gifted Arab women who haven't found they can reconcile their talents with the demanding roles of mother and wife, so they give up their work and writing in favour of doing the daily chores and keeping the family happy.

'I feel strongly that our political situation as Palestinians is imposing on me, as a writer, an unbelievable geographical reality which is causing my literary creativity to suffer. Both as a woman and as a writer I feel I need the unflinching will of Prometheus to be able to go on. What I find most disconcerting now is the periodic loss of everything I own and the need to start from scratch again. How many more times I can cope with this distressing experience I don't know.

'For example, as a child I collected children's books, and this library got larger as I grew up. In 1967 I had to leave it and start my life in Amman on a *hasier* with no books, no clothes, no bed, no past and little hope for the future. When I became a university student in Amman I amassed an interesting literary and political library which our neighbours were forced to set fire to when we were chased out of

Amman in 1971. After our expulsion the Jordanian government organised missions to burn revolutionary books and private libraries and
persecute their owners. In Beirut I decided not to start a personal library again because I couldn't cope with the inevitable loss of my precious books. Indeed, for about four years I didn't buy any books – but
you have to read and books accumulate as a result! I ended up with
over 6,000 books on every single subject I was interested in, plus
over 500 records which were my pride and joy. In 1982 I took nothing
out of Beirut except another nightdress, just like the one I had taken
from our home in Ariha back in 1967, and this time I took my children instead of my sisters as previously. I couldn't take anything else
with me, not even the tapes on which I had taped my children's first
words. Once again, my whole world was totally shattered.

'Throughout my life I have never thought much about clothes.
Clothes to me were only practical necessities and I was only margin-
ally smart. But after leaving Beirut I discovered I was fanatically in
love with a jacket and trousers which I used to wear often. I found out
that clothes symbolise the happy moments we spend while wearing
them. When I arrived in Damascus in 1982 with no change of clothes
I felt so naked that it seemed all the shops in Damascus could not possibly cover my nakedness. There were no clothes which belonged to
me and to which I belonged and felt at home in. I suffered a sudden
loss of memory, and to a certain extent, loss of identity. I had to forget that I spent most of my life trying to forget things dearest to me:
colourful Ariha, the old Jerusalem, my books in Amman and in
Beirut; I had to forget the records and the beautiful music I used to
write about. It is this urge to forget which turns Palestinians into
people with no memory and no past. I try to keep these memories and
this past very much alive in my writings. This has become my most
urgent task.'

'Would you like to see Arab women as free as Western women? Do
you approve of sexual freedom, for instance?'

'The Western woman is not free. She has achieved freedom in
some areas, such as the sexual arena, but essentially she is still
deprived of many basic rights and suffers from unbalanced relationships. Despite the fact that in the West there is hardly any social
stigma relating to liberated sexual relationships, within these relationships women are still subjected to blackmail, chauvinist authority
and oppression. There is clear evidence for this in the high numbers

of rapes and the blatant exploitation of young women as sexual objects and consumer targets. A woman's body in the West is still treated as an object. Internationally women are thought of in terms of fashion shows; they are marketed and priced according to their looks, figures and appearance. Men don't have to be fashionable, look after their skins or their figures, yet it is their values which dominate and direct women's lives. And these sexually liberated women could in an instant turn into whores or prostitutes in men's eyes; their sexuality remains a potential source of shame and social disgrace and it is still the most accessible means men have of subjugating them. Thus, in my view, Western values haven't changed much from values which exist in any male chauvinist society. Women's movements both in the West and in the East have still got a long way to go. I truly believe that sexual freedom in the West is only a cover for more strident forms of women's oppression and exploitation. Only when a woman becomes a free, independent individual who gets equal pay and equal opportunities can she enjoy an equal sexual relationship in which she is never used, blackmailed or maltreated.

'It is impossible for Palestinian women to make a distinction between the struggle for home and the struggle for women's rights, equality and emancipation. I fight to break the fetters of femininity which cage my soul and mind; at the same time I fight ferociously for the restoration of my homeland to its own people. The thousands of sacrifices which Palestinian women have already made make my struggle worthwhile and purposeful. My dream is to have a home, a country which I can call mine, an identity and a passport. I want to live in a secular, non-sectarian state in which men and women can achieve true equality through mutual love and understanding. My struggle for emancipation as a Palestinian is inseparable from my struggle for genuine liberation as a woman; neither of them is valid without the other.'

As Palestine is the one Arab country I am not allowed to visit I had to choose my Palestinian interviewees from the Palestinian women living in refugee camps in both Syria and Lebanon. Some of these women were forced out of their homes in Palestine after the 1948 war and the creation of the state of Israel. Others made their exodus from the West Bank and Gaza Strip after the 1967 war while still others arrived here in Syria as recently as 1982 after the Israeli invasion of

Lebanon. Like me, these Palestinian women are banned from the occupied Arab territories where they were born, while at the same time Israeli authorities encourage foreign-born Jews from Russia, America and Poland to settle there.

Mona, a Palestinian woman with a postgraduate degree in history, has been working in the Palestinian Cultural Centre in Damascus since 1982. She had lived under Israeli occupation in both Jerusalem and Ramallah up to 1977, waging her own battles against occupation until she felt she was top of the Israeli list for arrest. She fled to Beirut in 1977 and then to Damascus in 1982 where I held an interview with her that drove my imagination to the heart of Jerusalem which I still dream of visiting.

Our appointment was at ten o'clock in the morning. A thin, tall, firm-looking woman came through the door of her office and, with a very reserved smile, said, 'You must be Bouthaina.' We shook hands and exchanged casual greetings, while her left hand searched for a pack of cigarettes in her large bag. She seemed to be a very busy woman who had allotted me a certain amount of time and wanted me to make the most of it. She said: 'I understand the nature of your project and will try to relate my personal experience to you as fully as I can recall it. Whenever you see I'm going off the track, or that I'm providing you with irrelevant information, please do stop me.

'Perhaps the position of Palestinian women is unique. You might well find that many of the conclusions you have reached regarding the position of other Arab women are not applicable in this case.' Like someone who sees a glorious past compared with a shabby present she seemed to enjoy recalling past memories but made an effort not to make a link with the present unsatisfactory situation of Palestinians. When she failed to guard against making such a link she had nothing but regret and sadness to shower over the present.

The point I felt I had to stress before asking her any questions was that my book was not propaganda, either for Palestinian or for other Arab women, and that I was appalled by books about Arab women which contained clichés and stereotypes of women, written mostly by men. I stressed I was aiming to give an absolutely honest picture of the ordeals, struggles and aspirations of Arab women, to give a hearing to their inner voices which for centuries have been silenced by tradition, religion and social and political stigmas. She nodded with full approval and promised to give me an honest account of the plight of

Palestinian women in the occupied territories where she had lived until 1977.

'I was born to educated parents; my father studied in Cairo, worked in the field of education and was considered to be one of the most distinguished people in the Arab world. As such I am perhaps not a very typical Palestinian woman. My father never discriminated between boys and girls; in fact, he always showed a preference for girls. He took our education very seriously and tried his utmost to improve our performance. My mother was also educated; her English was excellent and she used to help us with our homework. The atmosphere at home was one of books, education and friendship between parents and children. Financially we were very well off, with the latest electrical gadgets. My father had a deeply ingrained interest in political events; he would listen to the news on all the radio stations. We followed his example, though our main concern was what was happening in Palestine.

'Originally we were from West Jerusalem, but after the 1948 war and the horrors of Deir Yassin's massacre we left our home and emigrated to East Jerusalem. I am sure you have read about Deir Yassin where the whole village had been requested by the Israelis to meet in the village's main mosque. The Israelis slaughtered men, women and children, just like sheep. Under constant pressure and harassment from the Israelis we had to flee West Jerusalem and leave places that were so dear to our hearts: Yafa Street, Al Aksa Mosque, Sakhra Mosque, Kaniesett Al Kiama (the church of doomsday), etc. Jerusalem, that lovely ancient town, had been dissected into East and West by a wall similar to the horrible wall in Berlin. My friends and I used to go to high places in East Jerusalem to be able to see our houses and lands in West Jerusalem which were often patrolled by Israeli cars. We felt extremely bitter and sad to have lost our homes, our lands and all that we possessed. My father had to start again from scratch; he had to work round the clock to support us and build us a new home. After a few years he was able to buy a piece of land and build us quite a nice house, this time in Ram Allah.

'That was in 1956. At that time we had a congenial, relatively quiet family atmosphere. We all went to Arabic schools where the Jordanian curriculum was taught. I went to Al Mamounieh school, one of the best Arabic schools in Palestine and the West Bank, and after my graduation I worked for a short period in teaching. When I got my baccalaureate I enrolled as a student of philosophy at Damascus University, but after the 1967 war and the occupation of the West Bank it was no longer safe for me to cross from the West to the East Bank to travel to Damascus. In 1967 Israel took over the whole of Jerusalem and the two parts of the city came under Israeli sovereignty. This meant that Arabic schools teaching the Jordanian curriculum in the Arabic part of the city were put under the Israeli ministry of education. The Hebrew language became the first language and the Israeli curriculum was very superficial in comparison with the Arabic curriculum. I'm talking about the educational system because it was my field, and I knew its ins and outs. At that time I decided to stay at home and refused to teach with the Israelis.

'After 1967, when the Israeli government allowed some movement between East and West Jerusalem, we pressed our father to take us to see our home about which our mother had told us so much. Eventually he agreed to do this. When we arrived there we found a Polish dentist living in the house. We told him that this was our house and we asked permission to look around it. He said that many people had come, saying that this was their house. But when my father gave him an exact and detailed description of the house's interior he was convinced. My mother collapsed in tears and nearly had a nervous breakdown. We were all crying bitterly; it was a horrible day. We went back to Ram Allah feeling we had to do something about the degrading situation in which we found ourselves.

'Shortly after this incident I got together with a few enthusiastic women and we decided to start a welfare society which we called "Jamiat Al Nissa Al Filistieniat" (Palestinian Women's Society) to help the families of the martyrs. We started touring round towns and villages, taking whatever people wanted to give away, and distributing what we collected to those who needed it. After the 1967 war the markets were flooded with Israeli products. We held a meeting and decided to impose sanctions. The market was full of Israeli biscuits, so we started making Palestinian biscuits which sold like hot cakes in all supermarkets. We wanted people not to buy the Israeli biscuits, and urged them to buy Palestinian biscuits instead. Most people responded positively. This was the beginning of our resistance to the occupation. We also urged all workers not to work in Israeli factories and planned to open our own factories. The greater the profits the more we expanded our domestic industry, until we catered for all that a Palestinian family would need in the way of food. We also started cooking for parties and special occasions, such as weddings and birthdays. We signed contracts with a few restaurants and regularly provided them with our traditional dishes. After our weekly meeting we would serve *tabouli* (a traditional Arabic salad with crushed wheat) and sold each plate for 50 *filis* (50p). We invented ways to make money, and in a remarkably short space of time were able to rent a suitable place and open a nursery and kindergarten where we offered children hot meals.

'Then we noticed that the Israelis were stealing some of our traditional handicrafts, such as embroidery and the making of the Palestinian national dress. So we decided to revive these crafts ourselves. We opened a centre for Palestinian embroidery, which was heartily welcomed by housewives who couldn't leave their children. We would give these women the materials, they would do the embroidery at home and bring us the finished products – for which they got paid, of course. We would sell them at auctions and make a lot of money for the welfare society. In no time at all we started courses to teach women traditional embroidery, canvaswork and dressmaking. We also opened a public library and a beauty salon. Our work expanded amazingly quickly, even though there were only 12 of us women and we were fully employed in teaching or doing something else, and only did voluntary work for the society in the afternoon. At this stage the society didn't have a single employee. Each of our factories was supervised by a member of the executive committee. Palestinians abroad knew about us and started sending generous donations. We also became experienced in choosing not only viable but profitable projects. With the financial help we received, and voluntary work, we were able to build a huge, complex building for all our activities, and this didn't cost us much.

'The Israeli government only allowed us two welfare bazaars a year. For the first we introduced the concept of an economic lunch. Tickets were priced at one Jordanian *dinar* (approximately £2) each. Women would cook a traditional dish, *Mjadara* (crushed wheat and lentils), which was served with salad and pickles. For most people it was like going out for lunch, but for us it was a profitable activity. The second annual festival was the welfare bazaar in which we would exhibit Palestinian crafts and traditional embroideries, woodwork, canvas work, sewing, homemade drinks and all kinds of domestic industries. It became a famous national occasion, just like carnival time with everyone in the West Bank turning up. The Israeli military governor attended it once; he was not invited, of course. We never sent invitations; we just announced the occasion in Arabic newspapers. We used to make huge profits which were used to start new projects.

'After the 1967 war our welfare society started a project which I am still proud of called ''Adoption by Spending'', which meant that wealthy Palestinians abroad adopted children in the occupied territories and spent money on them and their families. There was a real need for this project as many families had lost their sole breadwinner during the war and thousands of women had been left with a large number of children and no one to support them. We researched into the type of families we had in the distant villages, the number of children each family had, whether there was a man or woman supporting the family, and what these families needed most. So whenever we had some extra money we knew exactly what to buy and where to go. We also taught women to read and write, cleaned their houses for them, and told them about the importance of hygiene. When rich Palestinians came on holiday they would stay with their adopted children and families. In this way we solved financial problems for many families and created an emotional bond between Palestinians abroad and Palestinians at home. This was one way of keeping our identity and resisting the Israeli occupation; it was a women's way of doing things.

'There was also one other very important thing which our society did, and that was to collect folk songs and stories. We used to visit distant villages and ask people to meet in the village square to record their local popular songs. For example, I remember when the Egyptian leader Gamal Abdel Nasser died we called on a few villages where people had kept the ancient custom of making circles and competing in singing songs and telling stories which revealed the merits of the deceased, and we recorded all kinds of songs. Eventually we published a book of folksongs and tales of a village called Tormus Aia in Halhous and in Dir Bzeh. We also collected popular proverbs and issued a periodical called *Culture and Society* in which we published folksongs and stories. All this work was done exclusively by women. The occupation seems to have motivated women to examine their reality, explore it and ensure its rebirth.'

'What does that tell you?'

'Quite honestly, it tells me that women all over the Arab world must have a potential which could change the map and identity of the Arab world if it could just be brought to fruition by the right historical circumstances. Now you see a huge difference between the demands of Arab women in general and the demands of Palestinian women in the occupied territories.

'At this time I went back to teach and enrolled at the history department of Damascus University. I was teaching in Jerusalem where we had a daily confrontation with the Israeli enemy. Neither teaching nor daily work was ever predictable. Every day we had something new to do. We used to go to Al Aksa Mosque for protection as it is the House of God. It was only there that we were able to say what we wanted to say. Of course, the accusations against us were very much exaggerated. As a teacher of history I was able to draw parallels between what we had suffered under previous colonial rule and what we were currently suffering under Israeli occupation.

'Some historical sources claim that the Israeli army used the effective threat of raping Palestinian girls if their families didn't quit the land of Palestine. It has been reported that in 1948 some Palestinians raised the motto "Akhsar al Ard Wala Al ard" (lose your land rather than your honour, that is, your daughter's virginity). So how could Palestinian girls resist Israeli occupation under such circumstances?

'But in the 1960s and 1970s Palestinian girls were congratulated if they lost their virginity or were raped by Israeli soldiers. A family whose daughter was arrested was congratulated for bringing up a fighter. A girl's arrest or prison ordeal was regarded as honourable for both the girl and her family. So the concept of honour had been turned upside down. There are many Palestinian women who became national heroines: Leila Khalid, Lotfiah Houalis, Abla Taha, Fatma Bournawi, Dalal Mougrobi and many others led brave operations against the Israeli enemy. Other Palestinian women kept arms and weapons in their homes and passed them from one group to another. So they had an important role to play in every operation against the enemy.'

'Why did you eventually decide to leave the occupied territories?'

'I was quite an active member of our society and was active as a teacher of history. The subject I was teaching was very important, but sensitive. Through reading our past history and comparing it with the present and making parallels and inferences, I appeared to enthuse girls against the Israeli enemy. I reminded them of national occasions which we always marked by going on demonstrations or strikes or some such activity. Naturally, the Israelis were watching me closely and didn't like me. They started to chase me. On Land's Day we decided to go on strike, so I stayed at home. The Israeli military governor rang me at home and asked me to take my passport and go to the police. So I did. At the police station an Israeli man and woman took a very thick file out and started to ask me about everything for hours on end in a tense and terrifying atmosphere. This was meant to be a warning and a threat.

'I had got hold of some valuable Israeli documents which I wanted to escape with before being caught out. The Israelis had a project called the "Eighties" which aimed to make people ignorant; I managed to get hold of the original documents of this project. I also possessed a comprehensive study of old Jerusalem and its suburbs, done by my pupils, which was very precious to me. There was also a wealth of material relating to the educational system, which I was very anxious to secrete away from the Israeli enemy. However, I was watched very closely by the Israelis and I knew that it would be only a matter of days before they decided to arrest me. (In fact, it was only one day after I had left the West Bank that they went to my home trying to find me.) I went to Beirut in 1977 where I completed my BA and did my MA and PhD. I was working for the PLO, teaching and studying at the same time. In 1982 I started to do voluntary work with the Palestinian Red Cross. I cooked, cleaned and helped the wounded. I very much wanted to stay in Beirut but finally left one day before the Sabra and Shatila massacres.'

'How do you compare Palestinian women with Lebanese, Syrian or Arab women in general?'

'The Palestinian woman has her family, her work and her struggle to look after. Even illiterate Palestinian women are politically very conscious and speak about politics in a logical way. For the last decade, our presence in Beirut has left a marked influence on the Lebanese woman who has also become politically aware, particularly after the Israeli invasion of the South of Lebanon in 1982. You just have to visit the Palestinian camps to see how wonderful the women are, managing all kinds of jobs. Wherever you find oppression, aggression and occupation, women seem to perform brilliantly;

unfortunately, whenever the crisis is over, women in most cases are sent back home to resume their jobs as housewives – as if their brilliant struggles were performed according to a short-term contract. The Palestinian woman's role will, I hope, not diminish. I assure you that the position of women in the occupied territories is much better than the position of Palestinian women in exile. The struggle both for liberation and equality of the sexes is more genuine and more effective there than what you find in exile.'

'How do you compare the liberation of the Palestinian woman with that of the Western woman?'

'Actually, I always like to compare the position of the Palestinian woman with that of the Vietnamese woman, which I believe is the same. As for the Western woman, she is a working woman but apolitical. She is busy with her emotional and financial problems. The Palestinian woman has no time for fashion, beauty or skin care. She is a fighter who leads operations, and yet doesn't give up the right of being a wife and a mother. She has learnt to manage both roles under extremely difficult situations; with the loss or potential loss of father, husband and children, and with other additional hazards. I believe we have more respect for the family, parents and children than Western women have; we also have a more lasting interest in our children's education.'

'This is what most Arab women think. It seems to me that by saying this Arab women are holding Western women to be solely responsible for all their family problems. I agree, of course, that a congenial and happy family atmosphere is precious, but why do we always expect women to be responsible and pay the price for a peaceful family life?'

'You are right. Both men and women have to look after their children and work for the betterment of their family. But the Western woman is a bit selfish; she doesn't work as hard as the Arab woman does for the sake of her husband and children. The Western woman no longer believes in self-denial which is still the main tenet which regulates the lives of most Arab women.'

'Do you approve of sexual freedom for women?'

'Of course not! Sexual freedom causes all sorts of emotional and social problems, single parent families, the spread of venereal diseases, etc. When human relationships become mainly physical they lose their charm and mystery.'

'But how do you answer a Western woman who might ask you:

"How do you assume the right of an independent, sensible individual who fights, challenges and participates in the making of her country's future and yet denies herself the most basic right of all which is the right to her own body?" '

'Why not allow your body its sexual freedom within a marital relationship? If the marriage doesn't work you can always get a divorce and get married again. If you try to be sensible and thoughtful in choosing your partner you will most probably live a happy and fulfilled life. On the other hand, to have many sexual partners is to be an animal rather than a human being. A sexual relationship should be the culmination of an intimate, loving and caring relationship, not just the result of a cheap, physical desire to jump into bed with someone. Besides, so many women who choose this path become tired of changing partners. They get depressed and in most cases spend the rest of their lives longing for an intimate, loving and lasting relationship. Young girls might find sexual freedom great fun, but in the long run it is a sure way to loneliness, misery and depression. Sex within a decent and secure marital relationship is so much healthier and better for women. A change of partners doesn't provide any definite advantage for women; you change your clothes every day but you can't change the man you love and understand so easily. You have to consider the results. Is it good to enjoy sex for five or ten years and then spend the rest of your life despondent and lonely? I am against sexual liberation because I don't think it does women any good.'

When I heard about Nabila's story, a Palestinian woman and mother of four whose Tunisian husband was killed in one of the Israeli air raids on Beirut in 1982, I felt such pain in my heart and cold shivers in my body that I wondered whether I would be strong enough to talk to such a woman without shedding tears and making a mess of the interview. Her story, however, is typical of many Palestinian women's stories who lost their husbands and sometimes their children en route from one place of exile to another. When finally I decided to pay her a visit in a Palestinian refugee camp in Damascus I was truly surprised to sense the happy and congenial atmosphere that prevailed in her home and to find her children smiling, polite and extremely cooperative. A life such as hers is expected often to break a woman's resilience, in fact, though, it somehow made her stronger in that it provided her with an ability to face the daily ordeals of a permanent refugee. Although Nabila had been a widow for the last four years she still managed to seem bouncy and full of life, so much so that the loss of a husband – which I expected to be the main topic of conversation – seemed to be so irrelevant that I wondered whether I should mention it at all. I decided to start by asking her about her life as a Palestinian girl brought up in refugee camps.

'I was born in Amman in 1948 into a family of 14 children: seven boys and seven girls. My father was the only source of income but my mother was a great manager; she used to knit our woollies and make all our clothes. She must have been an excellent home economist to be able to manage a family of 16 people on my father's low salary. She was able to make an old, cold tent a happy and even cosy home for all of us. Having experienced the bitterness of poverty and the horrors of being a refugee I decided to become a member of the PLO because I was convinced that the only way to restore our land and regain our dignity was through armed struggle. In 1971 I got to know my husband as a comrade. I admired him because he was a Tunisian who felt so deeply about the Palestinian problem that he too decided to join the PLO. Soon afterwards we started a serious relationship which culminated in our marriage in 1972 in Beirut. He was my first and last love. I loved him dearly and we got on extremely well as comrades, friends and partners. Although during the ten years we lived in Beirut I was shouldering the main responsibility of our home and children I was very happy. I was happy in our love, togetherness, and deep understanding of each other. Though he didn't do much work at home he was always sympathetic, appreciative of what I did, and extremely pleasant. He always thanked me for what I did for him, for our home and for the children.

'In 1982, the political situation reached a very low ebb in Lebanon. A day before my husband was killed, the Israeli planes bombarded all the bridges around Beirut. That night he came back after midnight. I asked him about the situation and he told me it was very bad. The next day was my youngest daughter's first birthday, 17 July 1982. I woke up in a weepy mood; wherever I turned my face I found something to cry about. I said to my husband that I felt a hundred years old. He tried to leave, but my little girl wouldn't let him go. He had to carry her and she started smelling him and rubbing her face against his neck. That was a sure omen of something nasty. I am superstitious sometimes. He left to go to his office and I took my daughter and went to mine. About half an hour later the Israeli planes were over our offices, bombarding us and turning our day into a dark and miserable night. I collected my children from school, and how I found my way home I don't know. When the air attack stopped and he didn't turn up to ask after us I knew he had been killed. I couldn't look for him in the rubble. So I carried my children off and left the area. The children became my sole responsibility. Next day I went to the American University Hospital and found him stretched out as if asleep. Hundreds of wives, mothers and sisters were in the same boat as myself. There was nothing to say.

'However, when I see other women's tragedies I forget mine. There are illiterate women who have lost their husbands, have no jobs and no source of income, and a huge number of children to support and look after. I worry about other women and feel that my problem is a small drop of water in a large pond. Hundreds of Palestinian women face the problem of losing their husbands early on in their married lives and there are thousands of children with nowhere to go. So I now feel for Palestinian women and the Palestinian problem, much more than before. I can see now how well equipped for life women are. No man can manage his home, children, job and social life the way I and hundreds of other women do. At the end of the street where I live there is a Palestinian woman whose husband went abroad and never came back to her. She worked day and night, built a beautiful house, and brought up nine gorgeous children, all of whom are very intelligent, very polite, sociable and considerate. They adore and revere their mother. Suppose her husband were here and she caught a dangerous disease? He would have taken her back to her family and his children would perhaps have been vagabonds. But this woman was able to keep her family together and bring up her children to be healthy and productive individuals. So women are not just men's equals; in many instances they are their superiors.

'Although there is no doubt that Sabra and Shatila have been the most painful tragedies that have befallen Palestinians in their modern history they also stand as invincible proof of women's greatness. About one year after the massacres a woman from Shatila told me her story. She said that during the massacre there was a terrible shortage of water. She went out searching for water for her dying father. After many hours of searching and waiting she managed to get her jug filled, but just before entering her home she stumbled, fell and spilt the precious water on the floor which had already been washed with blood. That was the worst tragedy that could have happened to her. She went in to her father crying; he at once knew what had happened and died immediately, either from shock or thirst or from both. A day later her brother was massacred and she herself was pulled out from under some rubble by a Palestinian fighter with whom she had a lovely relationship which culminated in their marriage. She became pregnant. Her husband was desperate to see his child, but was killed in an Israeli air bombardment four months before her son was born. Her married life only lasted nine months and the loss of her husband came only a few months after the loss of her father and brother. She was just 25 when all these tragedies happened to her. Now her son and the precious, poetic photographs of the happy days with her husband are the two pivotal things in her life which keep her going. She is only one of thousands of women who move like black columns in Sabra and Shatila but who cherish their husbands' memory and do their utmost to bring up their children the best they can.'

'How do you reconcile this image of strong women with the idea of them as the weaker sex with brains only a quarter the size of men's?'

'I don't know, but I think that the concept of women as the weaker sex is inherited as the result of blind obedience to traditions and unquestioned habits. We are all brought up to think that the man is the master and the woman – however superior she might in fact be to him – his subordinate. Throughout history, particularly during critical periods, women have always proved themselves to be strong, efficient and trustworthy. What women have to do now is to organise and work assiduously through their organisations to make the world admit their worth.'

'I once had the theory that men who are intent on making women feel inferior do this basically because they are afraid of women's potential and abilities. This theory of mine found supporting evidence in an article published by UNESCO about women and Islam. The article argued that Islam found it necessary to suppress women's sexuality because of men's deep awareness of the vehemence of their sexuality. What do you think?'

'Yes. I have seen hundreds of women whose abilities far exceeded their husbands' and yet who accepted subordinate roles as wives because they wanted safe and secure marital relationships in which their children could grow up peacefully. Thus their marriages became a fate to which they resigned themselves. Women will do anything for the sake of their children; hence they appear to be weak and ineffective. As for the sexual problem: we live in a hypocritical society in which nothing is allowed to be done publicly but everything is permissible in private. Most people here live in two worlds: the private, which they enjoy and about which no one is supposed to know anything, and the public in which they are known and which is normally irrelevant to them. These are the most bitter problems in Arab societies: hypocrisy and our inability to be honest, either with ourselves or with others. I think we have either to do away with hyperbole about morality, honour, etc., or to lift ourselves up to become semi-angels. The gap between what we say and what we do is causing us to be schizophrenic, not only about sexual matters but also as regards social, moral, intellectual and religious issues. Feminists now are leading the move to a more honest way of life; they are voicing their views honestly and clearly. I think the time is not far off when everyone will understand and acknowledge what they are doing.'

'What is the most difficult problem you have had to face since your husband's death?'

'The most difficult thing is that I have no one to talk to, to feel angry with, or to complain to. Although I used to shoulder most of the responsibilities during his lifetime it was a great help having him around as a loving and genuinely interested companion. I don't encroach on other women's time or bother them with my problems. I can see that, like me, they are responsible for their children, home, work and their husbands, too. Many of the women I know think of their husbands as extra children; they worry about them and have to sort out their daily affairs. On top of all this they feel grateful that they have a man.'

'Doesn't it worry you that you keep your husband's name and bring up his children knowing perfectly well that he wouldn't have done the same for you had he been in your place?'

'No, it doesn't. I am sure he would never have done the same for me, but I still love him and feel quite happy about what I am doing. It pleases me a lot to think of him and to bring up his children. The idea of another marriage is totally alien to me. I want to be free to love him and think of him. I am sure I will never ever think of any other man. To be honest with you, it doesn't bother me in the least that he would never have thought in this way. This is my way of thinking; it is the way I feel. I am not doing it as a duty, so why should I expect him to be exactly like me? He has the right to be different. I have my own thoughts, my own life and my own values. These values, which perhaps are women's values, are so natural to me and so precious that I wouldn't like to exchange them for anything else in the world. The fact that men don't seem to hold or even esteem such values doesn't bother me in the least. All my comrades respect me now, but I know full well they would never forgive me if I ever thought of getting married again.'

'Suppose you turned up one day at work with a new husband? What would your comrades say then?'

'I don't know; they might reject me completely. As a widow I feel I am treated with great respect, as long as I'm prepared to sacrifice myself for my children, the family and the national cause; once I falter in any of these duties I am sure that my worth, both as a woman and as a comrade, would be in question. As long as I am working in the organisation, bringing up my children and keeping my family together, I am fine. But no one stops to think what I might need as a person in my own right. As a woman I am supposed to live for others; I have to be an inexhaustible source of giving and expect nothing in return. In fact it would be considered treacherous on my part to put my personal needs before those of my children and extended family. I believe that men deliberately project on to us an image of an infallible, strong, loving and supportive woman who has everything to give and needs nothing in return. Sometimes I feel sorry for myself. I feel I am a human being who needs love, affection, sympathy and even pity. I need to feel I can afford to feel weak and helpless and that there is someone who will take me by the hand. Women, especially widows, can't feel this, however.'

'How would you answer a Western woman who, after listening to all that you've said, would ask you: ''What about your life? What about you as a person? You are a full-time mother, PLO member, friend and neighbour, but what about that true self of yours, smothered among motherly, social and national duties?'' '

'I don't know how I would answer her. I would have to say that this is my fate; this is my society which I can neither change nor ignore. I envy the Western woman her liberation from social gossip and wicked looks.'

'How do you compare the position of the Western woman with that of the Arab woman?'

'Both the Arab and the Western woman enjoy advantages and suffer from some disadvantages. The Western woman has so far achieved most of her personal, social and educational rights, but sometimes these are carried so far that they undermine the family institution. This is because women are unwilling to make sacrifices for the family. Still, the Western woman is in a far better position than the Arab woman. We have a long way to go to achieve what she has achieved.'

Just then a short, fair man, preceded by his belly, arrived. My friend gave him a warm and friendly welcome. 'We are talking about women; what else?' she addressed him with a sweet smile.

'I have my own views on the subject,' he answered in quite a pretentious voice.

'Most men do,' I couldn't help commenting. 'But in most cases their views are totally irrelevant to the way women think and feel.'

The man started talking about Algerian women and comparing their position with the present situation of Palestinian women. After talking in a monologue for a long time he pretended to have just noticed my tape recorder and asked me to switch it off because he was not well prepared.

'I've already done that, I'm sorry to say,' I answered. 'Because my book is devoted to what women think; it is not about what men think of women.'

None the less, he was determined to say what he had already planned to say. So I asked for permission to leave, but just before I stepped out of the door he handed me an invitation to an exhibition of Palestinian women's handicrafts due to take place in two days' time. On seeing the card my interviewee looked askance and exclaimed: 'Where did you get that from?'

'We distributed most of them,' he answered quietly but firmly and left before I did with a sarcastic smile on his face.

There was no doubt that the 'we' referred to the strong, powerful and 'better' sex: the male sex. I started wondering why, if the exhibition was of Palestinian women's handicrafts and was set up by the Palestinian women's organisation, the men distributed the leaflets, and how my interviewee, who was an executive member in the organisation, could not have seen them. She looked extremely embarrassed and I didn't want to add to her embarrassment by asking such difficult questions.

The exhibition was held in the centre of the Palestinian refugee camp – Al Mokhiam in Damascus. The pedestrians in the exhibition's main street were predominantly male. 'They must be waiting for their wives,' I muttered to myself; perhaps they were not interested in women's handicrafts. But I was proved totally wrong when I arrived at the building and saw that most of the onlookers were men with a few women scattered here and there. I saw the husbands of the women I had either interviewed or talked to, but not the women themselves.

'Where is your wife?' I asked one of them.

'She stayed at home; I didn't expect women to turn up; otherwise I would have brought her with me,' the answer came back.

The building was choked with men, with a few women distributing sweets, drinks and posters. 'Bloody hell,' I muttered. 'This is an exhibition of female handicrafts held by a women's organisation in its own headquarters, and yet women are pushed back into a second position.' All the men rushed to the opening ceremony and a very limited number of women squeezed themselves in.

Despite men's desperate efforts to appear to be the masters of the earth, women's work in that huge exhibition hall stated one fact simply and clearly: women are the real creators. It was incredible to see how tragedies, massacres and sufferings were reborn as beautiful embroidered pieces. The traditional embroidery on the front of Palestinian dresses was turned into drawing on glass, pottery and into emotive political posters. Death in women's skilful hands was turned into soft, lovable cats, and the colour of blood was the only one used to make the striking Palestinian cushions which were supposed to make one feel comfortable. The handbag big enough to hold a bomb was also useful enough for a bunch of roses or for a present to one's beloved. A map of Palestine showed the traditional main crops in each area of Palestine, and was truly a magnificent piece of art. The Palestinian *konbas* (a long caftan men wear during the summer) and the Palestinian dresses were gorgeous. On the floor above there was take-away Palestinian food and some ready-made health food meals prepared by Palestinian women. Two women were demonstrating to inefficient women like myself how to cook *Moghrabiah*, which turned out to be a beautiful dish indeed.

The exhibition left no one in any doubt that Palestinian women are uniquely able to turn a tragedy into beautiful art. Blood became blossoms, the winter of a nation its spring and the tormented sigh in their hearts a brilliant idea. The exhibition demonstrated the depth of Palestinian women's feeling and the striking scope of their creativity. No wonder men were jumping around trying to prove themselves to be women's superiors. By the end of the exhibition my resentment of men's overwhelming presence had turned into a feeling of pity for the 'masters' who one day will have to admit that the subjects of their oppression are their equals, if not their superiors.

4   Algeria: Sharing the Struggle

Algerian women were acclaimed as heroines for their part in the war of liberation (1954–62) against the French colonists, who had ruled Algeria for some 130 years. Women carried messages for the FLN (National Liberation Front, which is still the ruling party of Algeria), hid guns beneath their robes, carried arms in battle. Several women were tortured by the French – Djamila Boupacha and Djamila Bouhired became household names round the world.

So women claimed their place in post-revolutionary society. Today half the students in Algerian schools and universities are female, there are women engineers, doctors, Members of Parliament, and one Government Minister is a woman. The National Union of Algerian Women, like the workers' unions and the students' union, is expected to play a part in the national political life, though this role is seen as subject to the overall authority of the FLN.

But there are also other forces at work in Algeria, as in other parts of the Arab world, and the influence of Muslim fundamentalists has led to the re-emergence of the veil on city streets and university campuses. The National Charter adopted in 1976 replaced the secular socialist principles of the State with an official commitment to Islam as the State religion, and since then reforms in family law have been slowed down and indeed some have been reversed. Thus in 1986 the Algerian parliament issued an edict confirming men's right to polygamy – subject to the first wife's consent!

Sharing the Struggle

Looking at a map of the Arab world from London our eyes always came to rest on Algeria, the young, liberated country that had bled so heavily and for so long to restore its national identity and independence. 'We should try to get jobs in Algeria and participate in fortifying this young revolution,' my husband and I used to say while we were finishing our PhDs. He applied for a job in Algeria from London and got one. A year later I too got my PhD and decided to join him there.

The flight was quite short, or so it felt. By the time I had eaten my meal, drunk my tea and read the *Guardian*, the stewardess was announcing that we were flying over eastern Algeria and that we could see the city of Constantine out of our windows. The first things I saw were beautiful hills and mountains, deep green valleys and lush forests surrounding the small town. As our plane started to descend, Constantine seemed to me a town carved out of rock. Two huge rocks on which the whole town rested were connected by multiple bridges and a very striking suspension bridge that seemed to extend so precariously over a deep, rocky valley that I felt safer in the air. Yet people did not seem to mind crossing the bridge and looking at the views through its railings. There seemed to be no barren ground; where there were no woods or greenery, there were the sharply contrasting colours of the Algerian soil, which I had not seen before – areas of deep red soil bordered by black, bordered in turn by a deep yellow or a pale grey. Later, travelling extensively in Algeria, I discovered that this colourful soil is a distinctive feature of an amazingly rich land; the French had good taste in wanting so desperately to settle in this beautiful country.

Mme Almnowar, when aged 51, had taken part in the Algerian revolution. Now she is a housewife with four children: two girls and two boys. Her elder daughter, Farida, is 31 years old, married with two boys, aged six and four; she was a postgraduate student of English, studying under me at Constantine University. Jamila, 28 years old and single, was also a postgraduate student of English.

I made an appointment to see them all at three o'clock. Farida opened the door and invited me in to a grand and expensively furnished room. The three huge bay windows and the soft, green curtains made the room feel comfortable. Farida is not only a student of mine – by far the most intelligent student I have ever taught at Constantine University – but also a friend. She is interested in her work and is serious and confident, with a great sense of initiative.

Over tea Farida's mother, Mme Almnowar, talked proudly about women in the Algerian revolution and compared the 1950s with the

1980s. She was very proud that women had realised their dream of an independent Algeria and that her daughter was now doing an MA at the university. Her daughter, however, had very different ideas.

'There is no hope for women,' Farida burst out. 'We are going backwards, not forwards. In my day we could invite our boyfriends home for tea or to play a record but now, particularly after the appearance of this Muslim Brotherhood, my brother won't even allow my sister to *speak* to a boy. How can things ever improve if the teacher at my son's school tells the children that God doesn't like women driving cars, smoking cigarettes or putting on make-up? So my son, who is only six years old, comes out of school demanding to go home with his friend because it is his friend's father who is driving the car and doesn't want to come with me because I am driving and I am a *woman*. Once home he says, "Mum, why do you smoke if God has asked you not to smoke? Why do you put on make-up if our religion disapproves of it?" How can my child's generation move forward on the woman question? Even to talk about contraceptives – let alone use them – is a sin according to men. Women should breed continuously to prove they are having good relationships with their husbands.'

I turned to Mme Almnowar and said, 'You are an Algerian woman who participated in the revolution, went to prison as a fighter, but after independence went back home to resume your duties as mother and wife. How did you feel on going back? Did you feel that the revolution had changed your social and domestic position, or did you have to go back to where you had left off before the revolution?'

'The time of the revolution was very special. Afterwards we went backwards, not as far back as we'd been before it started but still somewhat back on our revolutionary achievements. Before the revolution we were colonised. After the revolution we were free people. I took part in the revolution, although when we enrolled for revolutionary activities, we had no idea what we were eventually going to achieve. We never imagined that the French would do what they did to us. They imprisoned and tortured us, but the more we were tortured the more determined we were to carry on. When I was a young girl I was unaware of the complexity of the situation; I hadn't been taught about either the revolution or the French, but I understood just from the way we were treated by them how bad our situation was.'

'Were you married when you joined the fighters?'

'Yes, and I had Farida who was two years old.'

'What did your husband say to this?'

'We joined the organisation together. He encouraged me to do what he couldn't do. I could carry arms under my veil and get to see his comrade fighters (whom he couldn't see) and exchange information with them. I spoke French very well and had no problem talking to the French soldiers and crossing every checkpoint I wanted to cross. At one point they imprisoned and tortured me and started to imprison every member of my family. When I saw the terrible things they were doing to my people and country I realised we had entered into a battle in which there was no going back. I realised that the revolution was a question of life and death. I joined it in 1955. A year later we had the great students' strike. I started to send messages from the revolutionaries to the students to continue their strike. I also used to arrange medical care for those wounded in the towns or mountains, bringing doctors in to see them and providing medicines for them. In 1957 I became a fighter and started to carry arms. I used to walk with the fighters. I would carry arms under my clothes while the fighters walked unarmed beside me until we had crossed every checkpoint and had reached the mountains. We also managed to get identity cards for our fighters, which helped immensely in crossing checkpoints. I was sent to prison because some people who were almost tortured to death gave our names to put an end to their own sufferings. Colonial power has its way of getting to us, you know. The way they used to torture people is difficult to believe, even for those who went through it. When we remember things now we often ask ourselves, "Is it true that the French did this or that to us?" They put my whole family in prison, and each of us in a different town, leaving my two-year-old daughter with her grandmother. I was in prison for over a year, not knowing whether my husband and other comrades were dead or alive. Even my little girl was useful to the revolution. I used to put the documents which were very important to us in a plastic bag and insert them between her nappy and pants. Her toys were full of documents and important publications. My husband also spent two years in prison. After 1958 my house became a meeting place for the fighters.'

'Did the French treat women less viciously than men in prison?'

'No. They treated us all *kief kief* [in the same way]. They were just as cruel to women as they were to men. The other day I was talking to one of my previous comrades and we said it was impossible to believe that here we were alive and well in our own country with our children at university. It is difficult to believe that we survived everything the French did to us. I don't know how members of our household got away with all the activities we had going on there. There were some families who did much less and were wiped out completely. I suppose we were just extremely lucky.'

'Did you take on all these revolutionary activities as well as doing your domestic duties during the revolution?'

'During the revolution we forgot about domestic duties. Except when the fighters came down from the mountains when we would wash their clothes and cook for them – but they were fighters and so were we. Whether the fighters coming down from the mountains were men or women we did the same for them – and ''we'' here includes men as well as women. During the revolution it did not matter who did what; we were all the servants of the revolution which was going to liberate us and restore our identity. The men were hungry, tired and dirty and we were only too glad to receive them. There was a revolutionary spirit, a sense of solidarity.

'We did not read much. I came from a revolutionary family; my father used to write poetry against the French, so when the revolution started I recalled all this as well as my childhood and it helped me to face the enemy. When I remember the atrocities of the French I just wish we'd done a bit more; I just wish we in our turn had been a bit more barbaric and less civilised.'

'After independence you went back home and had more children. Did you feel any dramatic change in your life? Did you feel that the revolution had had any effect on your personal life as a woman?'

'During the revolution I decided not to have any more children because we were in and out of prison all the time. After Farida, who was just two in 1954, I did not have any children for eleven years.

'Women who were in towns served the revolution more than those in the mountains. After 1957, the leaders of the revolution started asking people to stay in towns, though women still went up to the mountains carrying arms. Personally I did not feel the revolution had had any effect on my private life. Our lives did not change. What changed was that we became free people. I saw my husband become a free man with pride in his society. I became a free woman. So socially our lives changed but my domestic life did not change at all.'

Here Farida turned to her mother, saying, 'I feel that the Algerian men used the Algerian women in the revolution. They used you as they used their weapons. You didn't get anything from the revolution; you got absolutely nothing.'

'No,' said her mother. 'I don't agree at all. Had we not fought the revolution you would not be here now doing an MA in English!'

'I am doing this in spite of the men, not thanks to them,' said Farida. 'You should see the men who work with us when we discuss something or express an opinion. They say almost to our face that it isn't our place.'

'This, I think is part of the bad heritage left to us by the French,' Mme Almnowar said. 'I don't think that after one or two generations you will find this any more. The average man at university, or anywhere else, considers the Algerian woman and wants her on the one hand to be like his mother who cooked and washed for him, and on the other hand to be a companion who goes out with him and socialises with friends and colleagues. He's got a problem. He can't choose between a servant and a companion; he wants both. It will take time before the Algerian man realises he has to make a choice between these two types of women.'

Farida countered this: 'I think the Algerian male is going backwards rather than forwards. I believe my father is better than my husband and my husband better than his son. My father saw French women and French people and accepted for his wife and children what the French accepted for their families. Since then, men have been going backwards.'

'I think what your mother said is true,' I said. 'Men are confused about the kind of woman they want to marry: the educated equal or the mother-servant. But in the meantime what does the woman think about this problem? The woman who has had an equal education and an equal job but who still has to go back home and cook, clean, wash and look after the children? I mean, do you suffer from this, Farida, or does your husband understand? If he came home and there was no meal ready for him, would it be a problem?'

'Yes,' said Farida. 'It would be a big problem. My husband was the only boy in his family. He had his mother and two sisters serving him all the time. If he finds his lunch isn't ready we have a row, and if he wants to wear a shirt which isn't ironed, there is another row. It is very hard, you know. He doesn't help me at all. As you see here today, he goes out and leaves the two boys for me to look after. I have to wait until nine o'clock when the children go to bed before I can do some reading or prepare some lectures and even then he says I shouldn't sit and read and leave him alone. He says I should do my work after he goes to bed. That my main job is to help him, and that the university should come after him. Algerian men consider women as objects, that's all there is to it.'

'But how can you live with somebody who considers you an object?'

'I wouldn't have lived all this time with that man were it not for my two boys,' said Farida. 'He's stopped me from doing so many things. I've been teaching at the university for eight years with just a BA. If I were not married (my children are no problem in this respect) I would have gone to England to do my MA, and PhD ages ago. Some of those who were studying with me at the time have already got their PhDs and here I am still struggling to do my MA!'

'You have only one woman in the government: Mme Zohor Wanisie. Is she genuinely representative of Algerian women?'

'Not in the least,' said Farida. 'The government put her there to shut us up. "Here is one of you who became a minister; what more do you want?" And then we have UNIFA (Union Nationale des Femmes Algériennes), the only women's organisation in this country, which does absolutely nothing for women. It even accepts that men are allowed four wives. UNIFA is an official organisation; that is why it doesn't do anything which the government might dislike, and the government is made up of *men*. Men aren't going to fight for us; we have to fight for ourselves.'

'What do you think is the solution for Algerian women?'

'The solution is for UNIFA to be infiltrated by educated women who are genuinely keen to work for women's emancipation. Some feminists, real ones, did join UNIFA once, but they resigned after a year or so because they discovered they could do nothing for women.'

Mme Almnowar spoke: 'Women should fight as we fought against the French until we achieved independence. I always tell younger women they should fight their battles as we fought ours. It is not shameful to do this. Rather, it is a battle which you have to fight sooner or later.'

Farida interrupted. 'You fought against an enemy: France. That was easy. How can you fight against your government? How can a girl fight against her father, brother or husband?'

Mme Almnowar replied, 'I tell you, time will help. But time is not enough. Education is the answer. It is the only way to liberate women.'

Farida was doubtful. 'Education liberates a woman from her own ignorance, but it doesn't liberate her from her social fetters. I feel free when I'm on my own, but I am not free when I'm with my husband and I am not free in society. When I'm sitting on my own late at night with a book I feel free. I think about what I want to think about and read what I want to read, but this freedom is limited and personal, or rather, perhaps, it is an internal freedom, because I can't *do* what I want. I can't even *say* what I want.'

'What is the solution? You have just said you could have done an MA and a PhD, and I am sure you could have done, but surely you are not the only Algerian woman who feels she could have done better things with her life? What do you think is the solution for all these women?'

Farida replied, 'The solution is to have a lot of courage and to throw everything out and begin a new life.'

'Are you saying that if we want to achieve what we are capable of achieving we have to sacrifice our family life?'

'Yes, certainly. I don't think there is any way of combining the two. I mean, for Algerian women it is very difficult. Most of my women friends who have good professional lives have sacrificed their family lives; they have been divorced.'

'But don't you think this is a very difficult choice to make?'

'Yes, very. Especially when you've got children. Because the man can be replaced, but the children . . . ! Then Jamila wants to marry a man she doesn't care about. He has no job, no flat, nothing. She pays for him to come to see her, and she wants to marry him.'

'Do you feel any social pressure to get married?'

'Yes,' said Jamila. 'That's why I want to get married. I feel I'm becoming an embarrassment to my family. Whenever neighbours or friends visit us they always whisper to my mother: "Poor Jamila, she's always been so successful in everything she's done but doesn't seem to be lucky so far as men are concerned." I really feel that whatever my academic or professional achievements might be, I shall always be pitied if I don't get married. This man has been hanging around me for ages and my parents seem to be quite pleased with him, so let it be. I can't be bothered to wonder whether he is the right person. I don't think I'll ever have the freedom to choose the right person or wait for him. I realise that in Algeria I can neither be free nor fulfil myself; all I'm free to do is exist, and what the hell does it matter what man I exist with. It is all the same. I just wish I'd been born anywhere else in the world other than Algeria.'

'You mean as a woman?'

'Yes, as a woman.'

'So you don't think Algeria is a good place for women?'

'Not at all; very far from it. In Syria, or Iraq, or any other Arab country, you have traditions and values. At least the inhabitants of these countries know where they stand. We are the only Arab country which seems to be lost between two totally different cultures. We sometimes entertain the illusion that we could be as free as French women because of the great French cultural and historical influence on us; on the other hand, the movement for reviving Arabic and Islamic culture in Algeria seems to return to the roots of Islam, and these have been outmoded in all Arab countries for the last two centuries. So we are neither Arabs nor Europeans, neither here nor there.'

'You are both teachers and MA students and yet you seem to be lost. What is the illiterate, ordinary woman going to be like under such circumstances?'

Farida responded. 'I think these women have different lives. They don't have our problems. When I go with my mother to Beskara and see all those married women with lots of money and jewellery they seem to be very satisfied with their lives. My uncle's wife, for example, is quite content, even though my uncle comes home at midnight every night. She has a very beautiful house, goes to Paris twice a year to get the latest fashionable clothes, has as much money as she wants – and she likes it. She appreciates what she has got but I *don't*. As you say "What do you want to be happy?" It depends on people. Some people are satisfied with material things. If you are searching for an identity it's a lot more difficult, however. Other less fortunate women are satisfied to be fertile breeders. I've talked to women who genuinely believe that their vocation in life is to obey their husbands and bring up their children. If you are *that* ordinary you might live happily in ignorance, but once you are aware of yourself, of your identity, it is a lot more difficult to settle for such a poor deal.'

'I was talking to another professional woman a while ago who said to me: "We have to make sacrifices for our children's sake. It is a battle we have to fight so our daughters won't have to suffer what we suffered.'' Do you agree with that?'

'No. I don't think so, because my generation is living in a better way than my younger sister's generation. I used to be allowed to have boyfriends whom I invited home for tea or to listen to music. Now, my brother won't allow my sister even to speak to a boy in the street. I don't think we're moving forward at all, and people who believe we are must be extremely optimistic.'

Mme Almnowar broke in. 'We still have some time to wait. A man wants his wife to work to bring home some money because everyone is under financial pressure, yet he still wants her to do all the work she used to do at home. This is impossible. A man has to understand that times have changed and he has to change with them. He does know this really, but refuses to admit or accept it. We have to fight to make him understand and accept change. I'm sure the next generation will see that the working mother can't be a super cook as well as cleaning the flat and doing the washing and ironing all on her own. The man will have to do housework as well. The coming generation will accept this as normal. Your children, when they get married, Farida, won't be like my children when they got married.'

Farida snapped: 'No, they'll be worse. When I go with my children on holiday to Tunisia or France we all go to the coffee shop and drink lemonade. Here I *can't* go with them to the coffee shop. They don't understand why their mother can go to a coffee shop in Tunisia or Paris but can't go to one in Constantine, her home town. So they are experiencing contradictory attitudes and values.'

Mme Almnowar spoke again. 'The time will soon come when Algerian women will achieve the same rights as Tunisian and Moroccan women.'

'No,' said Farida. 'That time is not coming. I am unhappy about the education my children are getting at school. What do you expect from a system in which the teacher tells the children that women should not drive cars, that Muslim women must neither smoke nor put on make-up? I have to fight the educational system, society and my husband! How much, I wonder, can I achieve? I have no hope for the future. How can my son's generation move forward on the question of women if the very first lesson the children learn at school goes like this.' Farida produced a text book in Arabic:

Mother is in the kitchen.
Father is in the farm.
Mother is going shopping.
Father is watering the trees.

'How are we going to get anywhere? I just don't know.'

I interrupted at this point. 'I have some Algerian friends who went to England on their own and did their MAS there, but once they were back in their fathers' homes they were not allowed to visit or even receive their women friends. I was a very good friend. They visited me regularly, but I never entered their homes; I was never invited. I don't understand how a father can allow his daughter to go to Europe on her own and yet not allow her to receive a woman friend in her own house. This is beyond belief. Can you explain this to me?'

'We have no standards,' Farida answered in her usual assertive manner. 'On the one hand the father wants to feel that his daughter has reached a certain educational level of which he feels proud from the social point of view. He can't know what his daughter has done in Europe – nor can anyone else who knows him as a neighbour. Once back home, however, all the neighbours have to know that members of the family are good, respectable Muslims. In Algeria, particularly in Constantine, we live only for society. You don't find any family living a life just as it wants to.'

'Yes, take me, for example,' said Mme Almnowar. 'I am a grandmother and I can't stay out late. Sometimes, like right now, I stay out with friends and relatives and I arrive home at about 7 or 8 in the evening. My husband then says: "You know I trust you and I don't need to ask where you have been, but what would the neighbours say about a woman who comes home at 8 when her husband is in?" We live for other people, for society instead of ourselves.'

'Or take me,' Farida resumed. 'When I wear my jeans my husband says: "The neighbours are going to say she has two young boys and she thinks she is still a little girl who wears jeans most of the time".'

'Does that mean that women have to fight to bring about social change?'

Mme Almnowar spoke. 'Personally, if I were one of these young, educated women I would fight to secure my place in society. We fought another battle, and we're tired and old. It is up to this new generation of women to carry on with the struggle and not give up.

Algerian women fought in the past and won. They should fight today. Educated women should join UNIFA and change what it is doing to what they want to achieve. It won't be easy, but then what is?'

Farida spoke again. 'But to join UNIFA we have to be affiliated to the Party, the FLN, the one political party in the country. I'm not a political woman; however, I would like to fight for women's emancipation. But I can't. I have to belong to the Party to be allowed to join the organisation. And once you are in the Party you have to abide by the Party's politics, to say what they want you to say, even about women. So why do this? This is not my objective.'

'Do you think the European woman is free?' I asked.

'Much freer than us. No doubt about that. She can go wherever she likes, and do what she wants without thinking about taboos, dogmas or society. When I go to London or Paris I enjoy going to a coffee shop and drinking a coffee. I can go out for a walk, or see a film or a play, without being escorted by a man. These are little things but they really do make life a lot easier. A bit of freedom is better than nothing.'

'Would you like to see Algerian women as free in the same way as French women?'

'Not in the same way. There are lots of French women who misuse their freedom. Here in Algeria we have all the drawbacks of the French and Arabic culture and the advantages of neither. We don't receive the respect which Arab women in Syria or Lebanon have. Women in Algeria are only considered as sex objects. The way men look at you and talk to you at the university is really awful.'

'Would you like to stay at home and enjoy the advantages of that way of life?' I asked.

'No,' Farida replied. 'But when I talk to women who stay at home they seem to me to be happy. They don't have to get up at six o'clock in the morning. They have a lot of time to cook their meals and then to socialise in the afternoon.'

'But what are they?'

'They are nothing,' said Farida. 'But they are happy. They are not under the same pressures. They don't have the same problems. I don't think that their way of life is really the solution to the problem, however. My husband keeps telling me that if I find my life too difficult I should stay at home. Why go to the university? I don't think a woman should choose to stay at home, despite the fact that her problems as a professional woman make her envious of the unprofessional woman. Were she to opt out and stay at home she would find her duties were doubled and her rights not even acknowledged. I would hate to see these motivated women leave their jobs and careers.'

'I think it is necessary for yourself, for your survival,' I commented, 'to leave home and participate in the outside world. I remember the first time I went to the university after three months at home on maternity leave. I felt as if I'd been let out of prison. I still feel that my work outside the house enables me to have a better relationship with my little daughter and husband. My work at the university provides an outlet for so much of the tension and frustration which mundane daily life causes.'

Farida interrupted. 'This is exactly how I feel. Every Thursday and Friday (the Algerian weekend) I feel in prison. Even if my job doubles my working hours I am still happier that way.'

By this time Farida's elder son was showing his book to Mme Almnowar, pointing to the pages which his mother had previously been criticising. Mme Almnowar suddenly looked furious and said: 'You have to revolt against this. It will take a revolution to get rid of this, just as it took a revolution to get the French out. It reminds me of the way French men used to describe French women as professional, educated and free, while they always showed the Algerian woman cooking, knitting or cleaning. Throughout the revolution we proved to be as good as men in all things, including climbing mountains and fighting a guerrilla war. How dare they throw this rubbish at us again! You have to fight, my girls. You just have to fight, even against the men closest to you. This battle has to be fought and won.'

Mme Hamdi, age 62, has four children of her own and five adopted children. The five adopted children all came from one family. Their father had died on the Tunisian border during the Algerian revolution, and their mother died in the mountains. At the time they were adopted the eldest was eight and the youngest aged one.

Mme Rashid was 57 with three children. She was a school teacher before the revolution. During the revolution her husband had joined the fighters in the mountains and she stayed with the children. When her husband was killed she left the children and went into the mountains to take his place. She also used to look after the children of other fighters.

My friend Leila, who contacted the two women on my behalf and in whose house we were meeting, seemed to have briefed them about the sort of questions I was interested in. Perhaps that explained why, the moment I switched on my tape recorder, Mme Rashid started to talk. 'Before the revolution we were working for educational reform. For us the revolution did not start in 1954; it started in 1930. Our families were quite progressive about the woman question; that's how we managed to become teachers before the revolution got under way. We were married to the men we wanted to marry and never really suffered from discrimination against us as women. We were trying to educate a new generation in Arabic-Islamic culture. In 1930, France celebrated its first centenary of occupied Algeria. Muhamed Abdo, the well-known Egyptian reformer, was here. When he went back to Egypt he was asked about Algeria. ''Algeria is a French country,'' he stated. It was then that we started our anthem:

> The people of Algeria are Muslims
> They belong to Pan Arabism
> Anyone who says they've forgotten their origins
> has told a lie.

In 1936 the committee of scientists and educationalists was launched. In 1945 educational reform started in earnest, and in 1954 we carried arms. We carried arms in towns and mountains, and were doing everything together with men.'

'I carried arms in towns,' said Mme Hamdi. 'I used to put weapons under my clothes and pass with the fighters from one area of the town to the other. In 1955 I was pregnant and was shot in the foot. I was in the operating room when the French authorities received confirmation that I was a fighter. I was taken from the operating room straight to prison but afterwards was released on bail. Even then I had to sign in every day at the police station. When I came out I found my comrades had made the necessary arrangements for me to leave for the mountains. I was with my husband then, but he went in one direction and I in another. We went out to fight; we didn't live together. We couldn't have lived together after seeing all the other families splitting up to fight for the revolution. For four years I was in the mountains, so when I came back my youngest boy didn't know me. We were fighting, planning operations and carrying them out. We were nursing children as well as blowing up bridges. While we were carrying out an operation I would carry a weapon to a particular spot. The man or I would shoot, and I would then carry the weapon back again. I was shot in the foot a second time. We were planning to kill a traitor and while rehearsing the various stages of the operation my comrade, not realising the gun was loaded, pulled the trigger and shot my foot. So it was an accident. They took me to hospital where a French doctor, who was in sympathy with our revolution, treated me. (In fact, many French people joined the Algerian revolutionary army and fought as well as we did against the French occupation of Algeria.) The doctor operated on my foot and after ten days a group of fighters who knew me very well was discovered. I had to leave the hospital and go into hiding. My doctor advised me that if I walked on my foot so soon after the operation my leg would never be straight again. I told him to just take the plaster off; I had no choice but to walk to the next town and look for a hiding place. I was three months pregnant then, and had to walk from Constantine to Batna (a good two hours' driving distance) and, as you see, I can't walk straight. The doctor was right, but I saved myself.

'Lots of women gave birth in prison. Once they started labour they were taken to hospital and as soon as they had delivered their babies they were brought back to prison again.'

'Did you take part in working out and planning the operations or did you just carry out the men's orders?'

'The men carried out *our* orders,' said Mme Rashid. 'We were the only ones who planned operations. The men didn't have a clue. There was very little they could do because of the way they dressed. The *fedayee* (the male fighter) was only a means to kill. We had a male comrade to drive the car but it was the woman who carried out the operations. Once a woman had to jump out of a car to escape the eyes of a French soldier and left her shoes behind. The French authorities gathered all the women of Constantine in the main square and made them try these shoes on to find out who the woman fighter was.

'Women were ingenious in discovering new methods to outwit the French enemy. We used to take someone to hospital, pretending that he or she was ill. Once they were in there we changed their clothes, dyed their hair and they went out the opposite door completely new persons carrying arms and ready for the next new operation. The town was divided into six parts. Mme Bouzien, for example, would come here from one direction wearing the veil and black shoes. She would come in, hold a meeting, plan an operation, then give her clothes and shoes to a man in the meeting and go out in another direction in a blouse and skirt with matching shoes and bag and uncovered hair. If she came in with black hair she would leave with red hair. We were constantly changing men's clothes, dyeing their hair and ours too, and doing our best to reduce the risk of being found out by the enemy. All this was thought of and carried out by women. The men had no idea of all these possible ways of hiding our identity and outwitting the French authorities.'

'After playing this great part in the revolution, what do you think the revolution has done for you as a woman?'

'It brought independence to Algeria,' answered Mme Hamdi. 'When the Algerian woman carried arms she was acting for her country. She took her children with her or left them behind and climbed mountains to fight for her country. This was *her* decision. No one asked her to do this. She wanted to see Algeria independent and how it is. What more does she want? Does she expect to be paid? None of us dared to hope to go back home alive. We fought for our future; for the future of Algeria. We had an ideal and the revolution was a public revolution. It was a great fight and we had a great aim. There was a woman whose son went up into the mountains. One day a French soldier knocked on her door and said: "We've brought your son, come out and see him." She went out to see her son lying dead. She keened and bent down to kiss him, saying: "Now I know you are a man; had you come alive I would have known you were a coward and I would have been ashamed of you." The French soldier hit her with his truncheon on her bent neck. She lost her husband and four sons fighting for the revolution, and now she is starving but she is neither bitter nor even angry. She says we worked for an objective. We wanted to fight. I wanted so badly to see Algeria independent. I never expected any reward.'

'If we hadn't had the revolution, you' – she turned to Leila – 'wouldn't have been at university now.'

'Perhaps this is true,' said Leila, 'but it is not enough.'

'We have only had twenty years of independence,' said Mme Hamdi.

'I agree,' I said. 'But the other day a Greek delegation from the Women's Union came to Algeria and was received mainly by men. The media referred to the head of UNIFA as "One of those who attended the meeting''. My question is: How could the Algerian women who fought and won a revolution ever have come to accept being treated in such a humiliating fashion? Why did they not run their own organisation?'

'We are at a transitional stage and we need the Party to look after our affairs,' replied Mme Rashid. 'The women's organisation is no more independent than the students' organisation and workers' organisations which do not deny their official affiliation to the Party. The women who fought in the revolution are unfortunately over 50, and the men here, like men everywhere, want women who are less than 25, so they certainly don't want us.'

'I am sorry, but I still don't understand,' I said.

'Now, I am going to talk to you frankly,' said Mme Rashid. 'After independence, the government of Ben Bella called on us to draft legislation for Algerian women. We didn't like what we saw but we thought this would be a transitional stage which wouldn't last very long. Our women were longing for freedom but were making a mess of it.

'In 1965 when we had Bou Median's *coup d'état* they again called us to Algiers. We held a meeting but there were some men who told the women exactly what they should say. In 1968 they again called us to Algiers to send telegrams to this and that country. We were trying to lay down laws for Algerian women. We had decided on the laws but the men told us we had to change them. Our laws relating to women were approved by the majority of Algerian women in 18 districts in Algeria. So naturally we said to the Prime Minister, "We won't change anything. This is what we promised the women we would say and this is what we actually said.'' They tried to bribe us with villas, cars and seats in Parliament if we changed the laws but we refused. They promised us three seats in Parliament instead of two but still we flatly refused to change a word. All the women were for our laws; we were the real representatives of women. In the end, though, there was no solution but to hand in our notice and leave. The men threatened us with imprisonment if we didn't shut up. They cut off our phones and virtually put us under house arrest.'

'Why did the men want to change your laws so badly?'

'Because the legislation which the women wanted didn't serve the men's interests. They wanted women to remain tools in their hands. They didn't want laws which encouraged women's ability and potential.'

'Didn't they know you were fighters?'

'Of course they did. They knew that only too well. Some of the women are partly to blame for the mess, too. Some wanted villas and cars and didn't give a damn about women's rights.'

'So are you sorry that Algerian women did not achieve what they should have achieved after the revolution?'

'Of course we are. We tried to work but when we saw that it was to no avail we left. We used to leave our houses and children to attend meetings and talk and talk, only to realise afterwards that the men always did whatever they wanted to do. After a while we lost interest and left. Everywhere, I think, not only here in Algeria, women fight and work for their country as much as men do but eventually they get very little out of it. Men don't like independent women with opinions of their own. We said to our Prime Minister: "You say this is white and we say this is black; you have either to convince us or we will convince you." Men don't like this kind of a woman. They want women who tremble and submit to authority.'

'All this is on the political level. What about the social level? Do you feel that women's social position improved after the revolution?'

'Oh, yes; it's much better now,' Mme Rashid replied. 'Women had no identity, no dignity and no liberty before the revolution. As for education, there is no question about it now. Parents are prepared to work day and night to pay for their children's education. I don't believe there is any Algerian father who refuses to send his daughter to school. This in itself is a big achievement. Our only regret is the loss of that absolute equality achieved during the revolution. As far as that's concerned, we seem to have moved backwards rather than forwards.'

'Mme Hamdi,' I said, 'did the revolution change your relationship with your husband in any way?'

'Oh, yes, dramatically,' was the reply. 'My husband came down from the mountains married to another woman. That was the last I saw of him. I stayed with my children. Now he has six children by her. Life was difficult, she was with him and it was a long time. He did not see me for four years. In more than one sense I feel I am a victim of the revolution, but I'm not the only one. So many of the fighters who spent five years in the mountains, and who could only have continued with the support of their wives and families, happened to get a good social or political position after independence. They divorced their wives and got married to stylish young girls who were good enough to attend reception parties with them or accompany them to France!'

'Are you talking about a few individual cases?'

'No. This was very common. In fact, it was the norm. There were lots of men who married their women comrades in the mountains. Once they came down, however, and got good positions or good jobs in the towns they divorced their comrades and got married to younger, more presentable, women. So you see women paid the price whatever the situation. If the man had tried to make his woman more sophisticated it would only have taken him a year or so to do this; instead he got married again. As women we paid the price from every point of view, and now they won't allow us to put our own laws on the market. I am convinced that all men are aware that women understand things a lot better than they do. That's why they feel inferior to us, and instead of having the courage to face us they try to keep us down. How long it will take us to outwit them, just as we outwitted the French, I don't know. Not very long, I hope.'

I was walking along the long corridor of the arts' building at the university when I met and was introduced to the newly elected head of the Institute for Foreign Languages, Mme Radia. I had already heard from some friends of mine that Mme Radia had fought all the battles which Algerian women had had to fight for the last forty years and that although she did not call herself a committed feminist she was nevertheless a very thoughtful and independent woman. After exchanging polite greetings with her, I said I would like to talk to her some time at length if I could.

'About the postgraduates?' she asked.

'No,' I answered. 'About Arab women and the problems they face, if you are at all interested.'

'Oh, yes! Of course I am interested,' she answered, her friendly smile lighting up the otherwise sad expression on her face. So we agreed to meet at ten o'clock the following Saturday.

At ten o'clock sharp I was at Mme Radia's office. She was busy sorting out the problem of a French teacher who had just been transferred from Batna University. She apologised and asked me to wait.

The clock struck 11 and I started to worry about my one-year-old daughter. She would soon be hungry, I thought. I had forgotten to ask my husband to give her a drink of water. I wondered whether he would think of doing that. Then I wondered whether he would prepare some lunch for her, or whether he would be cross with me – because I was certainly going to be late for both of them. Amidst these turbulent thoughts I suddenly asked myself, 'Why do we always live in fear? Why can't we ever stop worrying about husband, home and children and concentrate on what we are doing?'

Fortunately, I was saved from my own worries by Mme Radia's voice saying, 'Well, here we are. Where shall I start?'

Hastily collecting myself I glanced at my notes and said, 'I should like to hear from you about all the battles you have had to fight against both family and society, concentrating on the things which you think have happened to you because you are a woman.' So Mme Radia began to speak.

'I was one of seven girls who lived in a far-off village but who fought hard for schooling and education. I went to school at a time when girls were never seen out on the streets. As for my family, my father had already forced my two elder sisters out of school and made them wear the veil, but afterwards he seemed to have regretted that very much and was determined not to do the same to me. So, in a sense, my two elder sisters paid the price for me, although I must admit I often felt that the fate of my sisters was still looming over my head. It was the early 1950s and, as you know, we were under French occupation at that time. They were very difficult times, particularly for women. At the age of ten all girls had to wear the veil. So I had to fight two battles: one against the veil and another against ignorance to get my education.

'While I was at school I responded, together with most Algerian students, to a call from the National Front for the Liberation of Algeria (FLN) and went on strike for two years. After that I could not go back to school because my name had been circulated by the French authorities to all schools forbidding my attendance. So I had to study in what we call *L'Ecole Universelle* and had to support myself until I got my BA.

'Around that time, my father was tortured to death in prison and my brother had already joined the Algerian fighters in the mountains to fight the French occupation. After my father's death we had to start another battle, the battle of women who try to do men's jobs in a totally male-oriented society. There were only my mother, sisters and myself left. For a start, we had to fight a battle against the extended family. (Family in Algeria does not only mean the immediate family but also includes uncles, aunts, grandmothers and grandfathers.) All the family resented my doing men's work. I had to seek a teaching job with the French authorities so that I could support my mother and younger sisters. Such a thing was previously unheard of in our social circle, but I just carried on doing it. One has to remember that in those days women were literally locked in the house. Men were the only visible reality. Only they were to be seen out working in public and once a man stepped inside the house he was the supreme master. Women never used to eat in front of their husbands or fathers. You never saw women on the street and you never saw them at home; they were just not there.

'Once the Algerian revolution started, things became easier for me and for everybody else. With the revolution, women moved to the front lines and fought alongside men. We immediately rejected the veil and being locked up at home. We were fighting for a national cause, so women were not afraid to go against tradition or even against religion. It all started in the mountains and in distant villages where women had always done men's jobs and where Algerian women first became fighters. In these villages women used to work in the fields, ride horses and carry weapons, and so in the rural areas at least a certain equality had already been established between men and women. This is how Algerian women were able to become fighters. They started the trend in remote villages and mountains, and most Algerian women elsewhere soon followed suit. Women started fighting in towns; we formed groups and became more effective than men in helping mountain fighters. For the French army it was inconceivable that women could do what we were actually doing so we were not suspected. We moved quite freely between places – whereas men were subjected to frequent checks. Thus Algerian women became indispensable partners in the Algerian revolution.'

'Do you think this equality between men and women, so quickly achieved during the struggle against the French, was maintained and sustained after the revolution, or do you think there was a return to the pre-revolutionary mentality regarding women's position and rights?'

'The answer to this question can't be clear cut. The revolution changed most ideas regarding women. During the revolution a woman was equal to a man; she carried arms and fought as well as he did. After independence she managed to keep most of what she had won. For example, after the revolution there was no problem about women going out without the veil, or going out to work, to school or to university. Considering women's position before independence these were big achievements. As for legislation which should be issued to protect these achievements, the government is still studying this. Algerian society developed quickly and ideas underwent remarkably fast changes. Previously ideas had been very traditional. The French made it their business to keep us backward and ignorant. Today we still have backward groups and families within these groups, but we also have people who are advanced socially and culturally, together with an entirely new class which wants women to work and study while remaining veiled. Now in Algeria you can distinguish between the veil of the Muslim woman and the traditional veil of the Algerian woman in its various colours. Every area has its own veil. There is the white veil, the black veil, and in the South they have a coloured veil.'

'So the traditional Algerian veil is not a religious one?'

'As far as I know the Berber woman never wore a veil. The veil came with the Arab conquest and also, perhaps, with the Turkish occupation of Algeria. After the Arab conquest of Algeria 80 per cent of all Algerians became Muslims, and accordingly most of the women started to wear the veil. That is why you find in the far-off villages in the mountains (which were not reached by the Arabs) that the Algerian woman does not wear the veil at all. Yet the same Berber (non-Muslim) woman wears the veil when she comes to town, because she finds many women in town are also wearing the veil. In this sense, therefore, the veil has a social as well as a religious function. As for the colours of the veil: all veils were originally white and then each area for its own reasons changed to different colours. For example, here in Constantine, Saleh-Al-Bye, the *Wali* (governor) of Constantine, was killed by the French, so the women of Constantine decided to go into a state of mourning and changed the colour of their veil to black, and for two centuries now they have been wearing the black veil.'

'To return to you. Was your marriage your own or a family decision?'

'At the time of my marriage a woman had no say whatsoever in her marriage. Her father decided for her. But as I had no father or brothers, I had the freedom to decide for myself. I saw my husband before getting married to him but never talked to him at any length and never went out with him before marriage. It is only because he persisted in asking to marry me for many years that I decided to marry him.'

'Does your husband believe that women are equal to men?'

'No. No. No. No man in Algeria ever believes that woman could be equal to man.'

'With all the battles you have fought and won and with the position you have reached now, do you think, or does your husband think, *he* could have done any better?'

'He knows the truth but hates to admit it: he certainly never mentions it. All Algerian men believe that men are superior to women. Perhaps women are ultimately responsible for this because as mothers they should bring up their children to believe in the equality of men and women. Algerian men, however, do try their best to make sons believe that they are men, better and stronger than women and they believe this is absolutely essential for their manhood and pride.'

'I gather from this that your husband does not give you any help at home, and that you have to do your job here as well as cook, wash, clean and look after the children?'

'Of course I do. My husband believes that it is my duty to do all the work at home and that it is up to me to keep my job in the Institute or leave it. I find all this hellishly difficult, but what can I do? I feel it is my duty to keep and protect our marriage for the sake of the children. I do not want my children to suffer the consequences of a broken home and this is why I persevere in my marriage, knowing very well how unjust this is. My only hope is that my daughter will not have to fight the same battle or suffer the same things. We continue to do the work but are fighting against the injustice of it and, hopefully by the next generation we will have won. This is the problem for all Arab working women, now. They go out to work while still carrying the full burden of keeping homes and bringing up children. They are quite well aware, though, of what is being done to them by men and are trying hard to change the situation; but I don't think it is going to change soon enough for me to benefit from it. I hope the next generation of women will reap the fruits of both our struggles. This is the only hope that keeps us going. I do hope that by fighting our daily battles we are laying the basis for a better future. In the last few years, for instance, I've noticed a change in my husband's attitudes. He at least acknowledges that I'm tired, that I'm doing a lot and that I need a rest. He might even, very occasionally, give me a hand with something. Of course, I don't believe he'll ever cook a meal for us. It is extremely difficult to do all my work here at the university and then have to go home and do all the washing, cleaning, ironing and cooking in the evenings and at weekends.'

'Do you think, then, that women who stay at home and look after children have a better deal than working women? At least they have enough time to rest and sleep.'

'No. That is not right – because all women in Algeria who are supposedly doing just their housework and bringing up their children are in fact doing other jobs in the home. In Algeria we have a unique situation; 80 per cent of the population is under 20 years old and the average family consists of eight children. So at home women sew, knit – or do anything to bring in some money. I believe that if we made a study of this phenomenon we would find that 90 per cent of women who stay at home are doing some other job as well as housework. In the building I live in, for example, all the women do some paid work or else help their husbands with their businesses – this is in the case of educated women, of course. There is the very rich class where the women do not have to do anything, but this class makes up only a very small percentage of our society. So most women in Algeria work and yet receive no help at all with the housework, while men have only got their careers to look after. We are still fighting the most important battle of all which is to get equal opportunities for jobs, professions and careers. I really do believe that if women could devote the same time to their professions as men they would be far more creative than men. There is something else – and here I might be unfair to men. Whenever there is any change in any aspect of life a woman senses and feels this change before a man does. She is more open, more ready to accept changes and new ways of living, and this is what men do not allow. When Algeria was very backward women were nothing. When the revolution started the women immediately became fighters, and important ones at that. After independence the Algerian woman developed quickly. Her reality started to change every two or three years, and men did not like this at all. They do not like to think or believe that women are so capable of understanding things and responding to them so quickly.'

'So do you believe that part of the reason why men try to keep women under their control is fear of their ability and potential?'

'Oh yes! I believe this very strongly. Men, I feel, are always puzzled by the very readiness of women to develop and change, so they try to slow them down because of their fear that they might develop into people who they can neither reach nor even understand. They keep them under their control until they can feel the things women feel, understand and experience them themselves.'

'Do you think that men are also afraid that if women take control they might bring about a major social change?'

'Although I am for women's liberation, I feel that we, as women, have to be clear about the society we want. If women's liberation means we have to imitate European women, I am against it. I do not want to travel the route which European women are taking. I am against what I have seen in the West.'

'What have you got against European women?'

'European women fought for their education and their careers. We have done the same. These are very important achievements for women. But I do not like the fact that sometimes Western women identify their rejection of men's control with their rejection of marriage as such. In the West men and women are completely free to choose each other as partners but on the slightest whim they get a divorce and leave their children as victims of their failed marriages. I am against this. A woman's liberation should not mean she feels less motherly love and less concern for her children's welfare. Both the woman and the man should try as hard as possible to keep the family together as a unit. I am against the deterioration of the family unit in the West. What does divorce mean after all? Both the man and the woman are free – but what about the children? There is a whole generation of children in the West from broken homes. What kind of homes are these children going to make? Perhaps every society is unique; Western society maybe finds its own way of organising the family to suit it best. But as an Arab woman, as a Muslim woman, I am against women rejecting men's control by deciding to stay single, or by getting a divorce for the slightest reason. Ours is a developing society, and these particular Western ideas don't suit us. We have to find our own way; we have to make sacrifices.'

'But don't you think that women in our society are often the only people who do make sacrifices to ensure a reasonably peaceful life for their children? Men for their part, manipulate this sacrificial tendency in women to the full. They do not make sacrifices for the sake of their families or children. So we end up with women at the very bottom of the ladder again.'

'I agree with you. Men in our society are using us. I am very aware of men's manipulation of our willingness to make sacrifices. But what else can we do? This is a battle we are fighting. I believe we have to fight from within rather than from without the family structure. I do not lay the entire blame on the European woman for what is happening in her society. The man is to blame as well. But, as we say in Algeria, you can't clap with one hand, and as a woman I would like women to be citizens who play a major role in the progress of both the family and society. Obviously, the men have to do their share as well but here I am only concerned with women. I would like to see men and women living as equals and to see loving relationships between them. I do not want women to achieve their liberation by rejecting motherhood and thereby denying themselves the most wonderful feeling they are ever likely to have, or through directing all their resentment against men alone. I recently met a French woman who said she did not want to get married or have children because she travelled, had a job and did everything she wanted to do. Why should she want a husband and children? I think this attitude goes against human nature and is also rather selfish. It is true that women should learn to be a bit selfish but not in this kind of way. This is a selfishness which annihilates us.'

'I don't think there is any fear of annihilation of the population in Algeria with the birth rate the highest in the world! Don't you think that women should be encouraged to use contraceptives and control the birth rate?'

'Women in our society must fight for birth control and for a small family made up of two to four children. In this new society the man should work with the woman both in and out of the home and this requires social, political and legal changes. Men, government and society should all help women to be good mothers and good citizens. A single woman should be able to work the same hours as a man, but once married she should work only half a day. The man should also do part of the housework. The government should provide cheap and efficient nurseries for babies and children. In this new society every effort should be made to give the woman more time to be more creative and enjoy her family and children without having to spend sleepless nights trying to catch up with her career.'

It was now 12.40. The telephone rang. It was Mme Radia's husband. 'Where are you?' I could hear him shouting at the other end of the phone.

'I'm with Mme Shaaban talking about "la femme",' she answered in French.

'Oh, "la femme"! Come on now, I can't wait any longer.'

'We are finishing in about five minutes,' she said, and put the phone down.

'I'm terribly sorry,' I said, 'but I really wish he had prepared the lunch instead of making you feel guilty because you didn't leave your office and dash home to do it for him.'

'What can I do?' she said with a sweet smile. 'All that I can say is that this is part of our battle.'

As she was locking the door of her office I said: 'Why is he waiting for you, anyway? Don't you drive? I can give you a lift home.'

'Yes, I do drive,' she said. 'But he doesn't let me; he says it is not quite acceptable in our society.'

'Nonsense!' I answered. 'There are lots of women driving cars in Constantine.'

'Oh, but what can I do? I'm tired,' she said.

As we walked down the long corridor towards the exit, Mme Radia tried to interview me, and asked me to tell her about the battles I had had to fight. I thought it was only fair she should want to question me after she had poured her heart out to me for the previous two hours and I tried to tell her as much as possible about myself in the few precious minutes left to us.

Suddenly I was interrupted by a very loud horn sounding just outside the building. On hearing the horn, Mme Radia pulled me by the arm and said, 'Oh God, let's run, please.' We ran. As we came out of the building she pointed to her husband's car. He was driving crazily round the car park like someone just bitten by a snake. I felt sorry for her and said, 'I'll apologise to your husband for the delay.' She thanked me and on seeing us he made an emergency stop. I greeted him and said, 'I'm terribly sorry if you are very hungry. I am to blame for Mme Radia being delayed; we were talking about women, you see.' He just nodded his head without saying a word, as if it was unreasonable to expect him to settle for this insignificant apology. I don't think it would ever have crossed his mind that we had more reason to be angry with him than he with us.

I had an interview with a distinguished assistant at the university, Mrs Bouhanoun. Now 32 years old, and with two sons, aged seven and five, she had been married for nearly eight years. The first question I asked her was:

'What are the things that you feel angry about as a woman?'

'As a married woman I feel very angry because I don't have the freedom to do what I want to do. Suppose I want to go out for a walk – I *can't*. I have to ask my husband and he has to agree; I have to explain why or where I want to go. He nearly always agrees but I still have to ask him and he has to agree; I can't decide anything for myself. That makes me very angry, because sometimes I have to wait until my husband comes home and it is either too late or I've stopped wanting to do what I fancied doing two hours ago. Such a problem didn't exist before my marriage; when I was single I had the freedom to go wherever I liked. I didn't have to have my parents' approval. Now my mother is ill and I want to see her, but if my husband doesn't agree I can't go. If I ever do anything without telling him there's a lot of fuss.'

'Does the same apply to him? I mean, does he have to ask you when he wants to do something?'

'I never ask him why he is doing this or that. As for me, I can't do anything, not even visit you, without his approval. That is the problem. Suppose I were at home and you rang me up to come and have a cup of tea with you, I couldn't just come; I'd have to wait for him and ask his permission. That makes me very angry.'

'Do you feel angry because it highlights the difference between men and women?'

'Yes. And I've told him that. But he says: "You're my *wife*; you're a *woman*; you can't decide things without me." He was the eldest boy in his family. His mother loved him dearly and spoilt him a lot. Now he finds it impossible to accept me on equal terms with himself.'

'It worries me that most of the women I have talked to seem to blame other women (either their mothers or their sisters) for their husband's behaviour. Don't you see that our mothers cannot be held solely responsible for moulding our characters?'

'I don't blame my mother-in-law because she brought up her children according to the way she herself had been brought up – and she had no education at all. At that time boys used to be brought up like that. Now she realises that it was a big mistake to have stopped her daughters' schooling and education. The eldest girl had to leave school although she is very intelligent, and now she is very unhappy because she knows she could have done better things with her life. What annoys her most is that it was not her father but her uncle who stopped her from going to school. Because he didn't want to send his own daughter to school he stopped his niece from going as well, so that his daughter would not make a fuss about her lot.'

'Did any man in your family stand in the way of your education?'

'No, not really. I went to England to do my PhD but didn't like the weather! After I got married my husband was very keen for me to continue with my studies. He almost forced me to go to France to do my MA! He is very enlightened as far as issues he thinks important are concerned, but doesn't like me to decide anything on my own.'

'But how could he trust you to go to France on your own and not trust you to go for a walk or to see a friend?'

'I don't know. I don't understand. Suppose I'm at the university and a friend invites me to have tea with her. If he's not there I can't go.'

'Do you think that this particular attitude of his is the result of his believing that as a woman you are incapable of making the right decisions?'

'No. My husband behaves like this because of our society. He often says that if we were living in Europe or somewhere like that he would change his attitudes completely, and I believe him because when we go on holiday he behaves exactly as I would like him to behave – as an equal. But that's because he knows we are on holiday and no one knows us. Whereas when we visit his parents he treats me in a way which shows his parents that he is "the man". I understand that now and I understand the code and make allowances for it. But I do not respect him for that. He is not really honest.'

'I have heard this same story from other Algerian women. Once they are out of Algeria they say their husbands treat them quite differently. They let them go to the cinema or for a walk on their own. So is it Algerian society which is standing in the way of your emancipation?'

'Yes. But I think you can always do on holidays what you can't do at home. This is my country; people know me and my family, but when I am in a different country I don't care; I do what I feel like doing, and I think this is true of everybody. My husband works at a research centre and his friends are very reactionary. He says I have to behave in a way which is acceptable to them. They are his friends and I have to take their feelings into account.'

'Is it the society *per se*, then, that is limiting your chances of liberation, or are you saying all this to excuse your husband?'

'Yes, I believe we say all this to excuse our husbands. In my case, for example, my parents used to let me do what my husband forbids – yet we live in the same society. We had neighbours who used to say things about me, but my parents never cared so why should he care about what others say? In the end our neighbours understood that I wasn't doing anything wrong and eventually they stopped saying anything. In fact, it might have been good for them to see me doing things differently. I think if we start doing something different others will eventually follow. They might gossip at first, but eventually they will shut up and think straight. I'm sure that when people see a good example of a liberated, educated woman behaving in the way she wants to they are bound to be influenced by the experience in one way or another. But this, of course, needs a bit of courage to attempt to do. It needs courage to be able to say that I am sure of myself and that I am going to do what I think is right.'

'How do you compare your father with your husband as far as women's emancipation is concerned?'

'Well, my mother never had to tell my father that she was going out for a walk. In many ways she was a lot freer than I. My father used to tell my mother that she could do what she liked and that she didn't have to ask his permission each time. When I tell that to my husband he says that he is the way he is and that he can't accept my father's way of doing things.'

'How do you explain the fact that although your father is older and less educated than your husband he seems to have a more liberal attitude towards women?'

'My husband is liberal but not as liberal as my father. My husband's family are not educated. I think it has something to do with the way they have been brought up.'

'What do you do to make sure that your children have good attitudes towards women?'

'At home they see that my husband helps me and they understand they have to help me, too. For them it is natural to see a man working in the kitchen, cooking and tidying up. So I think they are learning that there is no difference between men and women. My husband helps me quite a lot at home. If there is no lunch in the fridge he doesn't complain. We start preparing food together when we get back from the university. If the ironing is not done he'll sit down and do it. I don't really feel that I am fighting a battle to keep both my profession and my home going at the same time. The only problem is the children. Who will look after them when we are both working?'

'So do you feel privileged to be an Algerian woman?'

'If I compare myself with other women I feel privileged. Take my sister, for instance. She is educated but her husband isn't. Her husband didn't like having a home help, so he asked my sister to stop working. She agreed to leave work for a year when she had her first baby, and then another year – and as the time goes by her going back to work seems to be less and less likely. Now she is really unhappy because she feels there is something missing. She has even lost the incentive to work. I don't think she could go back to work even if she wanted to, now. Her husband's family is very rich. Every day they want three-course meals and the house always has to be scrupulously clean. She has three children and is really exhausted. She is treated like a servant. Had I been in her place I would have left ages ago; years ago, in fact. I believe that if she'd taken a stand right from the start she could have changed things, but the more submissive she became the more aggressive her husband became, too. Every year they make big decisions – but nothing actually changes. Though they go on holidays together and appear with each other on social occasions they are not companions for each other; they are not happy.'

'Do you blame your sister and other women in similar situations for their lot or do you put the blame on society?'

'I blame both. I blame individual women and the society they live in. Women should revolt against the way they have been enslaved. They should shout, cause a row and make their views absolutely clear. My sister, for example, accepted being treated like a servant and now it is taken for granted that this is her role and that she has nothing against it. If I were in her place I would have revolted and made everybody understand that I wasn't going to let anyone tell me how to live my life.'

'But a professional woman I was talking to the other day said she gets no help from her husband whatsoever, that she has to do all the housework and look after the children, as well as keep her job. When I asked her why she didn't do something about it she said "Because of my children. I don't want them to suffer the consequences of a broken home." What do you say to that?'

'I think to have a mother like that, a mother who is afraid to raise her voice, is not a good thing for the children because they can sense when you are afraid or unhappy. If they feel you are under threat or deeply unhappy they cannot be really happy themselves. I think women have to stop finding excuses for themselves and start doing something about the way they live. Women have to start doing something in their own homes as well as form groups, and organise collectively to campaign against their unfair circumstances. My colleague at the university, for instance, who has five children, talks about her situation as if it were her fate. She complains that she has five children. Well it was up to her *not* to have five children. She knows about contraceptives. Why have five children if you only wanted two? She speaks about children the way our illiterate mothers used to. Even our mothers, though, advised us not to have a lot of children. They would stress that to have many children is neither good for the mother's health nor good for the happiness of the children themselves. So I find it very difficult to sympathise with women who put themselves in the role of pathetic victims of circumstance and seem to enjoy asking to be pitied.'

'You said women should do something collectively, could they do that through the women's organisation (UNIFA) in this country?'

'No, not really. UNIFA does not include educated women. Most women who belong work in offices and they are fighting to make people understand that women can do the same jobs as men. This is their prime aim because women here are not used to working outside the house. They have tried, and to some extent have succeeded, to make men accept that a woman is equal to a man as long as she can do the same job. But in other respects – in the social context, for example – they have not managed to change anything at all. They say they can't change anything in the social sphere because of tradition. But I think tradition is something you can both respect and change. Consider contraceptives, for example. It is a very important issue which these women haven't even begun to speak about yet. They have to tell women why it's no good having a lot of children. They have to explain to mothers why and how they could have both fewer children and better lives. They could have done something very important in that field. We can't educate or even properly sustain all these children. As you know, in Algeria we have the highest birth rate in the world and 80 per cent of the country's population is under 20 years old. I am sure the country is going to face terrible problems in the near future. Women who have many children are either weak willed or must want children. Unconsciously women here try to make you feel pity rather than admiration for them. They want you to say: "You poor women, how do you manage with all these children? If you didn't have so many children you would all have had brilliant careers!"'

'Some women who have accepted their fate say that there are limits to what we can do at this stage, but we hope that our daughters won't have to suffer what we have suffered. Do you accept that?'

'No. My niece, for example, is going to be like her mother. She can see how men behave and how women are treated. I think she is going to grow up bearing this in mind. From time to time she comes to play with my children and it seems unnatural to her that my husband or our children should help in the kitchen. She sometimes laughs. We try to tell her that it is natural but she says her father never ever helps in the kitchen. We say the reasons for this are because there are many women sitting at home doing nothing. She is too young now to understand, but I think when she is older she is not going to behave any differently from her mother if they continue to live the same way as they do now. So if women are going to fight a battle they should start right now rather than wait for the next generation and hope that their daughters will somehow escape the same suffering. We have to educate our children by setting examples. If you tell your children not to do something and yet they see you doing it, they will do it, too. If I tell my children not to cross the road without looking they are going to say: "Our mother asks us to look right and left before crossing the road but *she* doesn't. Perhaps she is telling us something bad, or something just for children, so we are not going to do it." If I want my children to live differently I have to behave differently myself.'

'You said that the women's organisation is not doing very much for women and you evidently want women to start doing something about their lives. How do you think they could set about doing this?'

'I am always angry because we do nothing. I think that educated women and feminists have to invade the women's organisation in this country and change it. Those women who are in the organisation just do paid work to prove they are equal, but they still accept the whole burden of work at home and never question their status as women servants. I must also stress the importance of fighting on a personal level, because organisations can never do all the work. Every woman has to start doing something on her own initiative about her own life.'

'Do you consider European women to be liberated? Or do you have some criticisms of women's liberation in Europe?'

'I have seen many European women who live in similar situations to the way women in Algeria live, the only difference being that their society is not so strict. They can do more things but that is not to say they are happier. They have all the normal problems. A working woman in Europe also has to look after the home and bring up the children. The only difference is that their husbands are more ready and willing to help than ours are. Even when our husbands help us they think they are doing us a personal favour.'

'Would you like to see Arab women following in the footsteps of European women, or do you have a different solution to the problem of women's liberation?'

'I have some reservations about us imitating European women. We have traditions which, while they don't have to be followed to the letter, nevertheless have to be respected. I must stress that to respect a tradition is not to be narrow-minded. We can respect our traditions at the same time as improving our position. To imitate any liberation movement blindly is bound to be bad for us. For example, I know some women who, because they know some European women who smoke, think that smoking will make for liberation. It isn't because I don't smoke myself, or because I have anything against them smoking, that I disagree with this. I just feel it is wrong to do something simply because European women do it. We have to find our own ways of doing things rather than imitate others. As Arabs we should not deprive ourselves of our own traditions.'

I decided to spend two days working in Constantine University library with two of my colleagues, Fatima and Zehra (both working in the law department). On the first day when we arrived there Zehra discovered she had left her library ticket at home. The porter played stupid and refused to let her in. A row erupted between them, during which I could hear the porter shouting at Zehra in a voice which must have been heard by everyone in the library. 'This is not your place. You'd better go home and cook a meal for your husband.'

'My husband is just like you, a male chauvinist who doesn't deserve to have his meal prepared by someone like *me*,' she answered almost as loudly. The stress she put on 'me' emphasised her self-respect and pride which I had always appreciated and admired.

Still, I was cross with her for bringing her husband into the argument.

'Why should you be cross with me?' she asked when we settled down to a cup of coffee in the arts' building. 'They are all the same – husband, porter, it makes no difference. They all treat me the same way, and I hate them all.' I tried to calm her down but she was so desperate to let off steam that there was no way of stopping her. 'My husband is very poorly educated and his attitude to women, including me, is not much better than the attitude of that porter. I have to cook his meals, wash and iron his shirts, clean his home, bring up his children, stop reading and writing when he feels like talking to me and, on top of all that, play the role of the weaker, submissive partner in social and family gatherings. Here we are, teaching at university and taking up court cases, with other women filling our schools, hospitals, engineering and medical departments, and yet in the eyes of our fathers, husbands and even porters we are small, insignificant human beings.'

'The chief reason for all this,' Fatima interrupted while Zehra was catching her breath, 'is because marriage is recognised in all Arab societies to be the sole aim of women's lives. Most Arab men, and a large percentage of Arab women, believe that outside marriage and children women just don't exist. Legally, no woman can be entered in the census of any Arab country. An Arab nation's citizens are all men – with daughters and wives as their property. When an Arab man gets married he is registered separately from his father, whereas his wife's name is just moved from the name of her father to that of her husband. If she gets a divorce, her name has to be re-registered under her father's entry, while her children remain under her husband's name. As for women who marry foreigners, they are crossed out of the country's registration books altogether. They have no right to pass their nationality on to their children, for the children's nationality is legally that of their father. I discovered only the other day that such women don't even have a legal right to stand for Parliament in their own country, because once they get married they are crossed off their father's constituency – and their husbands, of course, are foreigners.'

By now Zehra had drawn a deep breath and was holding her cup of coffee tightly with both hands in an obvious attempt to sound more calm and composed than she had been a few minutes ago. She said: 'The big problem is that this legal attitude reflects the social attitude towards women. It is still unacceptable for a single or divorced woman to live on her own, which in effect means that women are always caught between their father's authority and that of their husband. That is basically why we have a relatively lower divorce rate in the Arab world than in Europe. This is not because marriage is more blissful here – as some religious men would have us believe – but because women have less right to choose. For most of them the only choice they can make is the choice between a cruel husband and a malicious father. Are we to be considered privileged just because we have a degree in law? Like every other woman, we have no choice, no say and no social position.'

'I agree with most of what you've said,' Fatima intervened. 'But I don't agree that our problems are identical to those of illiterate and most ordinary women. Take any of your clients, for example, or mine; can you honestly say what it must feel like to be in Saaida's position? Can you imagine yourself forced into an arranged marriage and then forced out of it for reasons which have nothing to do with you as a person? Bouthaina is right; she should meet more ordinary women, and I am going to take her to meet Saaida.'

When we went to see her, Saaida (whose name in Arabic means, ironically, 'happy woman') was lying asleep on a small mattress in the one-bedroom flat which her old schoolfriend, Fatima, had rented with her elderly widowed mother. 'She is very tired,' Fatima whispered. 'For the last week or so she has been suffering from a terrible headache.' We sat almost silent, trying not to wake her up. All I could see was her dark, curly hair and a brown, serene-looking face. 'I feel so delighted when she falls asleep,' Fatima muttered almost to herself, 'because this is the only time she has to forget a little.'

The baby, of whose presence we had previously been unaware, moved under the cover, touched his mother's breasts and started to cry. Saaida was startled, jumped out of her sleep, and said before she had opened her eyes properly: 'Welcome; I knew you were coming and don't know how I fell asleep; I must have been very tired.' She went out, presumably to wash her face, and came back to greet us in the customary Algerian manner – four kisses on the cheeks.

She repeated phrases of welcome and seemed calm and thoughtful. 'Why do you want to hear my story?' she asked, surprising me with her sudden question. 'To tell it to other women? I don't think anyone will believe it, so why don't you tell them something which they find easier to believe? You hear of such things happening to other people, but never seriously think they could happen to you until you find yourself in the middle of the mess. I run over my story in my head a dozen times a day and still can't believe that all these things have actually happened to me.

'When I was 16 years old my mother came to me one day and said I was to be married off to the brother of my sister-in-law. I tried to argue that I was too young to be married and that I didn't know the man, but no one took any notice of what I said. My father gave me to understand that my marriage to this man would benefit my brother whose wife was creating problems for him. "Once you get married to her brother," my father kept reiterating, "she will have to stop pestering your brother, or else you will pester hers!" The result was that I was married off to this man, regardless of what I felt or said. Contrary to all my bad premonitions, however, my husband turned out to be a really nice man and I started to like him. I could even say we started to love each other. Within the year we had a baby boy and became a happy family of three. Just about this time my brother and sister-in-law were divorced. As anticipated, my family started to ask me to take reciprocal action. My husband, too, was subjected to the same kind of pressure from his family.

'We both refused to divorce, but in the end my family literally kidnapped me from my husband and refused to let me bring my five-month-old boy with me. Despite our desperate attempts to get back together our separation became an inescapable reality. Before getting married I used to be a very good dressmaker and embroiderer so I resumed these two professions and started to support my parents and my brother who had broken my own family life into pieces.

'In a few months' time my father found another man for me whom I had never seen before. This was even though I was still not legally divorced from my husband. It nearly drove me mad. I refused to cooperate, screamed and even made an abortive suicide attempt, but all to no avail. My father eventually led me like a zombie to this man's home and he married me, or more accurately, raped me. I later discovered that he married me because he expected me to have a lot of money and gold accrued from my embroidery and dressmaking. When he found out that I had nothing and that my family had already milked me dry before sending me to him he started battering me, locking me in the house for a day or two without food, and torturing me in all manner of ways to force me to leave him. But where could I go? My family made it quite clear that they didn't want me back, even as a corpse, because it was socially disgraceful for them to have a daughter who divorced and remarried annually. By now I was seven months pregnant and my life was becoming an utter and absolute hell. My first husband started a court case against me because I had committed bigamy. They say "It never rains but it pours". I felt as if all hell had contrived to pour all the misery it had over my head. Amidst all this chaos and my hard work doing embroidery (doubled at this stage in an effort to satisfy my husband's greed), my right arm became paralysed. Now, nobody wanted me. They all turned a blind eye and pretended it was all my fault; I was a burden and a social embarrassment to them all. So I left, carrying a baby and deep bitterness in my heart and came to live with my old friend out of the way and out of the marriage market. Legally, I am only married to my first husband, although my second husband received a religious sanction on the marriage contract between him and my father. Fatima is representing me in court and I am waiting for the court's ruling to find out what is going to happen to me. But already I can see that as a woman I am now regarded by my family, husbands, society and law as the guilty party. As far as the law is concerned, family pressure does not justify my doing what I did, for I am supposed to have had the freedom to choose.'

In December 1986 I was invited to go back to Constantine to give a paper at a conference about structuralism at the university. After the conference was concluded, the president of the Algerian Writers' Union, Al Arabi, asked all guests which parts of Algeria they would like to see. 'The Southern Sahara,' I said jokingly, reckoning that the trip would be far too difficult to arrange at such short notice. My colleagues (all male) showed signs of grave concern about my safety in that vast desert. They pointed out to me that most people in the tribes there did not speak Arabic, and those of them who did had a very strong accent which I would not understand, so it would be impossible for me to communicate with them. It was also pointed out to me that even after I had flown to the main town there (Tamnrassett) I would need to travel far and wide in the Sahara to be able to meet people from these tribes and so I would need both a car and translator. Only Al Arabi firmly maintained that it was all very easy; that there was a daily flight there and that he could arrange the trip for me. He said there was a decent hotel in which I could stay and as women were in full control there I might not want to come back. I was scared but fascinated. By the time the dinner party was over I had already made up my mind to go. The following day I was in the plane heading towards Tamnrassett, leaving all hesitations and calculations behind and enjoying for the first time the astounding Sahara scenery.

After about two hours' flight over the vast and amazingly varied Sahara, I felt as if my brain had become numb. I suddenly became aware that I was watching a great sand dune which looked exactly like a huge brain with finely marked veins. I wondered whether any painting could ever emulate the rich and varied dunes, the amazing shapes, and the fascinating thin veins which look as if they have been drawn by a sharp red pencil.

Only that same morning I had left women at Constantine airport, wrapped in their black *chaddors* and with their entire faces (except for their eyes) covered with white triangular cloths, to arrive here in Tamnrassett, still in Algeria, to find the men rather than the women were wearing the veil. It was neither a poster from the mysterious South nor a painting from the distant past, but a flesh and blood male approaching me who had actually covered his hair and face, leaving only his eyes uncovered, in what appeared to be a very large, thick, round veil. Walking beside him was a woman whose bare face was left open to the cool, refreshing breeze which accompanied the stunning Sahara sunset. Shaliefa was to act as my translator and the veiled man accompanying her was her husband, Mahmoud. That very first surprise was indicative of quite a few others lying in store for me on that short but immensely rewarding and fascinating trip to the Al Hoggar mountains, the historical homeland of the Al Tawariqu tribes.

I was driven by Shaliefa and Mahmoud to Tahat hotel, a single-storey building with long, winding corridors and isolated rooms. The receptionist gave me a double room with a fridge, television and telephone, none of which worked. The room was huge, cold and shivery, with no hot water for a shower after that long day. I felt hungry, cold and very dirty, the most unpleasant combination of things I've ever experienced. With no telephone in the room and two huge doors which opened straight on to the desert outside I expected the worst. Still, the people there were extremely kind. They heated a bucket of water for me so that I was able to have a strip wash, brought me dinner, a very welcome hot cup of tea, and two thick blankets. I was then able to sleep peacefully until the bright Sahara sun poured into what seemed to me then a warm, pleasant room.

A kind receptionist brought me an early breakfast and asked whether I would like to meet a Tarqui woman who was working at the hotel. 'I would love to,' I answered. He promised to bring her in when he came to collect the tray later. At about nine o'clock, a thin, brown-faced woman, who looked very Algerian with distinctive high-boned cheeks, deep dark eyes and frizzy hair, was sitting in my room gazing shyly at the floor.

Desperately wanting to start a conversation with a woman whose appearance, accent and way of life seemed somehow different, I found myself starting off with the question I hate to hear directed at women. Whether they are engineers, doctors or even ministers, women are usually classified solely according to their marital status: married or single; mothers or not mothers. And there I was, consciously adopting a chauvinist attitude, perhaps because I was certain the question was the most likely to be asked. So, knowing that Tita was only 26 years old I said: 'Are you married?'

'Not now,' she answered in a matter-of-fact tone. 'But I have been married four times.' I nearly fell off my chair at the casual tone and the mocking smile which accompanied her answer. While my blood pressure was jumping up and down at the thought of going through four marriages and four divorces and all the agony which this young woman must have gone through she looked at me with a curious smile, evidently guessing what was going through my head. 'Most women in Al Tawariqu tribes marry five or six times,' she said. 'We don't see anything strange in that.' She then relaxed and told me her life story which, with subsequent detailed investigations, I found to be typical of the lives of women in Al Tawariqu tribes.

'When I was about nine years old my mother left our home for that of another man whom she loved better than my father. I was left with my two younger sisters and my father. Although my mother paid us regular visits I missed her terribly. My father was also miserable because he hated her leaving, but he actually had no say in her departure. She simply said to him she no longer loved him and was in love with another man, and then asked him the terrible question: "Would he like her to stay with him under such circumstances?" He had to say no. In his turn, my father had to leave us for long spells of time and travel with the caravans crisscrossing the desert to Niger and Mali where they used to barter salt and *shieh* (a kind of herbal tea) for *albishna* (a kind of wheat) and clothes. He was in fact quite anxious to marry us off and relieve himself of his paternal responsibility. So when I was 14 he started pushing me to get married to a young man he liked. I didn't really want to, but although father didn't literally force me, he nevertheless kept pressurising me until he managed to extract a "forced consent". However, I only spent one night with this man – and never left my father's home.'

In Al Tawariqu all women spend their first year of marriage at their mothers' home (they actually say 'mothers' meaning 'parents') to have enough time to make their tents, their decorations and prepare themselves properly for their future married lives. Almost all Tarqui women have their first babies at their mothers' homes. In fact, a good percentage of them never move to their first husbands' homes – because they get a divorce before the year is out, not least because the parents usually interfere in their daughters' first marriages. Once the Tarqui woman gets her first divorce, however, she is free to marry whoever she likes without consulting anyone. The logic behind this (as a number of parents later explained to me) is that young girls who have never known men intimately cannot possibly choose their first husbands for themselves. Once they have had their first experience with the men, however, they can look after their own affairs very well. 'Hence,' Tita resumed, 'for most women here a first marriage is only necessary for shaking off family authority and marrying men of their choice.'

'But what about marriage and divorce procedures?' I enquired, unable to hide my anxiety.

'Well, marriage and divorce procedures are very simple. We don't register our marriages in government offices. You only have to take four witnesses with you and visit the nearest *Talib* (the local religious head of the tribe) and announce in his presence that you are going to marry or divorce this or that man.

'After divorcing the first man, another man told me he loved me. I was not very fond of him, but I was feeling quite lonely so I married him. After a year or so, however, I fell head over heels in love with our neighbour. The obvious thing to do was to divorce my second husband and marry my first true love, and that was just what I did. With this third husband of mine I spent the happiest two years of my life during which time I had my only two children. But before long, unfortunately for me, a beautiful young woman appeared in his life, so he divorced me and married her. Although I couldn't really blame him, because that was just what I had done with my second husband, I felt miserable. I remember promising myself never to get married again because I couldn't bear being so hurt. Yet two years ago I broke this promise and got married to a man whom I knew only very slightly. We had only lived together for a few months before he went off to Libya and never came back again. My only consolation was that I was always able to keep my children.'

Another Tarqui woman who had been listening to Tita's story asked her about her sister and whether she had a boy or a girl. 'A girl,' Tita answered shortly, evidently keen to change the subject.

Her obvious embarrassment incited my curiosity. 'Is your sister married?' I asked Tita.

'No,' she answered, rubbing her palms and looking at them sadly.

'How did she have a baby, then?' I asked naively. What I think I meant was: 'How could she have had a child outside marriage in an Arab country?'

'Well,' Tita answered. 'She had an affair with a man who turned out to be irresponsible; while my sister was quite serious about their relationship he was just having a good time. She got pregnant and had the baby; what else could she do? Now she is bringing up her baby with my children.'

'But what do other people say about her?' I couldn't help asking.

'Nothing; what can they say? On seeing the baby some people might mutter: "What a shame, the baby needs her father." On the whole, however, most people here look with deep contempt on the man who makes a woman pregnant and then refuses to father his child within a normal marital relationship. If anyone should be ashamed it is the man and not the woman.'

I was stunned at what I was hearing but tried to hide my surprise so that our conversation could continue. 'But doesn't anything happen to the woman?' I said.

'Well, what can we do? We try to help her bring up her child,' said Tita.

I tried to explain: 'What I mean is that in some other Arab countries, a single, unmarried mother might be persecuted; she might even be considered to have brought shame upon the honour of her family.'

'And if you think she is guilty of that you try to persecute her; in our tribe we always try to take reformist rather than punitive measures. A single mother can be a very good member of society – and a very good mother.'

It was a great surprise to find a place in the Arab world where social traditions seemed to deal reasonably well with unmarried mothers as a social group. Even so, what I'd just heard was so different from anything that I expected to find here. Yet this version of Islam seemed so simple, and in no way contradicted the ethics of humanity, love and true affection. Everything here, in fact, in this beautiful patch of the Sahara seemed pure, simple and easy to understand.

The next morning I woke up to a wonderfully quiet and sunny Sahara morning. The sun's beams were bathing the adjacent valleys and a long line of rocky, volcanic mountains, colouring them all with a warm, relaxing golden pink. Everything seemed so absolutely quiet that even the movements of my pen on paper somehow disturbed this utter stillness. It was the first time I had ever heard the loud noise of my breathing; as for footsteps approaching my room in the hotel, they sounded like thunder.

My translator and her husband were waiting for me in the car, just outside the hotel. Shaliefa was in a long, bright blue robe which looked very much like an Indian sari, the only difference being that the waist did not show. She had also put on blue make-up: blue lipstick, blue eye-shadow and even light blue cheek-colouring. Amidst this blue her large black eyes looked darker and deeper than any other pair of eyes I have ever seen. Her long, black hair was partly covered with a golden scarf which she tied behind her neck. Both her bright scarf and the bright silver which she wore round her neck, on her fingers and ears, seemed to match the bright pink beams of the sun. Her husband, Mahmoud, was wearing attractive black Tarqui traditional clothing (a large pair of trousers and a long, wide robe of the same colour embroidered round the neck, pockets and the brim) and had veiled his face completely with a white sash, leaving only his large dark brown eyes showing which made them look very alluring. He was tall and slim – as are most Tarqui men – while his wife was robust and stout.

As soon as the car started to move Mahmoud turned round to speak to me from the front seat, saying: 'Today we shall take you to Tigmar, Dirhinanen and, if possible, Askaram, so that you can see the authentic Tawariqus, not the emigrés from Niger and Mali who pose for the French tourists as Tawariqus and misinform French folk writers about our traditions, habits and ethics. I am taking you to see people from the dominant Kel Ala tribe who were the rulers of Al Hoggar so you can gather all the information you need from its original, pure source.

On the way we saw some deer and I asked Mahmoud whether Al Tawariqus relied on hunting as a main source of food. 'Yes,' he said. 'But there are very strict rules and regulations. For example, they won't hunt a female and hunting is altogether prohibited during certain months of the year (I think, October and November) when the female deer are known to be pregnant, just in case a misguided shot hit one of them.' He also told me that Al Tawariqus never eat the meat of their own camels even if they are starving. No Tawariqu would eat the meat of the camel on which he had travelled in the Sahara, and which he had fed and lived with for many years. He also explained to me the respect paid to animals, plants and land, which made me feel that for this group of people 'everything that is natural is holy'.

Tigmar was no more than 40 miles away, yet we spent over two hours battling with a really treacherous path in our strong but slow Landrover. No wonder, I thought to myself, that in the race which had been arranged two days previously between cars and camels, camels were the first to reach Askaram. Indeed, I would very much have preferred to be on a camel on this narrow, stony and extremely difficult path. I knew we were not going to reach Askaram, for by the time we had reached Tigmar I felt really ill and had terrible backache.

We stopped in the middle of a village of about 30 huts and five or six modern houses (made of clay or cement), and as soon as my companions got out of the car all the men, women and children of the village had surrounded us within seconds. We were invited to the house belonging to the eldest couple in the village and everyone seemed to follow. The house was built of cement but the huge front room we entered had the usual sand floor. Our elderly hostess quickly unfolded the traditional, colourful Algerian carpets for us to sit on, but I noticed that most people were pushing the carpets aside and enjoying rubbing their feet against the sand. Men and women together immediately divided into three large groups, with age being the only factor that decided the rough divisions. Ahmad, who had come with us from Tamnarassett and who seemed to be a good friend of the family, started preparing the tea, for making tea is men's rather than women's speciality in these tribes.

About ten minutes after our arrival a beautifully decorated, portable sink was passed around for people to wash their hands in with soap and water. The sink was a big round bowl made from brass, with two handles and a cover which rested about two inches below the surface. The cover had small openings which allowed the water to pass down. About half an hour later, three straw trays full of dates and three big bowls of yoghurt were brought in.

My hostess was quite an old lady, beautifully slim with an upright figure and a cheerful smile which revealed a life of fulfilment. She was of high descent and from quite a cultured tribe, Kel Ala, so she spoke Arabic fairly well. Only the men of religion and cultured people spoke Arabic for Al Tawariqus speak the Tarqui language.

'Madam,' I began. 'I wonder if you would tell me about your life as a Tarqui woman, both before and after marriage.'

'Well, let's first get one thing straight. I am not old; I feel extremely young (she must have been in her seventies), and would like to live for many years to come.' As she said this she held both my hands and squeezed them affectionately. 'So that makes you a baby, and you have to enjoy this beautiful life,' she added. 'Agreed?'

'Yes,' I said. 'I do agree.' I felt quite envious of her zest and verve.

'Well, young girl,' she continued, 'the first memorable day in my life was the day I had my first period. That was the happiest day I have ever had. The custom amongst Al Tawariqus is to celebrate a girl's first period. So when I broke the news to my mother she sent the word round quickly to all the principal women in the tribe telling them of the happy event and asking them to set a date for *Tendi*. (Tendi is a big party when Tarqui women appear in their best clothes, their best silver and sing and play music. They form a circle at the centre of which are two women sounding the drum and singing. All the other women clap hands and repeat the songs after them while the men folk, also in their best costumes and some on their camels, dance on the periphery.) So, on that memorable day I wore my best dress, put on my silver and was the star of a huge *Tendi* in which men presented me with lovely clothes, bracelets and leather. I still remember feeling extremely privileged to be a woman and I enjoyed the incredible love and attention I was given because I had reached maturity. Look at that girl, for example,' and she pointed to a young girl sitting by the door, 'she has not reached maturity. How do I know?'

'I have no idea,' I answered.

'Look at her. She is not wearing any silver and has no make-up on. Only after having their first periods do our girls put on make-up and wear bracelets, necklaces and earrings.'

'So a woman's first period is a very happy occasion for her?'

'It is an even happier occasion for the men,' she said, laughing wickedly. 'For another girl is added to the list of marriageable women in the tribe.'

'After this party I felt I had been officially admitted to the enchanting and esoteric world of adults. It was so lovely to feel my small heart growing bigger and to feel the longing to embrace another person. Before very long I started a love affair with my husband whom you can see over there' – she pointed to a relaxed-looking man in his seventies – 'and this affair lasted for seven happy years after which we got married. During these years we got to understand each other really well. Such a relationship is fairly normal in our tribes. Most young people have premarital relationships for three, four or even seven years before they get married.'

'Do the parents normally know about such love affairs?'

'Of course they do, particularly the mother who is always kept informed of the latest details. And a love relationship is not something you can hide. The whole tribe knows about it; it is a normal and ordinary part of people's lives here, just as marriage is. All young hearts are ensnared by passionate love – which turns out to be either passing or permanent.'

'Does this love affair at any point develop into a premarital sexual relationship?'

'Sex? No, never. Well, some of them must do, otherwise how can we account for all the single mothers we have amongst Al Tawariqus! The lovers are allowed to have everything they want except sex. They kiss, hold each other, caress, play together but never have sex. Tarqui young men and women know the rules and stick to their limits. Those who make love before marriage are not considered true and genuine lovers. If the lover asked his beloved for sex she would immediately reject and despise him because she would know that he was only idling away the time with her and was not serious in his intentions to marry her. So if she was well brought up she would generally put an end to their relationship there and then.

'There are so many things which lovers can enjoy without making love. The eldest woman in the tribe arranged *Essehar* for all the lovers in the community. This is a late evening party that often goes on all through the night. She invites all the lovers to her place just around midnight when all the other men and women have already gone to sleep, to sing, dance and spend the whole night together enjoying themselves under her guardianship. On other, quieter nights the lover waits until everyone is asleep and then sneaks to the tent of his beloved, slips into her bed and stays there until dawn, talking to her and caressing her and leaving only when light is about to break on the horizon. Her parents would, of course, be sleeping in the same tent and would know their daughter's lover was there, but this is accepted conduct. The parents are confident that neither he nor she would do anything outside the tribe's social and moral ethics. The memory of these happy and exciting years plays an important role in making the marriage a success.'

'Was this true of your own relationship?'

'Oh yes! I was so happy during those seven years that I have never stopped being in love with him, even now. I now arrange *Essehar* for young lovers because I know what a pleasurable activity it is for them and what a lasting effect it has on their relationships.'

As people started eating another elderly woman started to play the Tarqui's traditional musical instrument which is called *Al Imsad*. (This pear-shaped lute, its body tapering to its short neck, has four pairs of strings and is played with an eagle's quill.) I was told only women played while men sang for them. My hostess continued to tell me about the unquenchable thirst she still had for love and life. She had only two children (she does not know why this should be the case) who are now both married. She had no reason to complain, she could never want for anything else.

While lunch was being cooked and served my hostess had been talking to me; other women from the village had done the work. I had not heard her ask anyone to stay for lunch, but everyone did all the same; it seemed to be the natural thing to do. What struck me, though, was how little everyone ate; perhaps a few mouthfuls each. No wonder they were all so slim, particularly the men. You might find a robust, stout woman but the men were all slim, tall and extremely upright. When I asked my hostess about their diet she said: 'We eat enough only to survive, and when we eat we do not stuff our stomachs to the limit. As for our men being slim, we believe that being overweight is very bad for men. Women's bodies can cope with being overweight a lot better than men's bodies can. That is why you will find most, if not all, our men slim and delicate.'

In Otool, also in the Southern Sahara, one young, strikingly beautiful woman attracted my attention among all the women who came out to receive us in their Tarqui costumes. She seemed quiet and thoughtful so I made an effort to sit next to her and started smiling at her and asking her simple, general questions. Once she started talking she seemed to me even more attractive than before. After we had had the usual tea of dates and yoghurt I asked to hear her life story.

Fatima started with a deep sigh, 'I've had a really hard life; though I might not look very old I feel as if I've lived a hundred years. My father died when I was a year old, leaving my mother with my elder sister and myself. As we grew up to be quite good-looking girls my mother was anxious to marry us off as soon as possible. So she married me to a man 30 years my senior when I was only 14 years old. I had no idea what was happening to me; the only thing I knew only too well was that I hated the man. I lived with him for two really miserable years which still give me nightmares. Sometimes I wonder why I stayed with him all that time when divorce in our tribe is so easy. I don't know; I was very young and simply didn't know what to do. Eventually I just walked out with a forty-day-old baby and never looked back.'

'Why did you hate him so much? Was he violent?'

'No, never. But I could not stand the sight of him. He was a miserable, selfish old drunkard who couldn't have cared less about me or my needs. We used to have constant rows, and life with him was sheer hell.'

'Did he ever hit you?'

'Hit me? God, of course not!'

An old woman sitting next to us and obviously listening to our conversation, interrupted, 'No Tarqui male would ever lay a hand on his wife. I once heard of a Tarqui who was extremely angry with his wife and slapped her on the face. She went to *Al Talib* who made him pay her a goat in compensation and sign a document which said that if he should ever repeat this misconduct, divorce would be the immediate outcome.

'A Tarqui woman will never accept being battered; this is something which doesn't exist in our tribes – we only heard of it when we came into contact with urban society. To all Tarquis, both men and women, this is something shameful. If a man here happened to hit his wife for any reason whatsoever he would be so scorned by every member of the tribe that his life would subsequently prove to be impossible; the social disgrace would certainly make him something of an outcast and might very well lead to him leaving the tribe altogether. My mother used to tell me that if she cooked a meal for my father she would have the right to ask *Al Talib* for compensation. *Al Talib* would usually tell the husband that his wife was his wife and not his cook, so why did he ask her to serve his meals? Now, however, both men and women cook, work in the fields and look after camels and goats. Our mothers and grandmothers seem to have been better off than we were, and we might be better off than our daughters.'

I asked Kolla, another elderly woman, whether to her knowledge polygamy was known amongst Al Tawariqus.

'Although according to the Koran it is permissible,' Kolla answered quietly and thoughtfully, 'no Tarqui woman would agree to marry a married man and no woman would agree to stay with her husband once she was sure that he was interested in another woman. Hence, effectively, particularly with regard to respectable tribes such as Kel Ala and Dik Ali, polygamy is unknown. You might find it in lesser tribes, though it must be extremely rare. Personally I've never seen a

Tarqui male who had more than one wife. Even men whose wives get chronic diseases or never have children either decide to stick with them or else get divorced and remarried.'

'Are divorce procedures quite easy?'

'Oh yes,' answered Fatima jumping at the chance to join in the mainstream of our conversation again. 'If you don't like the man all you have to do is to put on your shoes and say goodbye. Later you can take your witnesses and inform *Al Talib* of your decision. When I was divorced,' she continued, 'I had the best time ever. According to our traditions the mother of the divorcee informs all the tribe's elders that her daughter is divorced and that she would like to celebrate her divorce on such and such a date. On that date the divorcee wears her best clothes and silver and make-up and is the star of the *Tendi* party, a party as good as her wedding party. People from all tribes turn up, also wearing their best clothes and bring her presents and silver. Traditionally, the divorcee does not take any of the presents home with her but gives them to the poor and needy. Most presents come from the men who would like to get married and who are glad to have another potential wife among the women of their tribe. At my *Tendi* divorce party I was presented with two camels – the best present any woman can receive. I offered one of them to the family of silversmiths, who, as craftspeople, don't keep animals, and the other to a very needy family. It is usually at this party that the divorcee is approached by one of the men who later on will propose to her. The only thing that religious teachings stipulate is that the woman has to stay single one hundred days after she is divorced. Apparently this time is necessary to decide who the child's father is if the divorcee happens to be pregnant.

'After that *Tendi* party four men went after me, asking me to choose one of them. I chose the one I was most familiar with at the time, and I am glad I did. He is my present husband and we have been together for the last 15 years. Thank God I have no reason to complain. I've been really happy with him. The only thing is that I haven't had any children by him, though I did have a boy from my first husband.'

'Doesn't he complain about not having children?'

'No, never. He never mentions the subject.'

'So, do I take it you are happy with your life as a Tarqui woman, or would you prefer to live like the urban women you meet in towns or see on television?'

'Yes, I am quite happy with my life as a Tarqui woman, but when I see women teachers and professionals I regret never having been to school. I can't help thinking that had I been to school I might very well have done something worthwhile with my life. Before the independence of Algeria in 1962 there were no schools at all round here. We were taught to write *Tifinar* (the written language of Al Tawariqu) by our mothers and we speak the Tarqui language but it is not the national language, the language of education, and it won't lead us anywhere. Thus I would like Tarqui women to keep their traditions, values and customs but also to go to schools and universities and become professional women.'

'What exactly are the things you don't like about the urban society you come into contact with?'

'Well, let me tell you this. The other day I was in Tamnrassett visiting a Tarqui friend of mine. As we were having tea and enjoying a pleasant chat her neighbour, a woman from Algiers, came in crying bitterly. She hugged my friend and then showed her her thighs which were dark blue from the blows she had received. She later told us that on that day her husband had come home from work earlier than usual but had not found her at home. She told him she had been visiting a friend of hers but he did not believe her and beat her violently, kicking her out of her home. My friend and I burst out crying from the shock of this. We could hardly believe what we saw and heard. It would be impossible for such a thing to happen in our society. If my husband arrived now, for example, and didn't find his lunch ready, then he would either have to wait or eat whatever he could find. And if I told him I was with a friend of mine he would never doubt my word.

'I also heard for the first time from these urban women about the importance of virginity for unmarried women. To us, this sounds absolutely disgraceful. What goes on between husband and wife is extremely personal and it is disgusting to hear the nature of these goings on bandied about publicly or considered as a family right or, worse still, a mark of honour. Whether or not the Tarqui woman is a virgin this has no bearing on her marital life.

'Another thing as a Tarqui woman I feel quite glad about is that we have such easy-going attitudes to divorce. There is no stigma or social shame attached to it at all. A woman who has been divorced five times stands as much chance of getting married again as an unmarried woman with the same looks and merits. A school teacher from Constantine who was a good friend of mine told me she was living through hell with her husband but did not want to ask for a divorce because she hated to be labelled a divorcee; it must be a horrid label to have in their society. To all Tarquis divorce is a natural facet of married life; it says nothing about the merits or demerits of the divorced couple. All that it means is that the two people in question were not compatible living together. So a divorced woman does not have to feel she is a failure, that she has committed a social crime, or anything of the kind. Even single, unmarried mothers stand a very good chance of getting married to someone who is prepared to bring their children up. Many men have brought up fatherless sons who have grown up to be the best of men, and fatherless daughters who have turned out to be the best of women.'

'How do you compare your position as a woman with that of the European women?'

'In the last 20 years our area has become a tourist attraction and many people, especially those from France and Germany, spend their annual holidays here. My brother is in fact married to a French woman, and I spent three months in Paris consulting gynaecologists about my apparent infertility. I was really shocked to find out how terrified European women are of rape, how many women actually do get attacked, and how many of those try to commit suicide. I found all this horrific because at its root there is a nasty view of women as helpless, defenceless sexual objects. Women in my society never feel they are sex objects; they are appreciated as companions and partners. Rape is unheard of in our tribes; it is so horrid and humiliating that I can't imagine how any society in the world could tolerate it.

'I also discovered during my three months' stay in Paris that there were places for battered women. I was really shocked to find that in Paris – or in any European country for that matter – women are battered, and this despite the magnificent progress which women have made in every field. This just does not make sense to me. It is incredible how much women put up with and how little they have achieved in terms of their most basic rights. In my opinion, the first and most important right for a woman is to feel she is a free and equal individual whose sex is neither a curse nor a privilege. It is true I feel privileged as a woman, but that privilege does not derive from my sexual nature but from a deeply rooted appreciation and even glorification of the woman's role in my society. Motherhood for us is something holy; our culture has been handed down through our mothers since the time of our great ancestress, Tin Hinan, believed to be the originator of Al Tawariqu tribes. In mothers, Al Tawariqus believe you find history, culture, education, values and ethics. We have a saying which runs: "If you want to know a people's culture try to understand the culture of their women." This does not mean that as women we do not make love, for we certainly do and we enjoy it, but that we are fully appreciated as responsible, sensible, decent and more than equal human beings rather than just as beautiful bodies. Did you know that in our tribes it is our mother's descent which counts, rather than our father's? A man, for example, whose mother is from a respectable tribe would be able to compete for any position he aspired to in Al Hoggar, whoever his father might be, but a man whose mother is from humble origins would never be considered for any post in his tribe, even if his father were from noble origins. So it is the mother who counts. Hence, I would not like to exchange my position as a Tarqui woman either with an urban woman or with a European woman. I am quite happy as a Tarqui woman, though, as I've said before, I would like to see young Tarqui women going to school and becoming professional women without giving up any of the advantages which their tradition, habits and religion have endowed them with.'

As Fatima was evidently enjoying teaching me this significant lesson about Tarqui feminism my eyes were fixed on the beautifully colourful leather bags hung on the wall opposite me, the size ranging between small and huge. There was so much art, craft and taste in the making of these bags that I decided to ask about their maker and find out if I could buy a sample to take home with me. 'These bags,' she said in answer to my question, 'are made by Tarqui women. Not all Tarqui women can make them, of course, but a good number of them can. You also might be interested to know that women here make tents, suitcases and pots from heated clay; they put up the tents themselves and handle most of the physically demanding jobs. Men handle the delicate materials such as silver from which they make finely engraved bracelets, rings, necklaces and earrings.'

'Oh dear,' I caught myself muttering to myself as I was leaving. 'Where does that leave our well-established theories of femininity and masculinity, I wonder?'

When the time came to leave the Southern Sahara I felt really sorry to part from the friends I had made. No fewer than three women stipulated that if I ever came again I should come straight to their homes and never consider going to the hotel again. As they bade me goodbye at the airport our eyes exchanged looks of warmth and genuine affection. It is incredible, I thought, as I went up the steps to the plane, that even in this vast Sahara one is able to build bridges of friendship so quickly with people who at first sight look so different from us. Perhaps this is what being 'human' is all about. In the plane I wrote a poem in Arabic; the first poem I had written for a long time. Once again, the language came to me as naturally as ever. It was just possible that these wonderful people with their relatively simple lifestyles and spontaneous actions had begun to heal the wound that had been bleeding inside me for years. The humanity, love, affection and values felt and held by people living in tents and huts taught me a new lesson about humanity and made me hate all the more racial or sexual discrimination.

On this trip I had been exposed to one of the most important experiences in my life. As a woman I found in Al Tawariqu society a unique type of women's emancipation which nevertheless derives its mores and logic directly from the same historical source as all Arab countries' laws, namely the Koran and the sayings of the Prophet Mohammed. But here, unlike in the other Muslim countries I have visited, male dominance has not been allowed to distort the ancient teachings to the detriment of women. I found a Muslim society where women were neither servants nor men's inferiors, and where reproduction is held in high esteem and even glorified, rather than taken as an excuse for oppression and subjugation.

5 And Now What?

Ten years ago, perhaps, none of the women interviewed would have said anything against their husbands or fathers, because that would have been deemed dishonourable to the family, whereas now all the women I talked to were able to see themselves as separate and independent of both husbands and fathers. This newly rising consciousness and stress on women's identity, rights and ordeals is the first step in the process of challenging the forces responsible for the oppression of women. Both observation and research confirm that a rising consciousness is rapidly spreading among Arab women; there has been a noticeable change in attitudes during the last few years. When I married my husband in 1981 against my parent's will, everyone regarded me as a social outcast. Even the Dean of Al Adab college at Damascus University said to me, 'Who forced you to marry an Iraqi and leave your family?' Now, in 1987, I hear only words of encouragement and praise for women who marry men of their choice, regardless of family pressures or social considerations.

One does not want, of course, to carry this argument as far as one of my veteran interviewees did. She voiced the belief that Syrian women had already fought and won all the major battles; all they needed to do now, she said, was to concentrate on their personal battles at home. This is far too optimistic. Although in the four Arab countries studied here women are assured equal pay and equal job opportunities, they are still not assured an equal right to a dignified and respectable life. In the Personal Status law which applies in Syria, Lebanon and Egypt, Article 70 states that the wife has to travel with her husband unless otherwise indicated in the marriage contract, or unless the judge has found a serious reason for her not to travel. It literally means that the wife has to follow her husband wherever he goes. Article 73 decrees that the woman cannot go out to work against her husband's wishes. If she does, he has the right to stop paying her maintenance and to neglect her, and she would be legally classified as *nashez* (disobedient), which would seriously affect her chances of getting a divorce in court. Paragraph D under Article 307 states that if a man finds that the woman he is marrying is not a virgin, he has the right to an immediate divorce and to the reclamation of the dowry. Another article in the Punishment Law – which is applicable in all four countries and which is still very much in effect in Arab courts – decrees that if a man catches his sister or mother in an adulterous sexual affair and kills her, he should be imprisoned for no more than six months because the crime was committed in defence of his honour. There are two further unwritten extensions to this article which have proved to be effective in a court hearing. The first is that even if the man commits the crime a year or more after he hears of the affair (the law stipulates that he must commit the crime the instant he hears of it), he is still treated with the same leniency. The second is that this article, which ostensibly applies strictly to brothers and fathers, in fact also applies to husbands who kill their wives.

Besides these clear-cut legal battles, many other more subtle but no less significant battles are still to be fought by Arab women. A huge percentage of professional and educated Arab women still have no right to choose or to lead an independent life. For women to shake off the burden of housework as their sole responsibility or to stop feeling guilty for pursuing a career might be more difficult to deal with than the right to work or to education. The domestic injustices and maltreatment stressed by Arab women in this book might be more difficult to do away with because they are so deeply ingrained in men's conception of womanhood.

If I seem to be lumping Arab women in Syria, Lebanon, Algeria and Palestine together, it is because their accounts show that, despite national and local differences, essentially they have the same problems. What women's experiences in these countries reveal is that women should not fight national battles without continuously stressing their own feminist battles. In the past, it has been almost a female rule to want to be the unknown soldier whose only reward is her personal satisfaction and inner peace. Throughout all the national battles women have fought in Syria, Algeria, Palestine and Lebanon, they have appeared to show no interest in obtaining political power, position or even prestige for themselves. And as a result, they have failed to reap the benefits of their own success. Lebanese women, for example, excelled in thinking up ways to fight the Israeli occupiers to such an extent that they started to demolish traditionally held views of women's weakness and coward`ce. Yet, despite the confidence of my Lebanese interviewees in the irrevocable nature of their achievements, women have recently become the prime targets of religious fanatics in Beirut. Indeed, no sooner did the religious fanatics gain power in the political arena than they started to send home women who wore trousers and order them not to go out again without the *chador*.

I believe it is time Arab women learnt not to fight men's battles while losing out themselves. I think our priority as women should be to help spread a feminist consciousness in every domain and across all social categories in order to be well prepared for struggles to come. My hope is that the ordeals described in this book might be considered interesting accounts of a bygone age by the time my daughters' generation comes of age.

Glossary

Alb Ishna	a kind of wheat
Al Dakhiel	the one who has to be protected
Al Hijab	a scarf that covers a woman's hair without covering any part of her face. It is normally tied under the chin.
Al Imzad	a pear-shaped lute
Al Izar	a huge piece of black material with which a woman wraps her body and her head, leaving only her eyes uncovered
Al Mokhtar	village master or chief
Al Okht	sister
Al Shari	a knee-high dress or coat with matching trousers and matching scarf that covers the hair completely. This costume is worn by Shiite women in Lebanon.
Al Shieokh	Muslim religious leaders who lead prayers and are heads of Mosques; the plural of *Shiekh*
Al Sofour	an adjective used to describe the state of a woman who goes out without covering her hair. The word implies a reminder that this is done in disobedience to the ethics of Islam
Al Tarqui	the people of *Al Tawariqu*, which is a Muslim group that counts over a million people in the Southern Algerian Sahara. *Al Tawariqu* groups are scattered over Mali, Niger and Algeria but their main base and leaders have always been in Algeria.
Bloudan	a summer resort on the outskirts of Damascus

Caffans   plural of *coffin*; white cloth in which dead
                       Muslims or Muslimas are wrapped. It is also
                       worn by those who want to show their
                       readiness for martyrdom.

Chador   a huge piece of black material which covers
                       a woman's head and body. Women usually
                       hold it closed under their chins.

Daber rasak   find your own way out

Dar   a one-storey Arabic house with a huge
                       courtyard open to the sky

Dar Al Tofl Al Arabi The House of Arab Children

Doulma   stuffed vine leaves, courgettes and
                       aubergines

Erwad   a small Syrian island in the Mediterranean
                       sea, near Tartus

Essehar   a late evening party

Falaful   a popular and cheap Arabic dish made of
                       boiled chick peas that are ground, made into
                       a paste, spiced and then cut into small pieces
                       and fried. It is served with yoghourt and
                       salad.

Fatat   daughter

Fedayee   male fighter

Gazala   deer

Genderma   a name given to the police force in Syria
                       during colonial times

Ghota   green woods to the west, south and east of
                       Damascus

Haji   any Muslim or Muslima who went on *Al
                       Haj*, that is to visit Mecca, Saudi Arabia, at
                       a certain time of the year

Haram   anything prohibited in Islam

Hasier   mattress made of straw

Homos   ground chick peas with olive oil and pickles
                       served for breakfast or with meat dishes

Ibn Halal   a decent man

Isharb   a large piece of thin material that partly
                       covers a woman's hair, leaving the front part
                       uncovered; it is usually knotted under the

chin. Many women wear *Isharb* in compliance with social habit rather than with religious rules.

Kassion	the name of a mountain at the brow of which the city of Damascus rests
Kebab	a dish made of mince meat, onion, egg and a little flour
Kief kief	the same way
Konbas	caftan
Mabrouk	congratulations
Makdous.	aubergines stuffed with nuts, pepper and garlic and kept in olive oil for winter
Maliki	queen
Men of Fatwa	the chosen few of the knowledgeable Muslim leaders who have the right to change Islamic law
Mjadara	crushed wheat and lentils
Moghrabiah	a Palestinian dish made of steamed dough and chicken
Mordiaha	a woman who is paid to breastfeed another woman's baby
Muslima	a woman whose religion is Islam
Nashez	disobedient
Salam	peace, the word is used to mean 'hello', or 'peace be upon you'
Samahat	the reverent
Shari	in harmony with the rules of Islam
Sharia	Islamic legislation based on the text of the Koran and the sayings of the Prophet Mohammed
Shawrma	slices of lamb pressed together around a skewer and barbequed. *Shawrma* is often eaten as sandwiches.
Shieh	herbal tea
Shiekh	see *Al Shieokh*
Sora	a section in the Koran, a chapter divided into subsections called *Aiehs*
Sour	a high wall
Tabouli	traditional Arab salad with crushed wheat

Talib	local religious head of the tribe
Tendi	a big party
Tifinar	the written language of *Al Tawariqus*; it can be seen only on stones; there is no written literature in this language
Wali	a governor of a province
Wilayas	provinces
Zatar	powdered sesame with other spices and ingredients; it is eaten with olive oil for breakfast

BOUTHAINA SHAABAN holds a Ph.D. from Warwick University and teaches English literature at the University of Damascus. She was a Fulbright Fellow at Duke University during the 1990-1991 academic year.